THE
LONDON

An authoritative
guide book to London theatres
compiled by
the British Centre of the
International Theatre Institute

in association with UNESCO

Published by
LONDON TRANSPORT
55 Broadway, Westminster
London SW1

First published 1980
Copyright © London Transport 1980
ISBN 0 85329 107 1
Let's make the most of London series

All rights reserved. No part of this publication may be reproduced, stored in a retrieval system, or transmitted, in any form or by any means, electronic, mechanical, photocopying, recording or otherwise, without the prior permission of London Transport.

Whilst every effort has been made to ensure the accuracy of the information contained in this book, neither London Transport nor the British Centre of the International Theatre Institute can take any responsibility for possible errors or omissions, and readers should note that changes in admission details, facilities, and travel details occur from time to time. The opinions expressed are those of the compilers, and are not necessarily those of the British Centre of the International Theatre Institute or of London Transport. Suggestions from readers for future editions are welcome, and should be addressed to the British Centre of the International Theatre Institute at the address below.

Published by London Transport, 55 Broadway, Westminster, London SW1. Compiled and edited by the British Centre of the International Theatre Institute, 31 Shelton Street, Covent Garden, London WC2. Phototypeset by Carlinpoint Limited (T U), 31 Shelton Street, Covent Garden London WC2, and printed in Great Britain by Staples Printers Limited, Kettering and London.

380/057RP/20

CONTENTS

Foreword, *by Glenda Jackson* 5
Acknowledgements 6
Introduction, *by Colin Chambers* 7

THEATRE LONDON

Notes 12
Index to Theatres 14
see this page for a full alphabetical index to all regular London venues

A Ticket for the Show, *by Vincent Burke* 138
What's Playing Tonight? *by Philip Ormond* 141

HOW-TO-GET-THERE MAPS

How to Use the Maps 144
Outer London Venues 145
Key to Central London Maps 149
Central London Maps 150
The Underground 160

OTHER VENUES

Introductory Note 162
Index to Other Venues 163
see this page for a full alphabetical index to occasional venues for the performing arts

Theatre Contacts 191
About the International Theatre Institute 193
For Further Reading, *by Simon Trussler* 194
General Index 197

FOREWORD

Hello, I'd like to introduce you to Theatre London. *This new guide to all London's theatres does something no other guide has done before — draws together in one book the big and the small theatres, the West End and outer-London, the brave innovators and the traditional stalwarts. It reminds us all that good theatre is going on all about us, sometimes in unlikely places at even unlikelier prices. The famous theatres are also here, as well as places where you can hear good music, or where theatre is just a small part of the activities of a lively community centre.*

London Transport and the British Centre of the International Theatre Institute — only two years old but already through this guide and in its many other activities making a major contribution to demystifying theatre — are to be applauded for producing Theatre London. *Even seasoned theatregoers will find new names in its pages and, more importantly, learn of interesting work going on that they might otherwise miss.*

Do use this book and try out the new theatres as well as keeping faith with the old. I hope that you will find it rewarding and informative, and that you enjoy theatre all the more because of it.

Glenda Jackson

Acknowledgements

The Editorial Board wishes to record its gratitude to the following, who assisted immeasurably in the compilation of *Theatre London:*

For preliminary research and fieldwork, the staff and students of the Drama Department of University of London Goldsmiths' College: faculty members Vera Gottlieb and Nesta Jones; and from the student body, Paul Blackman, June Gilbert, Wendy Hallam, Simon Hughes, Marco Johnston, Laurence Mackenzie, Colin Mortlock, Brian Mulligan, Eva Shipp, Charlotte Singleton, Nikki Townley and Patrick Ward; and the Geographers Map Company Limited for supplying large-scale street plans.

For painstaking assistance and careful checking of proofs at short notice, the managements and staffs of all the theatres and venues included in the guide.

For help, advice, and liaison, the Development Office of the Society of West End Theatre, and the London fringe theatre association, IMOFTA.

For researching and obtaining illustrations, Theatre Despatch; for creating the title-page montages, Richard Fuller; and for the 'In Exile' photographs Mark Cummins.

For continuous patience and perseverance in typesetting the book to a very demanding schedule, Steve Chambers and Jeanette Koch; and for seeing the guide through its demanding final stages, Catherine Arnott, Neil Newman, and the editorial team of *Theatre Quarterly* and TQ Publications.

And finally, for demonstrating beyond any doubt the need for such a book as this, the hundreds of professional theatre visitors to Britain who have received the help and advice of the British Centre of the International Theatre Institute.

Michel Julian *(Managing Editor)*

Colin Chambers, Liz Edwards, Debra Hauer, Nesta Jones, Michel Julian, Simon Trussler *(Editorial Board)*

INTRODUCTION

All the figures seem to prove it — London is the theatrical capital of the world. But what does that really mean? Take a closer look: because such claims are usually made with one eye shut. Yes, London can rightly boast more than fifty elegant 'picture-frame' theatres in under two square miles, with the intimate Duchess a stone's throw from the grand Covent Garden. Yes, its musicals can swing and its comedies sparkle. But open the other eye, and see what you are missing. Discover the hives of activity in the most unexpected places — in basements, pubs, sheds, halls, and clubs — different prices, diferent plays, yet indisputably theatre. It is this rich mix that makes London's theatrical life so attractive, and which provides the key to the thinking behind this guide.

Previous surveys of the London theatre scene have concentrated on the capital's traditional strongholds — the West End, along with the major publicly subsidized companies. Yet not only is this to ignore all the energetic (if sometimes short-lived and uncomfortable) experiments that have become known as 'the fringe': it also gives the wrong idea of London's history as a centre of theatrical life.

'Which tube to the Sheffield Crucible?' is not such a daft question if you come from Connecticut. And just who or what *is* the Pindar of Wakefield? These are the sorts of questions that for years visitors to London have been asking policemen and themselves — and the staff of the British Centre of the International Theatre Institute, who first responded to the clear need for a comprehensive guide such as this. Now, with the help of London Transport, the answers can be found between the covers of a single book: and, as the title *Theatre London* suggests, the guide covers *all* theatre and *all* London, whether you are heading north, south, east, or west, looking for the Theatre Royal Drury Lane or the Bush.

The Historical Background

It's nothing new for London theatre to mean something different depending on where you live — or on your social class. From the beginnings of English drama, when pagan and Christian traditions came together in street dramas and festivals, not only the townspeople — particularly those in the craft guilds — were involved. Popular entertainers with their own traditions of singing and juggling would also take part. Making their living 'on the road', and often turned out of towns as vagabonds, they needed the patronage and protection of powerful lords. By the time of Queen Elizabeth I, there was conflict between the City of London, which wanted the streets free of the strolling players, and the Court, which rather enjoyed their performances. Thus, the first permanent professional public theatre was in fact built outside the City limits, in Shoreditch by Finsbury Fields, in an area used for such recreations as archery. Former carpenter turned travelling actor James Burbage built The Theatre, as it was simply but accurately called, in 1576.

A year later, another theatre, the Curtain, was opened nearby. But local displeasure forced Burbage out: The Theatre was pulled down, and the timber used to build another, improved theatre on the south side of the River Thames, also outside the City's boundaries — the famous Globe, at which Burbage's son Richard first uttered 'To be, or not to be'. The area, called Bankside, flourished with pubs, bear rings, and other theatres such as the Swan and the Rose.

With the English Revolution came the Puritan Suppression of Theatres Act in 1642, and the social divisions in the theatre which arose with the Restoration are reflected still, however dimly, in the one-eyed view that sees only half of what London theatre has to offer. When Charles II returned he issued only two patents for running theatres — one for the Theatre Royal Drury Lane and the other (via Lincoln's Inn Fields) for the Royal Opera House, Covent Garden. But official interference did not stop there: restrictions were tightened up in a later Act of 1737 remembered chiefly for the introduction of the censor in the shape of the Lord Chamberlain, imposed because Walpole was angry with plays which poked fun at his Whig government.

Yet, alongside the 'official' theatre, there has always been the 'unofficial', from the early days of Goodman's Fields, of Sadler's Wells, the Haymarket and the Harlequinades to penny gaffs, the political drama of the 1930s, and today's 'fringe'. In the wake of the Chartist movement, the licensing restrictions were eased in 1843, but it was only after many more years of determined battle, which had their funny moments, that the Lord Chamberlain finally lost his powers — on 26 September 1968. The very next day, the rock musical *Hair* opened and enjoyed a long run which delighted thousands, including members of the Royal Family.

The Recent Change of Mood

By this time the theatre had changed dramatically. Although experimental theatres and companies had existed throughout the twentieth century — the Embassy, the Gate, Group Theatre, Unity — activity had never been on the scale that began to be seen in the 1960s. There was a radical mood in the air: people wanted to control their own destinies, and in the theatre this meant going out onto the streets, into the cellars, arts centres, or back rooms of pubs, converting old churches and warehouses — in fact, performing anywhere but in conventional theatres. Even an ice rink was pressed into service . . .

The fringe was dismissed as a passing fad, but its impact has proved enduring, though sporadic and uneven. Now, established professionals go back to the West End refreshed from having worked on the fringe, while the next generation of actors, writers, designers, and directors are learning their craft there. So if previous histories of London theatre have been written around such names as Drury Lane, Covent Garden, and the Haymarket, and on the work of 'newer' theatres, like the Garrick, the Coliseum, and Her Majesty's, future historians will have to consider the Round House, the Oval House, Soho Poly, the Kings Head, the Half Moon, and many more. Added to the roll-call of names like Kean, Beerbohm Tree, Bronson Albery, and Laurence Olivier must be those of the numerous touring companies, backbone of the fringe, such as Red Ladder, Pip Simmons, the People Show, Monstrous Regiment, and 7:84. As if to underline the message, two fringe shows — one presented by the Belt and Braces Company and the other by the Orange Tree Theatre, Richmond — were invited to play at the beautiful Wyndham's Theatre in the West End in the very year that *Theatre London* first appears.

New Theatres, New Threats

The 1960s saw another kind of expansion, as well: the opening of the Royalty, the first West End theatre to be built in London since 1931, was followed in 1962 by the Prince Charles, though this was subsequently turned into a cinema; Peter Hall starting the Royal Shakespeare Company and finding it a London home at the Aldwych; the birth of the National Theatre at the Old Vic, and work beginning on its new South Bank premises after 150 years of debate; and the massive Barbican arts project getting under way in the City, in the footsteps of the Mermaid.

But the theatre, having survived the onslaught of the 'talkies' and the blitz (losing more buildings to the cinema than to the bombs), then had to confront the challenges of bingo and bulldozers — not to mention television. Of the 50 theatres listed in the last London Transport theatre guide, published in 1959, five are no longer functioning. New regulations, however, were brought in to protect theatres after the demolition of the St. James' in 1957; and an Act of Parliament established the Theatres Trust, which has to be consulted if any building that is, or has ever been, used as a theatre is under threat. Many theatres — landmarks in their own right and as much a part of London's history as any of the other sights — have been given protection as listed buildings of special interest. But the leases of several theatres are coming up for renewal in the 1980s. Will they survive the unquenchable thirst of office-block developers? Despite the legislation, the outcome could be in doubt.

Thus, two theatres — the Shaftesbury and the Criterion — have only been kept alive by a massive campaign, including a picket, sponsored by the performers' union Equity. Called the Save London Theatres Campaign, it joined forces with local protesters, such as the Save Piccadilly Campaign, the Soho Society and the Covent Garden Community Association. Yet even this array of forces, plus MPs and the major grant-giving bodies, could not save the famous London Pavilion, which stands opposite Eros in Piccadilly Circus. It is due to be pulled down by a triumphant opposition.

Two important fringe theatres are also 'in exile' thanks to property developers: the Open Space is going to the courts, claiming that it has lost the new home it was promised, since the land on which the theatre was built in Tottenham Court Road has been taken over from the original developers; likewise, the Almost Free has been promised new premises. For the time being, they are both presenting shows elsewhere. These more obvious effects of the economic situation are reflected in the West End, where at least a third of the commercial theatres are under one kind of threat or another, and all have been hit by the imposition of Value Added Tax on ticket prices, while publicly-subsidized theatres of all shapes and sizes are in danger from the cuts in public spending.

Many of the familiar names in theatre management are small, anonymous companies whose main interest is not in the theatre, and possibly not even in the entertainments business at all. Of the 56 more traditional theatres usually considered to make up

London's theatre scene, only 35 are commercial; and only one, the Phoenix, is owned by a single family. By far the strongest family group is the Wyndham's, which runs the Albery, Criterion, Donmar (leased to the Royal Shakespeare Company as The Warehouse), Piccadilly and Wyndham's Theatres. The Greater London Council owns the freehold of four theatres, as well as that of the doomed London Pavilion, Christ's Hospital owns two, and the Crown that of the Theatre Royal, Haymarket. Lord Grade has interests in about a dozen theatres through various subsidiaries of his mammoth Associated Television Corporation, from Associated Theatre Properties and Stoll Theatres Corporation to Moss Empires and the Grade Organization. Theatres Consolidated Ltd has interests in four theatres.

And so the list goes on: from Capital Radio taking over the Duke of York's, and Peter Saunders running the Vaudeville and the St Martin's, to the Cooney/Marsh group's four theatres, and the resolutely anonymous-sounding Industrial Capital Holdings Ltd. However, few, if any, of the commercial managements could claim to be independent of the publicly-subsidized theatre. A glance at recent programmes shows the number of subsidized productions which have transferred to the West End. Mention has been made of the two shows at Wyndham's, but add to that the better-known names of *Equus* or *Bedroom Farce* from the National Theatre, *Wild Oats*, *Piaf* or *Once in a Lifetime* from the Royal Shakespeare Company, *Side by Side by Sondheim* or *Whose Life Is It, Anyway?* from the Mermaid, or even *My Fair Lady*, which toured before coming in to the Adelphi thanks to a large guarantee against loss from the Arts Council, which gets its grant from Parliament.

Theatre for All Tastes

Outside the commercial theatre and the major subsidized work of the National, the Royal Shakespeare Company, the Royal Court and the Old Vic lies the jigsaw puzzle of the publicly-funded venues, stretching to the outer suburbs. Apart from a handful of self-supporting ventures, the would-be spectator can choose from a maze of grant-aided theatres, from smart modern auditoriums such as the Ashcroft or Churchill, built by local councils as a cultural amenity in a large complex, to impressive amateur work at theatres like the Questors or the Tower, to the smaller-scale theatres and community centres that can often be found in an all-purpose hall. These offer the range of fringe touring groups, and are able to respond more quickly to local issues and to develop local skills, whether in drama and dance, or in music, photography, printing or pottery.

When it comes to the fringe and the 'non-West End' theatre, funded by a mixture of national, regional and local grants, the assortment of buildings used is matched by the variety of what happens inside them. Some are dedicated to one type of theatre — new plays, music hall, mime. Others switch from politics to puppets, inviting groups who work with the people about whom they are going to perform — old age pensioners, perhaps — or who look at society from a particular angle — feminist, gay, ethnic, youth. Then there are the shows in the open air, or late at night, or at lunchtime, or swilled down with good food and drink. The choice is so great that even *Theatre London* has had to leave out some — mostly because they are too local and irregular, plus a few which will not open until after the guide comes out.

An example of the problem for the guide's compilers (but a bonus for the visitor who unexpectedly finds an unlisted venue) can be given from the programmes of two fringe companies. The first 36 performances this year of Common Stock's tour of *Away From It All* took place in 34 venues. Only six of them have full-page entries in this guide, which covers more than 120 venues, and only one is included in the composite section at the end. The first 33 performances this year of a nuclear power play by the Covent Garden Community Theatre took place in 28 venues. Of those, only five have full-page entries — and only one of the 28 venues coincided with any visited by Common Stock, 17 being local pubs!

Theatre London, then, is not a gazetteer but a guide. It reflects the changed circumstances of the theatre in London, which itself is part of a constantly changing picture throughout Britain. It is designed to help you choose — your price range, your style of theatre, your part of London — you can even see theatre on the tube! You can also dress as you choose, by the way — dinner jackets and long gowns are not compulsory any more, even in the 'dress' circle.

A live show still holds its distinctive attractions, despite all the technological advances made by film and television — which rely on the theatre, in any case, for their future well-being. Sybil Thorndike once said that, at its best, theatre could illuminate aspects of humanity, of day-to-day existence and struggle, and could add to the quality of life as no other medium could. Hopefully, *Theatre London* will help you to enjoy such experiences in whichever of the many theatres you visit. Perhaps it will encourage you also to try someting new. But whatever it achieves, you will see, with both eyes open, that wherever you are in London, you are not far from a theatre.

COLIN CHAMBERS

Notes

Times: All times are given in the 24-hour clock form, as employed in London Transport and most other travel timetables. Thus 13 00 to 23 00 is used to signify 1.00 pm to 11.00 pm, and 24 00 signifies midnight. For example, the times 10 00-20 00 in brackets after a box-office telephone number indicate opening hours from 10.00 am to 8.00 pm. Where an entry states that a bar keeps 'pub hours', these are normally 11 00 or 11 30-15 00 and 17 00 or 17 30 to 23 00 (12 00-14 00 and 19 00-22 30 on Sundays).

Telephone Numbers: The STD prefix 01 should be dialled before the numbers given if calling from outside the London telephone area.

Admin: is followed by the phone number to be used for administrative enquiries — that is, other than for booking tickets.

AmEx: American Express credit card.

Attendant: indicates a cloakroom with attendant in charge. See also **Paralok**.

Barclaycard/Visa: holders should note that these two credit cards share facilities, and are interchangeable for booking purposes.

Cloakrooms: indicates storage facilities for coats and bags, not toilets. See **Attendant** and **Paralok** for different types.

Concessions: price reductions for students, parties, etc. See further pages 139-40.

Mat(s): matinee(s) — afternoon or early evening performances.

NCP: National Car Park, a paying parking lot.

OAPs: old-age pensioners (senior citizens), persons over 60-65 years.

p.a.: per annum, annual cost.

Paralok: a self-service chain-and-lock apparatus. See **Cloakrooms**, above.

s.a.e.: stamped, self-addressed envelope, which must be enclosed when making postal bookings.

Wheelchairs: The numeral indicates the number of places available, but this is always *by prior arrangement only*.

Underground: The rail travel directions at the foot of each theatre page or 'other venue' entry give the nearest Underground or British Rail station. A connecting bus is indicated where the theatre is a considerable distance away. Check your route by using the map section of this book (pages 144-160), and on arrival the 'You are Here' map of the immediate area in the ticket hall of each Underground station.

Bus: The details of buses list firstly the routes passing close by the theatre, and then, when appropriate, other routes within a reasonable distance. Use the free London bus map and list of routes to help you plan your journey.

Map: Central London theatres are keyed to a page number and grid reference (eg 155 M5) in the coloured map section on pages 150-159 (see page 149 for Key). 'Thumbnail maps' are provided on pages 144-148 for outer-London venues: thus, 148 **G** indicates map G on page 148.

THEATRE LONDON

Index to Theatres

Names in italic are alternative forms or nicknames, other than those used as main headings in the alphabetical sequence of theatres in this section.

Aba Daba Music Hall 87
Abeng Centre 16
Action Space 17
Adelphi Theatre 18
Africa Centre 19
Albany 20
Albany Empire 20
Albery Theatre 21
Aldwych Theatre 22
Alexandra Palace 23
Ally Pally 23
Ambassadors Theatre 24
Apollo Theatre 25
Arts Theatre Club 26
Ashcroft Theatre 27
Astoria Theatre 28
Barbican Arts Centre 29
Bear Gardens 30
Bee and Bustle Music Hall 95
Bromley Churchill 34
Bush Theatre Club 31
Cambridge Theatre 32
Casino 90
Chats Palace 33
Churchill Theatre 34
Cockpit Theatre 35
Collegiate Theatre 36
Collie 68
Coliseum 68
Combination 20
Comedy Theatre 37
Company of Three 38
Court 99
Covent Garden 100
Cottesloe Theatre 39
Criterion Theatre 40
Croydon Warehouse 41
Curtain Theatre 42
Donmar Theatre 127
Drill Hall 17
Drury Lane 113

Duchess Theatre 43
Duke of Wellington 110
Duke of York's Theatre 44
Earl Russell 45
Embassy Club 46
Factory 47
Fortune Theatre 48
Garrick Theatre 49
Gate Theatre 50
Gay's The Word 51
George Inn Courtyard 52
Globe Theatre 53
Greenwich Theatre 54
Greenwich Young People's Theatre 55
Grove Theatre 56
Half Moon Theatre 57
Hampstead Theatre Club 58
Haymarket 114
Her Majesty's Theatre 59
ICA 60
Institute of Contemporary Arts 60
Intimate Theatre 61
Jackson's Lane 62
Jeannetta Cochrane Theatre 63
Kenneth More Theatre and Studio 64
Keskidee Arts Centre 65
Kings Head Theatre Club 66
Lane 113
Little Angel Marionette Theatre 67
London Casino 90
London Coliseum 68
London Palladium 69
Lyric Theatre 70
Lyric Hammersmith and Studio 71
Lyttelton Theatre 74
Marylands 47
Mayfair Theatre 72
Mermaid Theatre 73
Mouth and Trousers 136
National Theatre 39, 74, 75

New End Theatre 112
New Inn Theatre 76
Old Red Lion 77
Old Vic Theatre 78
Olivier Theatre 75
Open Air, Regent's Park 79
Opera House 100
Orange Tree Theatre 80
Oval House 81
Overground Theatre 82
Palace (Victoria) 126
Palace Theatre 83
Palladium 69
Pentameters 84
Phoenix Theatre 85
Piccadilly Theatre 86
Pindar of Wakefield 87
Players Theatre 88
Polka Children's Theatre 89
Poly 108
Prince Edward Theatre 90
Prince of Wales Theatre 91
Queen's Theatre 92
Queen's Theatre, Hornchurch 93
Questors Theatre 94
RSC 22, 127
Railway 95
Regent's Park Open Air 79
Richmond Theatre 96
Riverside Studios 97
Round House 98
Royal Court Theatre 99
Royal Court Theatre Upstairs 118
Royal Opera House, Covent Garden 100
Royal Shakespeare Company 22, 127
Royalty Theatre 101
Sadler's Wells Theatre 102
St George's Theatre 103
St Martin's Theatre 104
Savoy Theatre 105
Shaftesbury Theatre 106
Shaw Theatre 107
Soho Poly Theatre Club 108
South Bank 39, 74, 75
Stage Centre 55
Strand Theatre 109

Stratford 115
Stratford East 115
Sugawn Theatre 110
Talk of the Town 111
Theatre at New End 112
Theatre Royal, Drury Lane 113
Theatre Royal, Haymarket 114
Theatre Royal, Stratford East 115
Theatre Space 116
Theatre-in-the-Square 117
Theatre Upstairs 118
Theatre Workshop 115
Theatro Technis 119
Three Horseshoes 84
Tower Theatre 120
Tramshed 121
Tricycle Theatre 122
Unicorn Theatre 123
Upstream Theatre 124
Vaudeville Theatre 125
Vic 78
Victoria Palace Theatre 126
Wakefield Tricycle 122
Warehouse 127
Waterside 128
Watford Palace Theatre 129
Wells 102
Wembley Complex 130
Westminster Theatre 131
Whitehall Theatre 132
Wimbledon Theatre 133
Windmill Theatre 134
Wyndham's Theatre 135
York and Albany 136
Young Vic 137

Abeng Centre

7 Gresham Road, SW9 7PH
Box Office: **737 1628** (11 00-17 00) Admin: **274 1291**
Performance Space: Hall undergoing modifications *Seating:* 300

Bookings: Postal (phone first) Phone (held to ½ hr before show) No credit cards.
Prices: £1 **Concessions:** Parties, OAPs **Perf Times:** Monday-Saturday 19 30 and lunchtimes 12 30 **Mailing List:** Free **Catering:** Hot & cold Caribbean food 12 30-14 00 Monday-Saturday **Bars:** No **Wheelchairs:** No **Cloakrooms:** No **Parking:** Municipal car park opposite **Other:** Bookstalls when available. Drama and music workshops, youth clubs, craft activities.

Policy: The Centre has its own resident drama and music groups which put on shows. It also acts as a venue for other Afro-Caribbean groups and touring companies whose shows emphasize the Centre's concern for improving community relations through a greater understanding of Afro-Caribbean culture.

Perspective: Tucked away behind Brixton Police Station in the multi-racial south London borough of Lambeth, the Abeng Centre, though little known, provides a valuable outlet for Afro-Caribbean arts. This is obviously important in such an area as Brixton but, as is too often the case, ethnic minorities and British-born non-whites suffer the general lack of facilities in an even more acute form.

Abeng aims to encourage contact across cultures and backgrounds. It was started in 1969 for young people and children, mainly of immigrant parents. As well as being a theatre venue, which could be used more by touring companies in a part of London that has almost no live entertainment outside pubs, it also acts as a centre where people can find out about jobs (when there are any) and get advice.

It is being reconstructed so that it can become a fully-fledged community centre. Alongside a range of ethnic arts, drama, dance and music, its theatre policy is to promote plays that help its audiences to understand and explore Afro-Caribbean culture. Its most recent success was Mustapha Matura's *Welcome Home Jacko,* a funny but hard play about the need to face up to being black in Britain instead of looking elsewhere, like Africa, for unreal solutions. (It had first played at the Factory — see separate entry). Other visitors include the Temba Theatre Company, founded in 1972 to give artistic expression to black culture.

Underground: Brixton (Victoria)
Bus: 2, 2B, 3, 35, 45, 50, 109, 133, 159, 172, 196, P4, or 37 to Brixton Road
Map: 145 **A**

Action Space

The Drill Hall, 16 Chenies Street, WC1E 7ET
Box Office: **637 8270** (10 00-20 00 Tuesday to Saturday) Admin: **631 1353**
Performance Space: Small basement theatre & large ground floor hall
Seating: 100 & 250, flexible seating in both

Bookings: Phone bookings for collection on day or in person on the day only. No credit cards. Sterling travellers cheques.
Prices: £1.25 -£2, including membership **Concessions:** No **Perf Times:** 20 00 Tuesday-Saturday. Some lunchtime shows at 13 00 **Mailing List:** Available for full members **Catering:** Egon Ronay recommended vegetarian cafe Monday 12 00-14 00, Tuesday-Saturday 12 00-20 00 open to public **Bars:** Opening autumn 1980 **Wheelchairs:** 3 in main hall **Cloakrooms:** No **Parking:** NCP Gt Russell Street. Streets after 18 30 **Other:** Bookstall for mags & pamphlets. Workshop Membership £2 p.a. or combined Theatre/Workshop Membership £3 p.a.

Policy: To take new and original theatre to the people and to promote the work of other theatre groups.

Perspective: Action Space began as a nomadic group formed in 1968 by artists working in different fields — music, video, theatre, film and 'structures' (anything from scaffolding to plastic inflatables). They toured anywhere, from parks to playsites, art galleries to OAP clubs, in Britain and abroad, trying to redefine the role that the arts have to play in society.

After having two bases, the group moved to the Drill Hall off Tottenham Court Road which had been used, as the name suggests, for military training. They were getting nearer to the sort of centre they wanted, and opened the basement theatre first (1976), followed by the ground floor hall. The resident artists still take their work out to all kinds of venues, and they are particularly involved with disabled people and the under-fives.

For touring companies, Action Space, as the centre has now become known, is a useful London venue which offers the range of committed fringe activity. The emphasis has been on seasons based around an issue (eg as an alternative to the 'Sense of Ireland' festival, a controversial programme was presented called *State of Emergency*, which coincided with the phones suddenly not working and files being stolen).

Sexual politics have been prominent in the plays shown here (eg The Women's Festival and The Gay Times Festival), from the pre-Edinburgh Festival showing of work by Heartache and Sorrow to Melissa Murray's *Ophelia* and Gay Sweatshop's play about Edward Carpenter, *The Dear Love of Comrades*. Exhibitions are interesting and the vegetarian food is recommended.

Underground: Goodge Street (Northern)
Bus: 1, 14, 24, 29, 73, 134, 176
Map: 151 D5

Adelphi Theatre

Strand, WC2E 7NH
Box Office: **836 7611** (10 00-19 00) Admin: **836 1166**
Performance Space: Proscenium arch *Seating:* 1,500 (3 levels, boxes)

Bookings: Postal (cheques to Adelphi Theatre) s.a.e. Phone (held 3 days) Credit cards (836 7358) AmEx, Access, Barclaycard/Visa, Diners. Sterling travellers cheques **Prices:** £3-£8 **Concessions:** Parties 20+ discounts. Student Standby when available **Perf Times:** Monday-Saturday 19 30, Thursday mat 15 00, Saturday mat 16 00 **Catering:** Foyer coffee/sandwich bar **Bars:** 6 **Wheelchairs:** Yes **Cloakrooms:** Yes **Parking:** NCPs St Martin's Lane & off Bedford St

Policy: Normal commercial West End Theatre, particularly suited to large spectacular musicals and revues.

Perspective: 'Let's all go down the Strand' meant something once when this part of London boasted many clubs and theatres, such as the Gaiety which has since been demolished. One of the survivors is the Adelphi, which dates back to 1806 when a successful colour maker built a theatre called the Sans Pareil to show off his daughter (who created the part of Black-Eyed Susan in 1829 at the Surrey).

Four theatres and as many names later, the present Adelphi was opened in 1930 under Charles Cochran with *Ever Green*, starring Jessie Matthews. It had been one of the most fashionable theatres in town: the novels of Walter Scott and Charles Dickens had been adapted, the first mechanical 'sinking stage' in Britain showed its mettle there in 1834, 'Adelphi dramas' had become a catch phrase in the 1880s and Sarah Bernhardt had appeared there twice.

The '30s were noted for revue and musicals. Ivor Novello's *The Dancing Years* ran for 969 performances after the original production at Drury Lane had been interrupted by the war. Jack Hilton's shows, starring names from radio and records, kept the Adelphi going until Woolworth's bought the lease. However, permission to convert into a store was denied while Beatrice Lillie was packing them in with *Auntie Mame*.

This success was followed by Lionel Bart's *Blitz!*, Dora Bryan in *Six of One*, another Bart hit, *Maggie May*, and the return of Anna Neagle in *Charlie Girl* (1965-71) with a little known actor Derek Nimmo who during the run became a broadcasting star. Musical revivals were obviously the ticket — *Show Boat*, *The King and I* and *Irene* followed and in a refurbished, plush auditorium, *My Fair Lady*, backed by the Arts Council. However, one tragedy lives on. Leading actor William Terriss was killed by a rival as he entered the theatre in 1897. Understandably upset, his ghost still haunts the Adelphi.

Underground: Charing Cross (Bakerloo, Jubilee, Northern)
Bus: 1, 3, 6, 9, 11, 12, 13, 15, 53, 77, 77A, 77C, 88, 159, 168, 170, 172, 176 or 24, 29 to Trafalgar Square.
Map: 155 N5

Africa Centre

38 King Street, Covent Garden WC2E 8JT
Box Office: **836 1973** (09 30-17 30) Admin: **836 1973**
Performance Space: Hall, moveable rostra, & small hall *Seating:* 150 (flexible)

Bookings: On completion of booking application forms only (cheques to Africa Centre) s.a.e Phone enquiries. Credit cards — Access, AmEx, Barclaycard/Visa, Diners. **Prices:** 75p-£2.50 **Concessions:** Reduced prices for members (see **Other**) **Perf Times:** Variable **Mailing List:** Free on application **Catering:** Calabash Restaurant Monday-Friday 12 30-15 00 & 17 30-23 00, Saturday 18 00-24 00 **Bars:** 2 (1 adjoining restaurant) **Wheelchairs:** Yes **Cloakrooms:** Yes **Parking:** NCPs Bedfordbury & off Bedford St **Other:** Films, lectures, workshops, exhibitions. Various membership schemes for reductions, newsletters & other facilities (Student £2.50 p.a., Ordinary £5, Affiliated Groups £7 & Corporate £25)

Policy: The Africa Centre exists to inform the British public about all aspects of African life and as a meeting place for Africans in London. It acts as a venue for amateur and professional groups with emphasis on productions concerning African affairs or portraying aspects of African culture.

Perspective: In the busy Covent Garden area, the Africa Centre offers not just an excellent and relaxed restaurant serving African dishes cooked by a Senegalese but also a chance to find out more about that important continent, whether you come from there or not.

The centre, was founded in 1964 as a focal point for African cultural affairs in Britain, offers courses on African subjects — literature, development, language, dance, early music, drama — as well as plays, films, discussions and exhibitions open to the public. The modern offices were once an 18th-century house, the elegant hall of which remains, with a wrought-iron gallery. It was also a glass warehouse, a book depository, an auction rooms and a fruit warehouse (as you would expect in this part of London). The centre was opened by Zambia's President Kaunda.

Theatre in the main and rear halls covers the range of the fringe and does not have to be related to Africa, although preference is obviously given to plays and groups concerned with Africa. One night you might find the Temba Theatre Group or the South African actress Yvonne Bryceland taking time off from the National Theatre across the river; another you might see the Women's Theatre Group or the Brixton Arts Theatre. Theatre of Contemporary Arabic Drama has also appeared here, presenting *Strangers Don't Drink Coffee* by Mahmoud Diyab.

Underground: Covent Garden, (Piccadilly)
Leicester Square (Northern, Piccadilly)
Bus: 1, 6, 9, 11, 13, 15, 77, 77A, 77C, 168, 170, 172, 176 to Strand or 24, 29 to Leicester Square Station
Map: 155 M4

Albany Empire (The Albany)

Creek Road, Deptford, SE8 3PU
Box Office: **691 4562** (10 00-18 00) Admin: **692 0765**
Performance Space: Hall, staging rostra *Seating:* 150 (tables & chairs on 3 sides)

Bookings: Members only 60p for six mths in advance & at door. Postal (cheques to The Combination Ltd.) s.a.e Phone & Ansaphone (held to ¼ hr before show) Credit cards — Access, Barclaycard/Visa. No travellers cheques **Prices**: £1.90 **Concessions:** Parties of 10+ Thursday and Sunday 60p, teenagers any show £1 **Perf Times:** 20 30 (Sundays 20 00) **Mailing List:** Members **Catering:** Hot & cold home-made buffet from 19 30 **Bars:** Yes, from 19 30 **Wheelchairs:** No **Cloakrooms:** No **Parking:** Car park **Other:** Every show followed by disco to 00 30

Policy: The Combination Theatre Group, lessees of the Albany, aims to use the building as widely as possible, not just as a theatre space but as a community centre offering concerts, workshops, dancing and youth activities. The theatre is also a venue where visiting groups can perform and where the local people can be encouraged to present their own shows. Emphasis is on issue-based plays, new works by resident writers, and the very popular cabaret performances.

Perspective: Set up by worthy Victorians to help the poor in south-east London, the Albany's Sunday school hall was completely refurbished in 1973, when it was opened as the Albany Empire by The Combination, one of Britain's first community theatre groups. The Combination had come to Deptford in 1971 after a period of touring which followed their departure from a Victorian school house in Brighton the year before. This had been their base for three years, and played an important part in the development of the fringe, presenting new shows (by such writers as Howard Brenton in his early days and John Grillo), discos, live bands, film and good food.

Since the move to London, the collective that runs the Albany has turned it into a busy local centre that encourages people to take control of their own lives and to express themselves creatively in so doing. A family squatting association and a claimants' union have come directly out of the Albany, and the community work covers all ages and concerns from pre-school to old age pensioner. The Combination Kids Co has put on shows such as *Journey into Outer Space* and *The Monster of the Blocks*, and the playscheme uses inflatables, tape recorders, puppets and much more.

The Combination has tried to revitalize theatre in the area with a variety of entertaining, popular productions from agitprop to pub shows and their own brand of music hall. The resident group is interested in plays about particular local issues (eg poor housing, racial problems) and invites political or socially-oriented touring groups to visit (eg Pirate Jenny, Monstrous Regiment, Gay Sweatshop, Women's Theatre Group). In 1978, the Albany was 'mysteriously' burnt down, and benefits for its reconstruction were held by other theatres and companies.

British Rail: Deptford
Bus: 1, 47, 70, 108B, 188
Map: 146 E

Albery Theatre

St. Martin's Lane, WC2N 4AH
Box Office: **836 3878** (10 00-20 00) Admin: **836 5650**
Performance Space: Proscenium arch *Seating:* 879 (4 levels)

Bookings: Postal (cheques to The Albery Theatre) s.a.e. Phone (held 4 days) Credit cards (379 6565, 09 00-20 00) Access, AmEx, Barclaycard/Visa, Diners. Sterling travellers cheques **Prices:** £3-£8 **Concessions:** Student Standby when available, Omega Party Bookings (836 3962) or to The Party Organizer, The Albery Theatre **Perf Times:** 19 45, Thursday & Saturday mats 16 00 **Catering:** Albery Lunch Bar Monday-Friday 12 00-15 00 **Bars:** 2 **Wheelchairs:** 3 **Cloakrooms:** 1 (Attendant) 4 (Paralok) **Parking:** NCP Upper St. Martin's Lane

Policy: Normal commercial West End theatre.

Perspective: The 30th theatre to be designed by W G R Sprague, the up-to-date New Theatre opened in 1903 under Charles Wyndham (on land acquired for Wyndham's Theatre). In 1941, it became the home of the Old Vic and Sadler's Wells companies, and in 1944, of the Old Vic alone (until 1950).

In 1973, the name was changed in memory of Sir Bronson Albery, head of the family group (Criterion, Donmar, Piccadilly, Wyndham's and Albery Theatres) whose mother Mary Moore had been married to Wyndham. Albery's grandson now runs it.

Listed as a building of architectural importance, it has a classical front, picturesque interior and a good view from most of the elegant Edwardian 18th-century style auditorium (brocade and velvet, panels, and a gilt emblem over the proscenium). Noël Coward's first produced play was staged here, but it is best known for its star shows and Shakespeare — John Gielgud's *Hamlet, Romeo and Juliet* with Gielgud and Laurence Olivier taking turns as Mercutio and Romeo, *As You Like It* (Edith Evans and Michael Redgrave), Ralph Richardson as Falstaff, and Olivier in *Richard III*.

Many women stars have trod its boards: Ingrid Bergman, Deborah Kerr, Katherine Hepburn, Mrs. Patrick Campbell, Peggy Ashcroft, Sybil Thorndike (St. Joan), and Fay Compton as Peter Pan. The theatre has also housed transfers from subsidized theatres such as the Mermaid, National, Royal Court and Royal Shakespeare Company, and changed its name during the latter's run of *London Assurance*, with Donald Sinden and Judi Dench — and written, appropriately, by Dion Boucicault whose son had become manager of the theatre in 1915. In 1977 *Oliver!* came back for more, having played 2,618 performances after its opening at this theatre in 1960.

Underground: Charing Cross (Bakerloo, Jubilee, Northern, British Rail), Leicester Square (Northern, Piccadilly)
Bus: 1, 24, 29, 176 or 3, 6, 9, 11, 12, 13, 15, 53, 77, 77A, 77C, 88, 159, 168, 170, 172, to Trafalgar Square
Map: 155 N4

Aldwych Theatre (Royal Shakespeare Company, RSC)

Aldwych, WC2B 4DF
Box Office: **836 6404** (10 00-20 00) Recorded info **836 5332** Admin: **379 6721**
Performance Space: Proscenium, raked stage thrusting beyond arch *Seating:* 1,004 (3 levels + boxes)

Bookings: Postal (allow 7-10 days, cheques to Aldwych Theatre) s.a.e. Phone (held 3 days) Credit cards (379 6233) AmEx, Access, Barclaycard/Visa, Diners **Prices:** £2-£7.50 **Concessions:** Student Standby £2 when available, parties 15+, OAPs & other special groups **Perf Times:** 19 30 eves, 14 00 Thursday & Saturday mats **Mailing List:** Full & Associated members (see **Other**) **Catering:** Snack bar for coffee & sandwiches (1 hr before show) **Bars:** 3 **Wheelchairs:** 2 (Dress Circle) **Cloakrooms:** 2 (Attendant and Paralok) **Parking:** Ample side streets after 18 30 **Other:** RSC Bookshop next door (Tuesday-Saturday 10 00-14 30, 17 45-19 45 Mondays 17 45-19 45); London Associate Membership £2 for limited priority bookings, leaflets and RSC Newspapers. Joint London/Stratford memberships also available.

Policy: The Royal Shakespeare Company aims to present Shakespeare with a contemporary awareness and, at its London venues (Aldwych and The Warehouse), to also stage those new plays and modern classics that have a strong sense of language and are best suited to the Company's disciplined approach to theatre. A core of associate artists, actors, directors and designers work together over long periods of time, ensuring the development of the Company's distinctive style.

Perspective: Before 1960 when the Aldwych became the London base of the Royal Shakespeare Company, it was best known for its '20s and '30s farces, mostly by Ben Travers with a team led by Tom Walls, Ralph Lynn, Robertson Hare, and Mary Brough. It was designed in 1905 by W G R Sprague as a pair with the Strand.

In 1911, the Stage Society presented the first performance in England of Chekhov's *The Cherry Orchard* — an appropriate foretaste of Peter Daubeny's World Theatre Seasons presented at the Aldwych by the Royal Shakespeare Company (RSC) from 1964 to 1975. The RSC itself has mixed new work, particularly Harold Pinter (eg *The Homecoming*) and David Mercer (eg *After Haggerty*), with revivals (eg *London Assurance, Wild Oats, Once in a Lifetime*) and, of course, Shakespeare's plays as they come year by year from Stratford-upon-Avon where the RSC is based.

Breaking world records for box-office success, the RSC has established itself as the foremost subsidized company in Britain, and its range of activity (four theatres, large and small scale touring, annual Newcastle season, West End transfers, television and film) is testament to the high standard of acting, design and direction. With Shakespeare, the RSC has led a revolution in production styles (from *The Wars of the Roses* to Peter Brook's *Dream*), and its more recent modern successes include *Destiny, Piaf* (both from the small RSC theatre started in Stratford by Buzz Goodbody), *Pillars of the Community*, and *Privates on Parade*.

Underground: Covent Garden (Piccadilly), Charing Cross (Bakerloo, Jubilee, Northern, British Rail), Temple (District, Circle)
Bus: 1, 4, 6, 9, 11, 15, 55, 68, 77, 77A, 77C, 168, 170, 171, 172, 176, 239, 501, 502, 513
Map: 155 M5

Alexandra Palace

Alexandra Park, Wood Green, N22 4AY
Box Office: **444 7203** (09 00-17 00 Monday-Friday) Admin: **444 7203**
Performance Space: 3 large halls with staging *Seating:* 6,000 The Great Hall, 350 The Edinburgh Room, 350 The Alexandra Room (all flexible)

Bookings: Postal (cheques to London Borough of Haringey) s.a.e. Phone (held 72 hrs) No credit cards or trevellers cheques **Prices:** Vary with show
Concessions: Variable **Perf Times:** Regular events: Thurs 20 00 Old Time Music Hall, Sunday lunchtimes jazz & children's shows. Other events variable
Catering: Restaurant facilities & bar snacks event-related **Bars:** Panorama Bar open normal pub hrs, 6 others, event-related **Wheelchairs:** Yes **Cloakrooms:** 2 (Attendants) **Parking:** Free for 2,000 cars **Other:** Guided tours of Alexandra Palace every Sunday Spring-Autumn

Policy: While used mainly as an Exhibition Centre, Alexandra Palace is also a venue for a wide range of professional and amateur events including music of all kinds, dance and occasional drama performances.

Perspective: What is the connection between Lenin and Real Ale? Answer: Alexandra Palace, that imposing tribute to Britain's imperial power which commands from its hill-top setting a picturesque, panoramic view of London. Lenin spoke there on May Day 1903, though recently Alexandra Palace (Ally Pally) has swung to different sounds — the London International Jazz Festival, guzzling at the Great British Beer Festival, scratching pen nibs at exam time, or the organ used for recitals.

Built on the site of a dairy farm by businessmen inspired by the Great Exhibition of 1851, the first palace was named after Alexandra of Denmark, who came to marry the Prince of Wales, and burnt down 16 days later. The second building, looking like a weird Gothic fortress, opened in 1875 but was only in use for 10 out of its first 25 years, and 5 of the first 8 managements went bust. In 1900, it was bought by the local authorities as a People's Palace, though it was not until 1974 that its future was put on a sound footing.

Even then, controversy raged. Should the 'jonah' be pulled down or used for the local citizens? The Alexandra Palace Action Group and Save Our Space campaigns were set up, and survive to keep an eye on the local Haringey Borough Council, which took over in 1980.

Ally Pally's long association with entertainment includes racing of all kinds — horse, penny farthing, roller, skate, boat, balloon and parachute — and the BBC's 40 years there (from the world's first outside broadcast and the arrival of mass viewing for the 1953 Coronation to the Open University). In 1971, Edward Bond's *The Passion* was played here as part of a CND rally. But as you stroll through the park past the pitch and putt and boating lake, think back to the extravagant firework displays of James Paine and watch out for the ghost of Blondin performing his high wire feats.

Underground: Finsbury Park (Piccadilly, Victoria), Wood Green (Piccadilly) then bus W3
Bus: 144, W2, W7 to Alexandra Park
Map: 146 F

Ambassadors Theatre

West Street, WC2H 9ND
Box Office: **836 1171** (10 00-20 00) Admin: **836 4797**
Performance Space: Proscenium arch *Seating:* 460 (2 levels, boxes)

Bookings: Postal (cheques to Ambassadors Theatre) s.a.e. Phone (held 4 days) Credit cards — Access, AmEx, Barclaycard/Visa, Diners. Sterling travellers cheques **Prices:** £2.50-£5.50 **Concessions:** Student Standby, Parties **Perf Times:** Vary **Catering:** No **Bars:** 2 (open ½ hr before show) **Wheelchairs:** 2 **Cloakrooms:** 1 (Attendant) 1 (Paralok) **Parking:** NCP Upper St Martin's Lane

Policy: Normal West End commercial venue.

Perspective: The stalls are found below ground level because the theatre had to be built low, so as not to interfere with the neighbours' view — a right known as ancient lights. the Ambassadors was planned with the St Martin's, but the second theatre had to wait 3 years to be finished — both were designed by W G R Sprague.

However, all history pales in the face of the slow burning but deadly effective time bomb of 25 November 1952 — the opening of Agatha Christie's *The Mousetrap*, which has notched up a string of world-beating records as the longest running show (the cast and direction changes, the words stay the same). Before that the Ambassadors had a reputation as the first theatre to stage an 'intimate revue' (it is a cosy place for a proscenium theatre). During the war, air raids led to daytime entertainments — Lunch Ballet, After Lunch Ballet and, naturally, After Tea Ballet, presented by Ballet Rambert and the London Ballet under the umbrella of the Arts Theatre Club.

Other 'firsts' include the debuts of Ivor Novello, and, in London, of Vivien Leigh. Paul Robeson appeared in 1925 in Eugene O'Neill's *Emperor Jones* — so perhaps it was appropriate that the first show of the new management after *The Mousetrap* moved next door took up Robeson's progressive tradition with two plays, *Sizwe Bansi is Dead* and *The Island*, originated in South Africa by Athol Fugard.

Underground: Covent Garden (Piccadilly), Leicester Square (Northern, Piccadilly)
Bus: 1, 14, 19, 22, 24, 29, 38, 176
Map: 155 M4

Apollo Theatre

Shaftesbury Avenue, W1V 7HD
Box Office: **437 2663** (10 00-20 00) Admin: **437 1872**
Performance Space: Proscenium arch *Seating:* 792 (4 levels, boxes)

Bookings: Postal (cheques to Apollo Theatre) s.a.e. Phone (held 3 days) Credit cards — Access, AmEx, Barclaycard/Visa, **Prices:** Vary with show **Concessions:** Coach & Party **Perf Times:** 20 00 & some mats **Catering:** Coffee from bars, confectionery, ices **Bars:** 3 **Wheelchairs:** Only if patron can make own way to seat from foyer **Cloakrooms:** 2 (Attendant) **Parking:** NCP Brewer St.

Policy: To provide a venue for shows requiring a medium-size West End theatre.

Perspective: In the turn-of-the-century rush of theatre building, the owner of the Apollo site offered a prize to anyone who suggested the name eventually chosen for the new theatre, which was built in 1901, the fourth in the recently opened Shaftesbury Avenue. Apollo was the Greek god of music, and the management wanted to stage mainly musicals.

To this end, the floor of the orchestra pit was hollowed and covered with a sounding board on which was placed a tiered rostrum. This helped achieve the right tone for each of the different instruments which occupied a different level of the rostrum. The badge of the first owner's family of German gypsies living in Poland can be seen in the dress circle.

In 1908, the Apollo became the home of the Pelissier Follies, while a different notoriety came 20 years later with the production of Robert Sherwood's *Idiot's Delight*, written in 1936 but foretelling the Second World War. Terence Rattigan's *Flare Path* had a remarkable run in 1942, but a mixed programme continued until the 3-year stint of the comedy *Boeing Boeing* (1962), which was followed by a transfer of another comedy *Spring and Port Wine*, then *The Flip Side*, John Gielgud in *40 Years On* and Gielgud again in a much-loved partnership with Ralph Richardson in David Storey's *Home*.

You can recognize the Apollo by its four statues, and, although there are no pillars, keep to the middle if possible and mind the steep balcony.

Underground: Piccadilly Circus (Bakerloo, Piccadilly)
Bus: 14, 19, 22, 38 or 3, 6, 9, 12, 15, 53, 88, 159 to Piccadilly Circus
Map: 154 N3

Arts Theatre Club (The Arts)

6/7 Great Newport Street, WC2H 7JA
Box Office: **836 3334** (10 00-20 30) Admin: **836 7541**
Performance Space: Proscenium arch *Seating:* 337 (2 levels)

Bookings: Members only (temporary at door 15p, monthly tourist 75p, annual £3.75) Postal (cheques to Arts Theatre) s.a.e. Phone (held 4 days) No credit cards. Travellers cheques **Prices:** Monday-Friday £1.60-£4, Saturday £1.85-£4.85 **Concessions:** None **Perf. Times:** Monday-Thursday 20 30, Friday & Saturday 19 00 & 21 15 **Catering:** Snack bar on stalls floor for salads, sandwiches, soups (12 00-20 30) **Bars:** 1 **Wheelchairs:** Yes **Cloakrooms:** No **Parking:** NCP St Martin's Lane

Policy: West End venue for visiting companies.

Perspective: The Arts was opened in 1927 with eating and drinking facilities as a club outside of the censorship restrictions operated by the Lord Chamberlain (whose powers lasted from George II's reign until 1968). The first notable production was *Young Woodley* by John van Druten (about an adolescent, which was banned). As well as being a lively and useful outlet for less commercial plays in an intimate proscenium theatre, the Arts played host to foreign companies, such as La Compagnie des Quinze with Michel Saint-Denis, brought over by Bronson Albery. During the war, it was the home of Lunch-Time Ballet.

In 1942, Alec Clunes took over, and with the Arts Theatre Group of Actors, for the next 12 years earned the title of 'a pocket National Theatre'. Peter Hall directed the British premieres of *Waiting for Godot* (1955) and *The Waltz of the Toreadors* (1956) and in 1962, with threats of demolition, film producer Nat Cohen took the lease, redecorated the theatre and introduced films and late-night entertainment, but not before the Royal Shakespeare Company had held its financially unrewarding but then daring experimental season of plays by Giles Cooper, David Rudkin, Maxim Gorky, Fred Watson, Boris Vian, Thomas Middleton and Henry Livings.

In 1967, Caryl Jenner's Unicorn Theatre for children (founded by her in 1948) moved in, providing shows for eight months of the year, the majority especially commissioned from established writers, and letting to other children's companies (including foreign ones) the rest of the time, while the Unicorn tours parks and playgrounds in the summer. In 1977 the Unicorn acquired a 20-year lease on the whole building, in which the Arts Theatre Club still has its members clubroom and bar, and messenger service.

Ed Berman's production of Tom Stoppard's double comedy bill *Dirty Linen* and *New Found-Land*, written as an ironic comment on the US 200th anniversary, transferred from the Almost Free in 1976 and became the longest running fringe show in London, beating Robert Patrick's *Kennedy's Children* which had also played at the Arts after its opening at the Kings Head.

Underground: Leicester Square (Northern, Piccadilly)
Bus: 1, 24, 29, 176 or 14, 19, 22, 38 to Charing Cross
Map: 155 M4

Ashcroft Theatre

Fairfield Halls, Park Lane, Croydon, CR9 1DG
Box Office: **688 9291** (10 00-20 00) Admin: **681 0821**
Performance Space: Proscenium arch *Seating:* 748 (2 Levels)

Bookings: Postal (cheques to Fairfield) s.a.e Phone (held 2 days) Credit cards (681 0578) Access, Barclaycard/Visa. **Prices:** £1.85-£4 **Perf Times:** Vary **Concessions:** Parties 1 free in 10 for 20 or more Combined dinner/show tickets **Mailing List:** £1.50 p.a. applications to General Office, Fairfield Halls **Catering:** Fairfield Restaurant (688 9291), licensed lunches Monday-Saturday 12 00-15 00, dinners Wednesday, Friday, Saturday 18 00-20 30. Foyer buffet, licensed, Monday-Saturday 10 30-21 00 for lunches, snacks, coffee **Bars:** 2 (Fairfield, Ashcroft) **Wheelchairs:** 3 **Cloakrooms:** Attendant **Parking:** Space for 1,800 adjacent to complex **Other:** Bookstall open before performances, during interval. All facilities open to public

Policy: Venue for a varied programme of plays, musicals, pantomime and amateur productions.

Perspective: Situated in a mixed outer suburb of south London, the Ashcroft Theatre is part of a post-war civic complex that falls into 3 main parts: the theatre, the Arnhem Gallery (which has many uses, from exhibitions and children's entertainments to conferences and fashion shows), and the Fairfield Hall, used primarily for concerts and recitals but also other activities, such as boxing and circus. These areas are separated, and soundproofed from each other, by six spacious lounges.

Taking up to 4,000 people at any one time, this arts and entertainments centre, which is owned by the local council, provides facilities for all kinds of pastimes, including dabbling with closed-circuit television or recording.

Locally-born actress Dame Peggy Ashcroft, after whom the theatre is named, appeared there in 1973 in a Harold Pinter double bill presented by the Royal Shakespeare Company. The theatre has interesting local productions and shows that go on to the West End.

The predecessors of today's patrons were, however, less culturally inclined. The annual Croydon fair, which started in 1314 and had changed from trading in sheep, cattle and corn to sideshows and travelling theatre, was banned in the middle of the last century because of rowdiness — a decision which itself led to rioting. Brighton Railway Company bought the site, which passed from being a goods yard to temporary offices and a car park before its traditional entertainment use was restored in 1962, at first housing the company which had occupied the Pembroke Theatre-in-the-Round.

British Rail: East Croydon or West Croydon
Bus: 12A, 50, 54, 64, 68, 109, 119, 119B, 130, 130B, 166, 166A, 194, 194B, 197, 233, C1, C3, C4, 403, 405, 408, 409, 411, 414, 455, 470, 483, 725, 726, OD853, 855, 857
Map: 148 **C**

Astoria Theatre (The Jam Factory)

157 Charing Cross Road, WC2H 0EN
Box Office: **734 4291, 439 8031, 734 4369** (10 00-20 00) Admin: **437 5757**
Performance Space: Converted cinema, open stage *Seating:* 1,141 (2 levels)

Bookings: Postal (cheques to Astoria Theatre) s.a.e. (held 3 days) Credit cards — Access, AmEx, Barclaycard/Visa, Diners. Sterling travellers cheques **Prices:** £2-£5 **Concessions:** Parties 10+ £1 reductions on £3, £4 & £5 seats Student Standby when available **Perf Times:** Monday-Thursday 20 00, Friday & Saturday 18 10 & 20 50 **Catering:** No **Bars:** 2 **Wheelchairs:** Yes **Cloakrooms:** Attendant (Circle) **Parking:** NCP St Martin's Lane **Other:** Foyer kiosk for souvenirs. Circle kiosk for souvenirs & confectionery

Policy: Normal commercial West End Theatre, concentrating on modern musicals.

Perspective: Built on the site of a jam factory — hence its nickname, the Jam Factory — the Astoria was opened as London's 'Supreme Cinema' in 1927. Then seating 2,000 with a ballroom downstairs (now a discotheque), it was designed by Frank Verity, the first specialist picture theatre architect. He was appointed by the Astoria/Paramount chain and pioneered the 'super de luxe' cinema at a time when there was a great rush for new cinemas, many of which are landmarks in their own towns and bear the stamp of their creators.

The Astoria had a wide Roman-style auditorium with a relatively modest proscenium arch, flanked by columns and a grill to hide the organ. The interior was changed in the '50s to accommodate the large screen needed for films like *Around the World in 80 Days*, with which the cinema re-opened. It was taken over by the Cooney/Marsh group, which had saved several theatres from closure — and without public funds — such as the Windmill, the Broadway, the Regent, the Kings Road, and the Shaftesbury Theatre (their different fates do not, however, paint a very bright picture).

With good backstage facilities and an open stage ideal for musicals, the Astoria opened in 1977 with *Elvis*, a tribute to the King that had 3 people playing him for the early, middle and late years of his life, and which saw this part of Charing Cross Road often besieged by Teds and Rockers dressed in the fashion of the '50s and '60s. Sunday night concerts were tried and *Elvis* was followed by *Grease*, and then by *Beatlemania*, with 4 look-alikes of the Liverpool lads. *Ipi Tombi* was transferred when the American Mersey sound failed to catch on.

Underground: Tottenham Court Road (Central, Northern)
Bus: 1, 7, 8, 14, 19, 22, 24, 25, 29, 38, 73, 134, 176
Map: 151 E5

Barbican Theatre (projected opening October 1981)

Barbican Centre, Cromwell Tower, Barbican EC2Y 8DO
Box Office: **subject to opening** (10 00-20 00) Admin: **638 4141**
Performance Space: Open stage with proscenium arch & Studio (The Pit)
Seating: 1,166 & 200

Bookings, Prices, Concessions, Perf Times: All subject to opening **Catering:** 2 main restaurants are planned, the Terrace and the Carvery, plus numerous buffets **Bars:** Numerous, incl a pub open normal pub hrs **Wheelchairs:** 8 (4 disabled + 4 escorts) + disabled toilets **Cloakrooms:** Yes **Parking:** 500 spaces in Centre; other nearby facilities **Other:** RSC bookshop, in addition to numerous other facilities outlined below, in foyer

Policy: Integral to the Barbican Centre policy is that the principal London operation of the Royal Shakespeare Company should transfer to its premises and that the RSC's existing policy will apply to its programme of performances at Barbican. The theatre may also be occasionally used by visiting companies or for conferences.

Perspective: The Barbican Centre for Arts and Conferences has been in the pipeline since 1955 when a firm of architects submitted a plan for redeveloping a war-devastated part of London near the City called the Barbican (a barbican is an outwork for the defence of a drawbridge in a fortified town. A street of this name was built partly on the site of a barbican in front of Aldersgate).

In 1964, the City engaged Anthony Besch, a leading theatre producer, to write a report on the proposed plans, and he suggested the involvement of a major company — which became the Royal Shakespeare Company (RSC) — and an orchestra, which became the London Symphony Orchestra. These would be linked to the Guildhall School of Music and Drama, which was having new premises built in the complex. Work began on the site in 1972 and the estimated cost is already £80.6 million. Regular public performances are scheduled from the autumn of 1981.

The centre also contains a 2,000-seat hall for concerts and conferences, a theatre (designed in consultation with the RSC), a studio theatre called The Pit, three cinemas (each fully equipped for conference use), an art gallery, a sculpture court, a library (lending music, records and children's books), five conference, meeting and seminar rooms, special function and catering areas, two trade exhibition halls, foyers, restaurants and car parks. When open, it will be the largest centre of its kind in Europe.

Underground: Barbican (Circle, Metropolitan), Moorgate (Circle, Metropolitan, Northern, British Rail), St Paul's (Central)
Bus: 4, 141, 279A, 502, or 8, 22, 25, 501 to St Paul's Station
Map: 157 R4

Bear Gardens Centre

1 Bear Gardens, Bankside, Southwark SE1
Box Office: **928 6342** (10 00-17 00) Admin: **928 6342**
Performance Space: 17th-century theatre replica *Seating:* 120

Bookings: Members only (+ guests) nominal charge, available in advance or at door. Phone bookings only (cheques to The Bear Gardens Museum & Arts Centre Ltd.) **Prices:** Max. £1 **Concessions:** No **Perf Times:** Variable with productions **Mailing List:** Free on application **Catering:** Tea, coffee, biscuits during show **Bars:** No **Wheelchairs:** No **Cloakrooms:** No **Parking:** Surrounding streets **Other:** Elizabethan Theatre History Museum open Friday-Sunday 10 30-17 00 & Wednesday & Thursday by appointment. Lectures, guided tours, slide shows — all bookable.

Policy: To provide demonstration and workshop performances of Elizabethan drama and Renaissance music, puppetry and dance. Productions by visiting companies, drama students and schoolchildren. Emphasis on educational work and Shakespeare.

Perspective: The Bear Gardens Muscum and Arts Centre was founded in 1972 to draw attention to the theatrical importance of an area on the south of the River Thames known as Bankside which runs from Blackfriars Bridge, opposite St Paul's Cathedral, down to Southwark Cathedral and London Bridge.

In the 16th and early 17th centuries, people would flock here by horse, boat or foot to see the plays of Shakespeare and his contemporaries performed at the Swan, the Rose or the most famous, the Globe. This was built by the son of former carpenter and travelling actor James Burbage, who had constructed what historians have called the first permanent professional public playhouse in the modern world.

This theatre was across the river in Shoreditch, also out of the City's bounds, but was pulled down in 1598. Its timber was used to build the Globe near to the Bear Ring, the success of which had given Burbage the idea of trying out a stationary theatre originally. The popular 'sport' of bear baiting lives on in the name of the Museum, which also celebrates the role this area played in the development of London as a trading city in the 19th century.

The performances and the permanent exhibition deal with the history of English theatre up to the start of the civil war period. It is hoped to redevelop the area further and preserve its warehouses. The locality is still fascinating and full of history. The best-known pub to try is the George Inn at Southwark which also serves as a theatre (see separate entry).

Underground: Cannon Street, (Circle, District, British Rail) or Mansion House (Circle, District) then walk across Southwark Bridge. London Bridge (Northern, British Rail) then bus 18
Bus: 95, 149, 176A
Map: 156 U3

Bush Theatre

Bush Hotel, Shepherd's Bush Green, W12 8QD
Box Office: **743 3388** (18 30-20 00) Admin: **602 3703**
Performance Space: Small room above pub, flexible staging
Seating: 90 (wooden blocks)

Bookings: Members only (+ 3 guests) 30p p.a. in advance or at door. Postal (pre-payment large parties only, cheques to The Alternative Theatre Company Ltd.) Phone in advance for collection & payment on night (held to ½ hr before show) No credit cards **Prices:** £2 **Concessions:** £1.75 Students, OAPs **Perf Times:** 20 00 Tuesday-Sunday **Catering:** Pub snacks **Bars:** As for pub, drinks can be taken into theatre **Wheelchairs:** Yes **Cloakrooms:** No **Parking:** Ample in streets behind Shepherd's Bush Green **Other:** Reciprocal membership with most other London club theatres. Occasional publicity mailings to members living in Hammersmith.

Policy: To present new plays by contemporary playwrights as a producing company hiring actors, designers and directors for each of its 6 to 7 annual productions. It also acts as a venue for touring companies.

Perspective: This cramped but friendly box of a theatre was set up by Brian McDermott in 1972 in what had been the dining room of the old Bush Hotel, standing on the corner of a large island of grass known as Shepherd's Bush Green in west London. The room had been used by the BBC for rehearsals, as it was just down the road from its Lime Grove studios, and as Lionel Blair's dancing studio. Now run by the Alternative Theatre Company, its versatile space has provided a home for many outstanding productions by new writers, the power of whose work has been enhanced by the close conditions (though not by the uncomfortable seating).

Early successes at the Bush included *Hitting Town* by Stephen Poliakoff, and his *City Sugar* which went into the West End and was broadcast on television. As well as being an important outlet for new writers like Robert Holman, and those who get short shrift elsewhere (eg Snoo Wilson), the Bush has also acted as a venue for new foreign plays in English, such as Franz Xavier Kroetz's *Stallerhof,* and for touring groups — Hull Truck, Women's Theatre Group, People Show, Lumiere and Son, and Wakefield Tricycle. It has also made a policy of staging Irish plays, because of the large Irish community. There are several cheap restaurants nearby (eg Balzac Bistro in Wood Lane), and Albestine's Wine Bar, Wood Lane.

Underground: Shepherd's Bush (Central, Metropolitan)
Bus: 12, 49, 72, 88, 105, 207, 220, 237, 295, 790
Map: 145 E

Cambridge Theatre

Earlham Street, WC2 9HU
Box Office: **836 6056** (10 00-20 00) Admin: **836 7183**
Performance Space: Proscenium arch *Seating:* 1, 280 (3 levels)

Bookings: Postal (cheques to Cambridge Theatre) s.a.e. Phone (held 3 days) Credit cards (836 7040) Access, AmEx, Barclaycard/Visa, Diners. Travellers cheques with identification **Prices:** Monday-Friday £2.50-£7.50 Saturdays £3.50-£8.50
Concessions: Parties 10+ discount; OAPs & Nurses (Mondays-Thursdays) when available; Student Standby **Perf. Times:** Eves, some mats **Catering:** Coffee, sandwiches in main bar; confectionery **Bars:** 4 with main & champagne/wine bars in stalls **Wheelchairs:** by prior arrangement if patron can be moved into seat
Cloakrooms: 2 (Attendant) **Parking:** NCP Upper St Martin's Lane.

Policy: To provide a venue for shows requiring a large theatre, mainly musicals, ballet and revues.

Perspective: Off Cambridge Circus (and not to be confused with the Palace which is on the Circus itself) this theatre with its *art deco* auditorium was built at a time of much theatre construction, in a once slum district of Covent Garden called Seven Dials (because seven streets met at a pillar with sundials, now moved to Weybridge, Surrey).

Standing on a corner, very modern, simple, symmetrical in design, with ribs across the ceiling getting nearer each other as you look toward the dress circle and each concealing lighting, the theatre was refurbished in 1950 with gilt chandeliers. Non-stop variety was at first the order of the day, opening with Beatrice Lillie in *Charlot's Masquerade*. There were then many transfers in a mixed programme that included visits from the Comedie Francaise, Sacha Guitry, and a season of Shaw.

In 1946, the theatre became the headquarters of the New London Opera Company under Jay Pomeroy, who had presented there earlier New Russian Ballet with a choreographer from the Moscow Opera House. After ballet and opera and Pomeroy's Sunday concerts, came new management, revue and the more obvious West End fare — *The Reluctant Debutante*, the stage version of *Billy Liar* (which ran from 1960 to 1962) and Tommy Steele in *Half a Sixpence*.

Subsequently a bumpy history has included visiting companies (69 Theatre, Prospect, National), revivals and musicals (notably, *Chicago*), which have kept the ball rolling, and after John Curry's Olympic success, an ice rink was put in for his balletic mixture of art and sport. The theatre also has a fine collection of Picasso prints.

Underground: Covent Garden (Piccadilly), Leicester Square (Northern, Piccadilly)
Bus: 1, 14, 19, 22, 24, 29, 38, 176
Map: 155 M4

Chats Palace

42-44 Brooksby's Walk, Homerton, E9 6DF
Box Office: **986 6714** (11 00-18 00 for phone bookings, from 19 15 in person)
Performance Space: Hall, flexible staging *Seating:* 150 (raked)

Bookings: Members only (+3 guests) 20p p.a. in advance or at the door. Postal (cheques to Homerton Community Centre Project) s.a.e. Phone (held to ½ hr before show) No credit cards or travellers cheques **Prices:** Max £1.20 **Concessions:** OAPs, children half-price **Perf Times:** Thursday-Saturday 20 00 **Mailing List:** £1 plus club membership entitles use of bar & various activities of the centre **Catering:** Hot & cold snacks Thursday-Saturday 19 00-23 00, Sunday 12 30-14 00 **Bars:** Members only. Real ale **Wheelchairs:** 5 + disabled toilet **Cloakrooms:** No **Parking:** Ample streets after 18 30 **Other:** Art exhibitions, drama workshops, & various community centre activities.

Policy: To provide good entertainment that will, first and foremost, reflect the interests of the multi-racial population of the area.

Perspective: A number of local organizations, including the committee which organizes the annual Hackney Marsh Fun Festival and Freeform, a local community arts group, set up a community/arts centre in the old Homerton Library, which had been vacated after the opening of a new building. The name Chats Palace came from the market (most weekdays and Saturdays) known as Chats, because it lies in the Chatsworth Road, which leads out of Brooksby's Walk. Chats Palace has a range of theatre activity from a regular programme of old-time music hall, social evenings, folk, jazz and rock music and productions by the resident theatre workshop. It is, in addition, a venue for performances by touring fringe theatre companies.

The Homerton Community Centre Project, which runs the centre, offers many other activities including a mothers' and toddlers' group, a youth club, a senior citizens' club, a supplementary school, and, from time to time, dance and other classes. Allow 75 minutes from central London.

British Rail: Hackney Downs then bus 38, 55, 106, 253 or walk to Urswick Road for bus S2
Map: 146 A

Churchill Theatre

High Street, Bromley, Kent BR1 1HA
Box Office: **460 6677/5838** (10 00-20 15 or when no show 10 00-18 00)
Admin: **464 7131** *Performance Space:* Two rolling stages *Seating:* 785 (2 levels)

Bookings: Postal (cheques to Churchill Theatre Trust Ltd)) s.a.e Phone (held 3 days) No credit cards **Prices:** £1.40-£3.40 **Concessions:** Parties (1 free seat in 10) Student Standby £1, OAPs £1, Thursday & Saturday mats **Perf Times:** Eves & Thursday/Saturday mats **Mailing List:** £1 p.a. for exclusive priority booking, 5-6 times p.a. **Catering:** Full-service restaurant (Monday-Saturday lunch & dinner plus Saturday tea) Combined dinner & theatre ticket Monday-Thursday £6.45, Friday £6.85 **Bars:** 1 (pub hrs); 1 (show times) **Wheelchairs:** 9 + disabled toilet in theatre **Cloakrooms:** 2 (Paralok) **Parking:** Car parks in Queens Rd, Lownds Ave, Elmfield Rd, Swan Hill Car Park at top of Beckenham Lane **Other:** Kiosk with posters, souvenirs, etc. open all day. Churchill Theatre Youth Section — 13-19 yrs youth theatre workshops. Churchill Concert Society — Sun concert series

Policy: A varied programme making full use of the technical facilities of the theatre, including concerts, new plays, revivals, pantomimes and musicals. The Churchill also aims to encourage good amateur groups.

Perspective: The proud history of the now defunct New Theatre, Bromley, went back to 1889. As the Grand Hall, which was advertised as 'pleasing alike to the aristocracy and the democracy', it offered plays, pantomime, lectures, lantern slides, minstrel shows, music hall, and, with the seats out, a dance floor that itself could be removed to make way for a swimming pool.

For the first 30 years of this century it flourished as a cinema, and during the war became a warehouse for the welfare services, with the swimming bath serving as air-raid shelter. Backed by film giant J Arthur Rank, it prospered as the New with weekly rep, attracting names such as Bryan Forbes, Noelle Gordon, Kenneth Williams and Nicholas Parsons. Actor Peter Goss and director David Poulson took it over in 1955 and progressed to three-weekly rep with more famous actors — Cicely Courtneidge, Margaret Rutherford, Jack Hulbert, Veronica Lake, Frankie Howerd, Sheila Hancock, Michael Bentine and, for the first time on stage, Cliff Richard.

The New was burnt out in 1971, having been threatened with closure in a redevelopment scheme blocked by local protest. It was suggested that the theatre could be rebuilt in a complex that was to house a new library and six shops, and this was approved only after ratepayers' objections and a Public Enquiry. The Prince of Wales opened the new building in 1977, since when it has not been free of management controversy but has presented a solid, all-round programme of professional theatre ranging across the board from *Cinderella* and *Sleuth* to Alan Ayckbourn and a one-man show about Bernard Shaw.

British Rail: Bromley North or Bromley South
Bus: 47, 61, 94, 119, 119B, 126, 138, 146, 227, B1, 402, 410, 705, 706, 725, 726
Map: 145 G

Cockpit Theatre

Gateforth Street, NW8 8EH
Box Office: **402 5081** (10 00-20 00) Admin: **262 7907**
Performance Space: Flexible *Seating:* 120, 180 or 240

Bookings: Postal (cheques to Cockpit Theatre)) s.a.e Phone (held 3 days or to ½ hr before show) No credit cards **Prices:** £1-£2 **Concessions:** Parties, students, OAPs 10-20 per cent discount **Perf Times:** 19 30 or 20 00 **Mailing List:** Free — contact theatre **Catering:** Coffee bar, snacks, open before & during show **Bars:** No **Wheelchairs:** 4 **Cloakrooms:** Paralok **Parking:** Street after 18 30 **Other:** Cockpit Education Publications (scripts, resource materials) from main office. Workshops for 18-24 yrs in drama and music with public shows (£1.50 p.a. under 18, £8.75 p.a. adults)

Policy: The Cockpit rents the theatre space to amateur semi-professional and professional groups which will benefit from its use and support its educational outlook. Other groups are invited to use the theatre as guests of the Cockpit.

Perspective: The Cockpit was built in 1967 on the site of the Gateforth Primary School and opened in January 1970 with a 3-month festival. It was the first arts workshop to be purpose-built by London's local education authority, a pioneer in the country. The theatre, modern, flexible and with good acoustics, forms part of an interlocking set-up, the broad concern of which is to bridge the gap between secondary school activity and out-of-school leisure time. The groups that use the Cockpit and the productions that arise from within the centre promote this educational idea (eg a summer youth production called *The Yeast Factory* looked at pacifism and explored the need for tolerance and concern for one's fellow workers).

The Cockpit operates as a teachers' centre, a youth centre (encouraging participation in different arts), a place to stimulate ideas that can be followed up in the classroom or college, a springboard into the community, a workshop in which artists in different media can work with young people, and as a renowned theatre-in-the-round. Dance, music, art, can be found alongside the theatre events, which include a permanent theatre-in-education team started in 1972 as part of a local education plan.

The Cockpit works with the Curtain Theatre in the east of London, Greenwich Young People's Theatre in the south-east, and Group 64 in the south-west. It is the main venue for the annual London International Mime Festival, which brings outstanding artists, such as Nola Rae, to a wide public. Nearby in Lisson Grove, off the Marylebone Road, is one of London's best fish and chip shops, *The Seashell*. There is usually a queue, so be patient and be prepared.

Underground: Marylebone (Bakerloo, British Rail)
Bus: 159
Map: 150 D1

Collegiate Theatre

15 Gordon Street, WC1H 0HH
Box Office: **387 9629** (10 00-20 00) Admin: **388 3363**
Performance Space: Proscenium arch *Seating:* 560 (2 levels, well raked)

Bookings: Postal (cheques to Collegiate Theatre) s.a.e Phone (held 3 days) No credit cards. Sterling travellers cheques **Prices:** Vary according to show **Concessions:** OAPs, students, children under 14, claimants 50p off or half-price according to show **Perf Times:** Normal student productions Thursday-Saturday term-time, other prods Monday-Saturday, particularly summer months. Eves 19 30 or 20 00; occasional mats **Mailing List** Free on application to Collegiate Theatre Mailing List **Catering:** Coffee bar open daily, serving quiches, snacks eves from 18 00 **Bars:** 1 open 45 min before show **Wheelchairs:** 6 **Cloakrooms:** 1 (Attendant) **Parking:** Ample streets after 18 30.

Policy: A mixed-media university theatre operating an educational policy for half the year, when its facilities are used by the University of London student societies, and hosting a variety of touring events at other times. There is a strong musical bias with emphasis on ballet, opera, concerts (including lunch-times), rock and jazz. The theatre is available for external hire for mid-March to end-September and during the Christmas vacation.

Perspective: Well-equipped and comfortable, the Collegiate Theatre was opened in 1968, and only came to be hired out to visiting companies (for six months of the year) because of financial problems. In 1974, the Collegiate housed the revival of *West Side Story* which then transferred to the Shaftesbury. The following year, Lindsay Kemp presented *Flowers* and David Wood brought his children's show *The Owl and the Pussycat*, though nowadays at Christmas there is the *Magic Circle Show*.

Other notable theatre events have included, in 1976, a season of international theatre that presented, among others, *The Amazons, The Sacred Flute,* and *Ondeki-Za*. In 1977, Steven Berkoff presented *Metamorphosis*, and Belt and Braces tackled the impossible with a political musical, *A Day in the Life of the World*. The theatre scored a 'first' in 1979 with the opening season of the British-American Repertory Company, set up mainly through the hard work of Ed Berman and the two performers' unions either side of the Atlantic. The company staged *Dogg's Hamlet* and *Cahoot's Macbeth*, two funny squibs by Tom Stoppard.

As well as providing an outlet for opera and ballet, both classical and modern, the Collegiate also is used for television and radio events. Tchaikovsky's *Atilla the Hun*, therefore, appears in the same theatre as David Frost, Prokofiev next to Michael Parkinson. Jazz, with Cleo Laine and Johnny Dankworth, for example, is also popular alongside rock. The rest of the year, the Collegiate operates under the aegis of University College London.

Underground: Euston Square (Circle, Metropolitan)
Bus: 14, 18, 24, 29, 30, 68, 73, 77, 77A, 77C, 134, 170, 176, 188, 239
Map: 151 D5

Comedy Theatre

Panton Street, SW1 4DN
Box Office: **930 2578** (10 00-20 00) Admin: **839 5522**
Performance Space: Proscenium arch *Seating:* 820 (4 levels, boxes)

Bookings: Postal (cheques to Comedy Theatre) s.a.e. Phone (held 3 or 4 days)
Credit cards — AmEx, Access, Barclaycard/Visa. Sterling travellers cheques
Prices: Vary **Concessions:** Parties 15+ price reductions. No Student Standby
Catering: No **Bars:** 3 **Wheelchairs:** No **Cloakrooms:** 1 (Attendant) **Parking:** Avis
24hr multi-storey Orange Street **Other:** Souvenir Kiosk when available

Policy: Normal West End commercial theatre.

Perspective: The area round the corner from the Theatre Royal, Haymarket, off Leicester Square had a low reputation up until the 1880s when the Royal Comedy Theatre opened (it was to have been called the Lyric or Alexandra). The first years saw a mixture of comic opera, for which the theatre was built, drama and farce. Many then famous names were associated with the theatre and Beerbohm Tree first tried his hand at management here. The word 'Royal' was dropped in 1884.

With the turn of the century came the 'new drama' and Frank Benson's company. John Barrymore made his first London appearance, and Gerald du Maurier made his name as the gentleman crook Raffles. A steady run of good productions kept the Comedy alive up to and through the war. In 1954 it underwent more thorough renovation than its previous reconstructions and redecorations, which had left architect Thomas Verity's Renaissance style more or less undisturbed (it had the oldest Victorian auditorium until the '50s modernization). *The Threepenny Opera* and Brendan Behan's *The Quare Fellow* were among the opening productions.

In 1956, the New Watergate Theatre Club was formed at the Comedy to present US plays that had been banned by the Lord Chamberlain (eg Arthur Miller's *A View from the Bridge*, *Cat on a Hot Tin Roof* by Tennessee Williams). Membership rose to 68,000 and this played a part in weakening the censor's authority.

Peter Shaffer's *Five Finger Exercise*, directed by John Gielgud, was followed by the Royal Court transfer of Ibsen's *Rosmersholm* with Peggy Ashcroft. Successful transfers or revivals of modern plays have been the keynote since — Spike Milligan in *The Bed Sitting Room* and *Oblomov*, the Open Space production *Fortune and Men's Eyes*, set in prison, the Mermaid's *Let's Get a Divorce*, *A Girl in My Soup* (which notched up over 2,500 performances), Paul Scofield in Christopher Hampton's *Savages* from the Royal Court, David Hare's *Knuckle*, Stephen Poliakoff's *City Sugar*, Simon Gray's *Otherwise Engaged*, Alec McCowen in *St Mark's Gospel* and *The Rocky Horror Show*.

Underground: Piccadilly Circus (Bakerloo, Piccadilly)
Bus: 3, 6, 9, 12, 13, 15, 53, 88, 159 or 14, 19, 22, 38 to Piccadilly Circus
Map: 155 N4

Company of Three

Fountains Abbey Pub, 109 Praed Street, W2 1RL
Box Office: **723 2364** (11 00-15 00 & 17 30-23 00) Admin: **723 2619**
Performance Space: Upstairs pub room *Seating:* 60

Bookings: Phone (held until ½ hr before show) In person. No credit cards **Prices:** £1.30 **Concessions:** Students, OAPs **Perf Times:** 19 30 **Catering:** Pub food incl eve meals **Bars:** Pub downstairs **Wheelchairs:** No **Cloakrooms:** No **Parking:** NCP in Harbet Rd (off Edgware Rd) **Other:** 10p membership gives seat price reductions

Policy: The pub theate is used by the resident Company of Three to present classical plays not normally seen in the repertoire of larger theatres, with concentration on the actors and the text, rather than elaborate scenery and sets.

Perspective: Anthony Homyer and James Gilhouly created the Company of Three out of their mutual dissatisfaction with commercial theatre, and their common belief that many classics that are left to get dusty on library shelves are in fact worthy of productions and of great dramatic value. Gilhouly trained and worked in his early career with Joan Littlewood, and went on to develop a strong reputation for his modern *mise-en-scene* of 17th and 18th century revivals.

In 1976 Homyer and Gilhouly first collaborated on *Lover Come Back* by James Dawson at the now-defunct Little Theatre. They were so encouraged by the reception of their work that a permanent venue was set up in Hounslow, where they presented work ranging from melodrama to Euripides. Such fare, while attracting an audience from central London, was not involving the Hounslow community, and it became clear that a central London venue was required. Their one year in a Hammersmith pub is best remembered for the Japanese Noh plays that were put on there (among the first to be seen in Britain), until they settled at the Fountain's Abbey, Paddington in February 1979.

Beginning with lunchtime shows, the Company of Three proved so successful that the landlord soon offered them evening performances, which have included such rarely seen pieces as Oscar Wilde's *The Florentine Tragedy*, Seneca's *Thyestes* (which Michael Billington said 'put Roman tragedy back on the map') and a Chinese opera called *Butterfly Dream*. The pub itself offers a warm setting, with a wall-tile picture of a scene from *As You Like It* and a continuously burning log fire.

Underground: Paddington (Bakerloo, Circle, District, Metropolitan)
Bus: 7, 15, 27, 36, 36B or 6, 8, 16, 16A, 18, 18A, 176, 616, 708, 719 to Edgware Road Praed Street
Map: 150 E1

Cottesloe (National Theatre)

Upper Ground, South Bank, SE1 9PX
Box Office: **928 2252** (10 00-20 00) **928 2256** (24 hr recorded booking)
Admin: **928 2033** Other information: **633 0880**
Performance Space: Rectangular box *Seating:* 350-400 (3 levels)

Bookings: Postal (cheques to National Theatre) s.a.e Phone (held 3 days) Credit cards (928 3052) Access, AmEx, Barclaycard/Visa, Diners. Sterling travellers cheques **Prices:** £3 (unnumbered; sometimes cheaper) **Concessions:** Student Standby 45 mins before show £1.20 **Perf Times:** Normally 20 00 **Mailing List:** See **Other** in National Theatre entry **Catering:** Snack bar & NT Restaurant **Bars:** 1 from 18 00-23 00 **Wheelchairs:** Yes (633 0880) **Cloakrooms:** 1 (Attendant) **Parking:** NCP under theatre **Other:** See National Theatre entry

Policy: Based on the belief that many important changes in the theatre begin on a small scale and before a limited audience, the Cottesloe aims to provide the National Theatre complex with a future-oriented venue where such changes may be accommodated, and enjoyed by the enquiring theatregoer.

Perspective: Contrary to rumour, the small, experimental auditorium of the National Theatre complex was always part of the plans — but it was also very much at the bottom of the ladder. The last of the three theatres in the complex to open, it has its own entrance and facilities, round the back past the stage door serving all three theatres. The Cottesloe began with great promise in March 1977 — one year after public performances had started in the first of the theatres to open, the Lyttelton (see separate entry under National Theatre).

The launch saw a visiting company occupy the flexible, smoothly finished box of a theatre for 12 hours at each performance — Ken Campbell's Science Fiction Theatre of Liverpool with their cult show *Illuminatus*. The first new play presented by the National here was *Strawberry Fields* by Stephen Poliakoff, but thoughts of the Cottesloe becoming a vigorous centre for experiment were soon dimmed; and Shane Connaughton's *Sir is Winning*, a documentary treatment of a case involving new educational methods that had become national news, had a rough passage.

However, under Bill Bryden, who has gathered together a core of actors led by Jack Shepherd, a style has emerged based on a series of highly popular promenade productions (*The Passion, The World Turned Upside Down, Lark Rise* and its companion *Candleford Down.*) The actors move among the audience as the play develops, switching from one part of the theatre to the next. If you are not careful, you get knocked down by the village postman.

Underground: Waterloo (Bakerloo, Northern, British Rail)
Bus: 1, 4, 55, 68, 70, 76, 149, 168A, 171, 176, 188, 239, 501, 502, 503, 507, 513
Map: 155 N6

Criterion Theatre

Piccadilly Circus, W1V 9LB
Box Office: **930 3216** (10 00-20 15) Admin: **930 0991**
Performance Space: Proscenium arch *Seating:* 592 (3 levels, boxes)

Bookings: Postal (cheques to Criterion Theatre) s.a.e. Phone (held 3 days) Credit cards (379 6565) to Wyndhams Theatres Ltd — Access, AmEx, Barclaycard/Visa, Diners. Dollar & sterling travellers cheques. US dollars accepted **Prices:** £2.50-£6 **Concessions:** Omega Party Bookings (836 3692) for parties 12+, Student Standby when available **Catering:** No **Bars:** 2 **Wheelchairs:** 1 (Paralok) **Cloakrooms:** NCPs Whitcomb St & Brewer St

Policy: Normal commercial West End Theatre; plays and reviews.

Perspective: A huge restaurant called The Criterion was built in 1837 on the site of a posting inn that had stood in Regent Circus (as Piccadilly Circus was then known) since the late 17th century. At the last minute, it was decided to convert the middle of the building, which was to have been a concert hall, into a theatre — but one with a difference: it was underground, and air had to be pumped in. Charles Wyndham made it fit for human use in 1884 (bringing in electricity and sunshine), and it was redecorated in 1902/3.

Today, it still has that cosy late-Victorian feel, with pink a predominant colour. It has also kept its wall decorations and tile work, and, apart from the entrance and foyer, everything is below stairs. The first shows were light and comic (and apparently one 'from the French' shocked the critics) and this reputation was confirmed in the First World War when one of the big hits of the day, *A Little Bit of Fluff*, played for 1,241 performances.

The Criterion's 'leading lady' Mary Moore took over in 1919 when her husband Wyndham died, and her great-grandson now runs the theatre. Farce and comedy continued to rule, with Mary Tempest appearing in many shows in the '20's, and Terence Rattigan's *French Without Tears* running for 1,039 performances from 1936. Afer a short spell under the BBC, the theatre reopened in 1945 with Edith Evans as Mrs Malaprop. Its recent successes include *A Severed Head, Mrs Wilson's Diary, Brief Lives, Flint, Butley, Absurd Person Singular* and *Bent*.

Underground: Piccadilly Circus (Bakerloo, Piccadilly)
Bus: 3, 6, 9, 12, 13, 14, 15, 19, 22, 38, 53, 88, 159
Map: 154 N3

Croydon Warehouse Theatre

62 Dingwall Road, Croydon CR0 2NE
Box Office: **680 4060** (10 30-20 30) Admin: **680 4060**
Performance Space: Upstairs studio, variable *Seating:* 70-80 plus

Bookings: Members only (+ 1 guest 30p six months or £5 p.a. for groups & at door) Postal (cheques to the Croydon Warehouse) s.a.e. Phone (held to ¼ hr before show) No credit cards **Prices:** £1 Tuesday-Thursday; £1.50 Friday-Saturday **Concessions:** Students 30p reduction. OAPs, Equity Usually 19 45, occasional lunchtime & Sundays **Mailing List:** 50p p.a. for 3 mailings **Catering:** Snack bar ½hr before & after show (lunchtimes & eve) & intervals **Bars:** No **Wheelchairs:** No **Cloakrooms:** No **Parking:** NCP in Dingwall Road **Other:** Membership offers reciprocal membership with other fringe theatres. Associate membership (for groups) allows any part of the group to attend.

Policy: The Croydon Warehouse is a producing company staging new and rarely performed plays to a largely local audience. There is no resident company and new productions are staged every 3 weeks.

Perspective: Not to be confused with the Royal Shakespeare Company's Warehouse in Covent Garden, this adventurous fringe theatre to the south of London (near the Ashcroft) was started before the other Warehouse in May 1977 by three professional actors. They felt the need for more relevant and modern work in the area, and have expanded considerably since they spent £500 on converting an old electrical warehouse that was then also a night club. Premises (not productions!) are still a little primitive, but the theatre is developing all the time, having redecorated, built a box office and moved on from lunchtime-only shows to evenings as well.

The Croydon Warehouse started with backing from local firms and was given a grant from the public purse. Co-founder and artistic director Richard Ireson sees the future of the company as lying in regular audiences from the neighbourhood, and hopefully a theatre-in-education team will be launched. Already there are workshops and 'teach-ins'.

The concentration so far has been on British plays — *My Girl* and *Abide With Me* by Barrie Keeffe, *Double Double* by James Saunders — but not exclusively, Athol Fugard's *Statements* was seen here recently, as was the Temba Theatre Company and a group called Camouflage presenting *The 1980 Spit and Polish Girlie Show*. A musical was staged to commemorate the 50th anniversary of Amy Johnson's flight from Croydon Airport to Darwin, Australia, and another recent show was *Dracula*, using the original 1927 script which had the Count baring his fangs in — guess where — Croydon.

British Rail: East or West Croydon
Bus: 12A, 50, 54, 64, 68, 109, 119, 119B, 130, 166, 166A, 194, 194B, 197, 233, C1, C3, C4, 403, 405, 408, 408, 411, 414, 455, 470, 483, 725, 726, OD853, 855, 857
Map: 148 C

Curtain Theatre

26 Commercial Street, E1 6LB
Box Office: **247 6788** (10 00-20 00 on perf. days) Admin: **247 6788**
Performance Space: Proscenium arch *Seating:* 355

Bookings: Postal (cheques to Curtain Theatre) s.a.e. Phone (held to ½ hr before show) No credit cards or travellers cheques **Prices:** £1-£2 variable according to show **Concessions:** Normally children & OAPs half price **Perf. Times:** Thursday & Friday 19 30 for most amateur productions; some Saturday mats of school prods; other times for visiting companies **Catering:** Cafe from 18 00 on nights of show **Bar:** No **Wheelchairs:** 1 **Cloakrooms:** No **Parking:** NCPs Aldgate East Station & Commercial St, Streets after 18 30 **Other:** Courses & projects in educational drama work.

Policy: Courses and projects for schools, colleges and institutes. The theatre has its own company of professional actor-teachers and directors, and hires in other professionals for its schools productions, performances of which are sometimes available to the public. The Curtain also acts as a venue for amateur productions and occasionally for visiting professional companies.

Perspective: In London's East End, near streets made notorious by Jack the Ripper, stands the home of the Inner London Education Authority's stagecraft centre, the Curtain Theatre. Appropriately, the area is also associated with a different, if less well-known, bit of history, one very much connected to the theatre.

It was in 1577 that the first Curtain Theatre was opened, taking its name not from drama but from Curtain Close, on Finsbury Fields, a name which survives today in nearby Curtain Road, Shoreditch. The site of the theatre adjoined a favourite spot for recreation, especially archery, was next door to the first permanent, professional public playhouse, built in 1576, called simply The Theatre, by former carpenter and travelling actor James Burbage.

The present building was opened in 1938 as the Toynbee Hall Theatre, and was used by professional and amateur companies until 1950. The Greater London Council took it over in 1964 when it became the Educational Stagecraft Centre of the education authority, running useful courses in all aspects of theatre craft as well as performing its own educational shows. The theatre-in-education team works in association with similar local authority ventures in Greenwich (south-east — see separate entry), Fulham's Group 64 (south-west) and the central theatre, the Cockpit in north-west London. The Curtain's most notable recent use by outside companies was by an emerging Bengali drama group and during the impressive International Festival of Puppets in 1979. Round the corner in Whitechapel is Bloom's, the famous Jewish restaurant, and Tubby Isaac's renowned jellied-eel stall.

Underground: Aldgate (Circle, Metropolitan) Aldgate East (District, Metropolitan)
Bus: 9, 10, 15, 22A, 23, 25, 40, 42, 44, 67, 95, 253, 723
Map: 157 S6

Duchess Theatre

Catherine Street, Covent Garden, WC2B 5LA
Box Office: **836 8243** (10 00-20 00) Admin: **836 0943**
Performance Space: Proscenium arch *Seating:* 477 (3 levels)

Bookings: Postal (cheques to Duchess Theatre) s.a.e. Phone (held 2 days) Credit cards (836 8243) Access, AmEx, Barclaycard/Visa, **Prices:** £2-£7 (variable) **Concessions:** According to show **Catering:** Confectionery, ices only **Bars:** 2 **Wheelchairs:** No **Cloakrooms:** Paralok **Parking:** NCP Bedfordbury (back of Strand)

Policy: West End commercial theatre.

Perspective: Planning problems and the depression had kept a site vacant for some years just down the road from the Theatre Royal, Drury Lane. Architect Ewen Barr, however, overcame local objections by designing a theatre on two levels, with the circle narrower than the stalls and supported by steel hangers from roof-level girders. This gives a good view all round in one of the West End's snuggest theatres, though an appropriately cosy forerunner to *Oh! Calcutta!* called *The Intimate Revue* (1930) had the shortest run ever when the curtain came down before the end of the first night.

The '30s were not all bad for the Duchess, with its 'modern Tudor Gothic' exterior of three jutting bays and panels under the windows. Successful productions by the People's National Theatre were followed by an all-women *Children in Uniform* with Jessica Tandy, written and translated from the German by women.

J B Priestley was associated with the management for a couple of years, and several of his plays have been staged there (eg *Laburnum Grove, Eden End, The Linden Tree*). The hit of the decade was the thriller *Night Must Fall*, starring and written by Emlyn Williams (who had appeared in the theatre's first show). His *The Corn is Green* played until the war stopped productions.

One of the first shows after re-opening was the transfer of Noel Coward's *Blithe Spirit*, which held the record for the longest run of a play until overtaken by *The Mousetrap*. Other transfers include *Murder in the Cathedral*, Harold Pinter's *The Caretaker*, *Alfie, Wait Until Dark*, and, of course, *Oh! Calcutta!* which was still thought very daring when it transferred from the Royalty in 1974.

Recently the auditorium was overhauled and a new lighting system installed.

Underground: Covent Garden (Piccadilly), Charing Cross (Bakerloo, Jubilee, Northern) Temple (Circle, District)
Bus: 1, 4, 6, 9, 11, 13, 15, 55, 68, 77, 77A, 77C, 168, 170, 171, 172, 176, 188, 239, 501, 502, 513
Map: 155 M5

Duke of York's Theatre

St. Martin's Lane, WC2N 4BG
Box Office: **836 5122/3** (10 00-20 00) Admin: **836 4615**
Performance Space: Proscenium arch, domed auditorium *Seating:* 641

Bookings: Postal (allow 7 days, cheques to Duke of York's Theatre) s.a.e. Phone (held 4 days) Credit cards — Access, AmEx, Barclaycard/Visa. Sterling travellers cheques **Prices:** £2-£6.50 **Concessions:** Student Standby when available. Parties 20+ discounts **Perf Times:** Eves 20 00, Wednesday mats 15 00, Saturday 17 00 **Catering:** Coffee, sandwiches from bars **Bars:** 2 **Wheelchairs:** 1 (Royal Circle) **Cloakrooms:** 1 (Attendant) **Parking:** NCP Upper St Martin's Lane, Trafalgar Square, Bedfordbury

Policy: Normal commercial West End Theatre.

Perspective: The theatre was taken over by Capital Radio and reopened early in 1980 with Glenda Jackson in *Rose* following a gala opening which included a chorus line of actors who had played Peter Pan (which was first produced at the Duke of York's).

The original theatre, called the Trafalgar Square Theatre, was built on the back of the Garrick and was the first in St Martin's Lane. The pretty auditorium, with its imposing chandelier in the dome, was warmed by three fires. Its custom of keeping some seats unreserved remains.

Reconditioned after the war when it was damaged, the theatre was redecorated to a design by Cecil Beaton. Two names recur during the early years: the American manager Charles Frohman encouraged exchange between his country and Britain, and ran a repertory season which included plays by the second outstanding name associated with the theatre — J. M. Barrie.

Apart from *Peter Pan*, many of his plays were first staged here — for example, *The Admirable Crichton*, which caused a sensation because on the first night the scene shifters went on strike and the cast had to move scenery themselves.

Most recently remembered of many notable productions are the revue *One Over the Eight*, a revival of Coward's *Private Lives*, Anouilh's *Poor Bitos*, *The Killing of Sister George*, Alan Ayckbourn's *Relatively Speaking* and Arthur Miller's *The Price*.

And there is a ghost — not of Puccini, who saw a one-act play there called *Madame Butterfly* and turned it into an opera, nor of Charlie Chaplin, who played in *Sherlock Holmes* yet was too insignificant then to be invited to the Royal Retiring Room. The ghost is that of Violette Melnotte, one half of the acting team that first ran the theatre, who lived there and was described as difficult. Just after 22 00, you can hear her closing an old iron fire door, long since gone — but you have to be quick.

Underground: Charing Cross (Bakerloo, Jubilee, Northern)
Leicester Square (Northern, Piccadilly)
Bus: 1, 24, 29, 176 or 3, 6, 9, 11, 13, 15, 53, 77, 77A, 77C, 88, 159, 168, 170, 172 to Trafalgar Square
Map: 155 N4

The Earl Russell

2 Pancras Road, NW1 2SY
Box Office: **537 5503** (09 00-23 00, enquiries only) Admin: **837 5503**
Performance Space: Upstairs pub room *Seating:* 60 (flexible)

Bookings: At the door. Phone enquiries only **Prices:** Vary with show **Concessions:** Variable **Perf Times:** According to show **Catering:** Bar snacks **Bars:** As for pub
Wheelchairs: No **Cloakrooms:** No **Parking:** Pancras Road

Policy: Newly opened venue for hire to fringe theatre groups.

Perspective: It is always good to see a newly-opened venue. This one, to the back of King's Cross, can be found in a pub that dates back to the 1860s, when it served thirsty railway workers coming from St Pancras or King's Cross. It has an old fashioned appearance with its original facade, although it was redecorated between November 1978 and January 1979. It is cheap to hire and welcomes amateurs or professionals, and can also be used as a rehearsal space; the large carpeted room used as the theatre may accommodate a platform or whatever staging and seating arrangements the performing group provides. To date, shows have included *Foreplay* with the One in Ten Theatre Company and a production by a Birmingham gay theatre group.

The policy of the landlord is to 'play by ear' the evolution of the Earl Russell into a regular theatre pub — for the time being it seems to be one of the most straightforward and accessible venues available to low-budget groups for central London performances.

Underground: Kings Cross St Pancras (Circle, Metropolitan, Northern, Piccadilly, Victoria, British Rail)
Bus: 14, 18, 30, 45, 46, 63, 73, 77, 77A, 77C, 168A, 214, 221, 239, 259, 263
Map: 151 B6

The Embassy Club

7 Old Bond Street, W1X 3TA
Box Office: **499 5974** (24 hrs) Admin: **499 5974**
Performance Space: Discotheque area *Seating:* 200 (incl at tables & bar)

Bookings: Members only (£75 p.a. UK residents; £20 per month for overseas visitors with free admission, or £25 p.a. paying entrance fee in addition) Membership 48hrs in advance. **Prices:** Free for members up to 23 00, £4 thereafter and for guests **Concessions:** No **Perf Times:** 21 00 & 02 00
Mailing List: Free for members **Catering:** Full restaurant meals round-the-clock, incl breakfast 03 30-10 00 Monday-Saturday, tea 15 30-1800 Monday-Friday **Bars:** Monday-Friday 12 30-1500 & 18 30-0300. Saturday 20 00-03 00 **Wheelchairs:** Yes, ground floor **Cloakrooms:** 2 (Attendant) **Parking:** NCP Old Burlington Street & ample street after 18 30. **Other:** By May 1980 the Embassy intends to be open 24 hrs and open to non-members for breakfast & tea (non-licensed hours) with piano entertainment

Policy: To establish a venue for high-quality avant-garde revues and cabaret using untapped talent, in a spontaneous and relaxed atmosphere

Perspective: Built as a theatre club after the First World War (and by the present management's own definition, as a 'Noel Coward-type venue'), the Embassy Club has a colourful history peopled by famous names and 'beautiful people'. Amongst its many claims to fame is the fact that it was at the Embassy Club that Edward first met Mrs Simpson and the royal romance began. For many years, Thursday night at the Embassy Club was considered to be London's most prestigious and exciting way of spending an evening out on the town. The Embassy is also the home of a famous cat who wanders freely throughout the club, a tradition that has been maintained for years.

Currently the Embassy is working to return the club's atmosphere to the period for which it is best remembered, both in terms of its decor and its programme policy. In late 1979 the Embassy Club presented *Bits of Lenny Bruce* which had formerly played at the Open Space and Kings Head theatres, and at Christmas they had a disco-pantomime called *Discoella*. For the future it is hoped to present 2 shows nightly of first-rate cabaret, as an integrated part of the club's atmosphere. Further plans include re-exposing the double-glass dome over the main dance floor, and providing a 24-hour venue for eating, drinking and live entertainment.

Underground: Green Park (Jubilee, Piccadilly, Victoria)
Bus: 9, 14, 19, 22, 25, 38
Map: 154 N3

The Factory

1 Chippenham Mews, London W9 2AN
Box Office: **286 1656** (08 00-22 00 Tuesday-Saturday) Admin: **286 1656**
Performance Space: Large downstairs room, smaller upstairs, both with flexible raised staging *Seating:* 300 & 150 (level & raised)

Bookings: Postal (cheques to Maryland Community Association) s.a.e. Phone (held to ½ hr before show) No credit cards or travellers cheques **Prices:** 50p-75p members of MCA, £1 non-members **Concessions:** Parties, when available **Perf Times:** Check with box office **Catering:** No **Bars:** Members only 19 30-23 00 **Wheelchairs:** Yes **Cloakrooms:** No **Parking:** Side streets **Other:** Membership of the MCA entitles cheaper seats, all facilities of building, use of bar & bi-monthly newsletters

Policy: To provide a social and creative focus for the culturally diverse people of the area. The centre aims to initiate workshops and festivals and to include professional theatre and cabaret performances, dance and puppetry.

Perspective: The multi-purpose Marylands Community Centre in west London (behind Paddington) is known as the Factory because that is what it was until 1973, when a group was formed to convert the building into a community centre serving a highly populated area that has poor facilities. Instead of making taxi meters, the Factory now makes links with the locality. It has taken time to get off the ground because of conversion work which has been going on since the centre was opened.

Improvements, including sound-proofing, completed this process in March 1979 when the Factory was re-opened as a permanent, modern, split-level centre, offering theatre, day nursery care, dance and drama classes, live music, a craft workshop and a place to play dominoes. (The music rehearsal room is being turned into a community recording studio by The Who pop group.) A Youth group, Sukuya, based at the centre, researched African tribal wear and music, and created their own costumes. The centre also takes part in the most famous theatre activity of this area, the Notting Hill Street Carnival, which occurs every August Bank Holiday.

The two theatre spaces play their part in making art relevant to the local people in an attempt to bridge cultural and ethnic backgrounds, and to help meet some of the problems posed by the alienation of young people in London. The Factory's opening show, by resident writer Mustapha Matura, who comes from Trinidad, dealt candidly with how you have to face up to the reality of life in Britain as it is. *Welcome Home Jacko* was so successful that it was toured — to south London's Abeng Centre, to the Riverside Studios in west London, and to the Theatre Royal, Stratford East, in east London (see separate entries). Excellent food at Greek restaurant opposite, plus fish and chip shop or health food at That Tea Room in Westbourne Park Road. The Needle Arms is on the corner.

Underground: Westbourne Park (Metropolitan, British Rail)
Bus: 18, 18A, 28, 31, 36, 36B
Map: 148 B

Fortune Theatre

Russell Street, WC2B 5HA
Box Office: **836 2238** (10 00-20 00) Admin: **836 6260**
Performance Space: Proscenium arch *Seating:* 432 (3 levels, steeply raked Upper Circle)

Bookings: Postal (cheques to Fortune Theatre) s.a.e. Phone (held 2 days) Credit cards — Access, AmEx. Travellers cheques with identification **Prices**: £2-£6.50 **Concessions:** Parties; Student Standby Monday-Thursday if available **Catering:** Coffee at mats, confectionery, ices **Bars:** 2 **Wheelchairs:** 2 **Cloakrooms:** Paralok **Parking:** NCP Drury Lane

Policy: To provide a venue for shows suited to a comparatively small West End theatre.

Perspective: Facing the colonnades at the side of the Theatre Royal Drury Lane, the Fortune was built in 1924 on the site of the Albion Tavern, a pub frequented by actors and named after the Fortune Theatre at Cripplegate, burnt down in the early 17th century. The theatre was to be called the Crown because it is above, below and along one side of a passage that leads to the Scottish National Church in Crown Court (making the title of the first production, *Sinners*, curiously appropriate). J.B. Fagan presented Sean O'Casey's *Juno and the Paycock* and *The Plough and the Stars* in 1926, but such a bold start came to little. A usual West End mix followed, with Frederick Lonsdale's comedy *On Approval* doing well (469 performances), until Nancy Price started the People's National Theatre there in 1930. Sybil Thorndike appeared in *Dark Saint* and *Fire* (1939), but during the war the theatre was used for Sunday Club and amateur performances, and occupied by the services entertainment unit ENSA.

Professional entertainers, like Joyce Grenfell, came mainly in the summer or at Christmas, until 1956. But there was no stopping the small theatre after Michael Flanders and Donald Swann presented their intimate revue *At the Drop of a Hat* (1957 for 773 performances), and the '60s satire *Beyond the Fringe* followed (1,184 performances).

Then came a string of successes, such as Alexei Arbuzov's *The Promise* with Ian McKellen, Judi Dench and Ian McShane, and transfers like E.A. Whitehead's *Foursome* from the Royal Court, a play that won the George Devine Award for new writing in 1970. The theatre was renovated and redecorated in 1960.

Underground: Covent Garden (Piccadilly), Charing Cross (Bakerloo, Jubilee, Northern, British Rail), Temple (District, Circle)
Bus: 1, 4, 6, 9, 11, 13, 15, 55, 68, 77, 77A, 77C, 168, 170, 171, 172, 176, 188, 239, 501, 502, 513
Map: 155 M5

Garrick Theatre

Charing Cross Road, WC2H 0HH
Box Office: **836 4601** (10 00-20 00) Admin: **836 9396**
Performance Space: Proscenium arch *Seating:* 700 (3 levels — Gallery no longer used)

Bookings: Postal (cheques to The Garrick) s.a.e. Phone (held 3 days) Credit cards — Access, AmEx, Barclaycard/Visa. Travellers cheques with identification **Prices:** £2-£6.50 **Concessions:** Parties of 15 and more **Catering:** Tea at mats when applicable, confectionery, ices **Bars:** 2 **Wheelchairs:** Yes **Cloakrooms:** 1 (Attendant) **Parking:** NCP Whitcomb St

Policy: To present plays suitable for family entertainment. The majority of plays are new, with some revivals. Plays run as long as their popularity lasts, the average being 3 productions per year.

Perspective: W S Gilbert had the idea of building a theatre at the Trafalgar Square end of Charing Cross Road, but little did he realize that the excavation would unearth a river. He should have asked the Romans, who knew all about it. Instead of leasing out fishing rights, he went ahead and opened in 1889 a classically late-Victorian theatre with a long Portland and Bath stone front.

You enter at dress circle level, passing a copy of a missing Gainsborough oil portrait of the famous actor/manager David Garrick, after whom the theatre is named. In the early years, it was controlled by a series of actor/managers, and this tradition was repeated in 1945 when Jack Buchanan took over, remaining in control until his death in 1957.

The first play, *The Profligate*, produced by the author, Arthur Wing Pinero, marked a new fashion which stressed the role of the writer rather than that of the stars. Neither made much impact here, and in 1934 retired music-hall veterans were wheeled out, also in vain. Various schemes fell through, from turning the theatre into a cinema to making it the Forces Theatre in the war, but Wendy Hiller hit the headlines in *Love on the Dole* (1935).

After Buchanan's reign, light drama held the stage, with notable runs from the Theatre Workshop (*Fings Ain't Wot They Used T'Be*), *Rattle of a Simple Man*, seasons of Brian Rix dropping his trousers and the transfer of *Side by Side by Sondheim*. At this theatre, the critics have to beware, because the Garrick is haunted by the ghost of actor/manager Arthur Bourchier — the first on record to ban a reviewer (in 1903).

Underground: Charing Cross (Bakerloo, Jubilee, Northern), Leicester Square (Northern, Piccadilly)
Bus: 1, 24, 29, 176 or 3, 6, 9, 11, 12, 13, 15, 53, 77, 77A, 77C, 88, 159, 168, 170, 172 to Trafalgar Square
Map: 155 N4

Gate Theatre Club

Prince Albert, 11 Pembridge Road, W11 3HQ
Box Office: **229 0706** (15 30-20 00) Admin: **229 0706**
Performance Space: Large upstairs pub room *Seating:* 70 (raked & flat)

Bookings: Members only (+ 2 guests) 25p p.a. & at door Postal (cheques to The Gate Theatre Club) s.a.e Phone (held up to 19 30 on the day) No credit cards **Prices:** £1.75 **Concessions:** Groups of 10+ £1.50 plus 25p group membership **Perf Time:** 20 00 **Catering:** Sandwiches, snacks in pub **Bars:** Pub (can take drinks into theatre) **Wheelchairs:** No **Cloakrooms:** No **Parking:** Street after 18 30 **Other:** Occasional bookstall (performance-related) Saturday afternoon readings of new plays (check with box office)

Policy: To fill the need for high quality, local fringe theatre in the Notting Hill Gate area with a programme of new and experimental works of a high standard.

Perspective: In the west London of Notting Hill, once synonymous with social and political experiment, it is surprising to find so little surviving fringe theatre. The Prince Albert, always a popular pub, and renowned as boxer Jack Doyle's life-long drinking spot, is largely frequented by BBC actors. Now the Prince Albert has regular theatre provided by the Gate Theatre Club which has been in operation since February 1979.

The emphasis has been on adaptations of novels, such as George Orwell's *Down and Out in Paris and London* and Flann O'Brien's cult book *At Swim Two Birds*. Neighbouring schools found these two shows very interesting and this has helped build the local audience. The Gate's other focus has been reviving neglected foreign plays — very much collector's items. The first was *The Empire Builders* by the French iconoclast Boris Vian and the second, *The Bedbug*, a musical play based on the satirical comedy of the same name by Vladimir Mayakovsky. In April 1980 the Gate premiered 3 John Antrobus plays: *Hitler in Liverpool, Up in the Hide* and *One Orange for the Baby*, with the latter two playing in repertory until mid-May.

Underground: Notting Hill Gate (Central, Circle, District)
Bus: 12, 27, 28, 31, 52, 88, 710, 715, 790
Map: 152 F2

Gay's the Word

66 Marchment Street, WC1N 1AB
Box Office: **None** Admin: **278 7654** (11 00-19 00 & Thursday 11 00-22 30)
Performance Space: Back-room area of bookshop *Seating:* 70-80, some at tables

Bookings: In person on the day only. Arrive early (19 30) to ensure getting a seat
Prices: Free **Concessions:** No **Perf Times:** Thursday 20 00 or 20 30, usually 3 times per month **Mailing List:** Newsletter £2 p.a. **Catering:** Coffee, tea & fruit juices
Bars: No **Wheelchairs:** Yes (ground floor) **Cloakrooms:** No **Parking:** NCP Marchmont St, after 18 30 **Other:** Workshops/discussion groups open to general public, free of charge, themes for discussion determined by those present (usually 2nd & 4th Tuesday of each month, 19 00-22 00)

Policy: To provide a showcase for non-sexist, non-racist gay entertainment in a relaxed setting. Everyone welcome.

Perspective: With a wide London gay scene (see the weekly *Gay News*) you might have thought that there would be several venues devoted to gay plays — but not so. Outside the drag pubs and cabaret spots, there were only a few theatres that presented gay plays or booked Gay Sweatshop's two touring companies (one based on men, the other on women). That is, until Gay's the Word started up. First of all, a bookshop was opened, in January 1979, in a building that used to be a bakery and a children's clothes shop. In March of that year, entertainment began, hitting its peak during Gay Pride Week when there was a performance every night. The shop became a focal point, which really established it, and from there on the theatre side has expanded. Performers appear free of charge, and there is no charge at the door to get in.

Apart from workshops with gay authors and discussions on different topics (all open to the public), members of Gay Sweatshop have appeared there. One of the directors of Gay's the Word, Roger Baker, was a founder member of Gay Sweatshop, which pioneered plays that dealt openly and honestly with all aspects of gay life. The group, for example, had performed a play that looked at the nazis and gays. (However, when Martin Sherman's play *Bent*, on this theme, was produced at the Royal Court and was transferred to the West End, it still caused a shock).

As Gay Sweatshop had to develop out of its male preserve, so Gay's the Word is trying to avoid a similar concentration excluding women. It makes the point that discrimination against gays is just one part of a much wider set of descriminations, and is therefore keen to present plays that avoid prejudice and stereotyping.

Underground: Russell Square (Piccadilly)
Bus: 68, 77, 77A, 77C, 170, 188, 239
Map: 151 D6

George Inn Courtyard

77 Borough High Street, Southwark SE1 1NH
Box Office: **703 2917** or **703 6311 x 359** (10 00-17 00) Admin: **703 6311**
Performance Space: Open-air pub courtyard, elevated stage *Seating:* 100 (& standing)

Bookings: Postal to Box Office, Southwark Entertainments, 28 Peckham Road, SE5 8PY (cheques to Southwark Corporation) s.a.e. Phone (held to 1 hr before show) In person from George Inn 1 hr before show **Prices:** £1 **Concessions:** No
Perf Times: Sats only May-July 15 15 **Catering:** George Inn resturant (407 2056), Wine Bar, Old Bar for hot & cold snacks during pub hrs **Bars:** Pub hrs only
Wheelchairs: Yes (easy access) **Cloakrooms:** No **Parking:** Small car park

Policy: A 13-week summer season of Shakespearian plays commencing in the last week in May and organized by the Entertainments Department of the London Borough of Southwark. A new play is performed each Saturday by a different amateur group or drama school. There are no professional performances.

Perspective: Situated in a fascinating part of London, full of theatre history— and of hostelries — the George Inn Courtyard is the last galleried coaching pub in London and can be traced in the records as going back to 1554. This area south of the River Thames was known as Bankside, and flourished as a centre for Shakespeare and his contemporaries at the Globe, Swan and Rose Theatres (see Bear Gardens Centre entry). The St George and the Dragon Inn, as the George was then called, must have been doing good business too.

The freehold was acquired by Guy's Hospital in 1849, and transferred to the Great Northern Railway in 1874. In 1937, the George was bought by the National Trust. The changes it has undergone during its many years of constant use are reflected in the mish-mash of architectural styles — oak, plaster, steel and glass — but it remains a picturesque sight with a lot of 'atmosphere'.

Many famous names are associated with the George Inn, from Chaucer and the Elizabethan and Jacobean playwrights, including Shakespeare himself, to Dr Johnson and Charles Dickens (a version of whose *David Copperfield* has been presented there). Plays have been performed in the courtyard since the 1930s when they were confined to 23 April, Shakespeare's birthday. On that day in 1936, the great actor/manager Ben Greet made his last public appearance. The summer season is now maintained by the local council, taking advantage of this unique building. The Inn itself serves Whitbread bitter and Bass real ales, and has a 200-year old beer engine resembling a cash register. Another item to note is the Parliamentary clock.

Underground: London Bridge (Northern, British Rail)
Bus: 10, 21, 35, 40, 95, 133 or 8A, 18, 43, 44, 47, 48, 70, 501, 513 to London Bridge Station
Map: 157 U4

Globe Theatre

Shaftesbury Avenue, W1V 8AR
Box Office: **437 1592** (10 00-20 00) Admin: **437 6003**
Performance Space: Proscenium arch *Seating:* 907 (3 levels, 4 boxes)

Bookings: Postal (cheques to The Globe Theatre) s.a.e. Phone bookings depending on ticket availablity. Credit cards — Access, Barclaycard/Visa Travellers cheques, sterling only **Prices:** £2-£6 (£7 if musicals) **Concessions:** Student Standby, etc. all subject to availability **Perf Times:** 20 00, Wednesday and Saturday mats
Catering: Tea & coffee in foyer during intervals **Bars:** 4 (from ½ hr before show)
Wheelchairs: 2 (must be able to move into seat) **Cloakrooms:** 2 (Attendant)
Parking: Very difficult

Policy: The Globe operates a strictly commercial policy of presenting plays with a wide appeal and running as long as popularity is maintained. The Globe is generally associated with 'quality Comedies' from writers such as Rattigan, Coward and more recently Ayckbourn and Nichols.

Perspective: The Globe was built in 1906 as the Hicks Theatre, named after Seymour Hicks, who was a partner in the building as well as the producer and half author of the opening show. The architect W G R Sprague also designed the Queen's, which occupies the other corner of the block in Shaftesbury Avenue.

The foyer is famous for its circular 'Regency' staircase and the French influence — Sprague designed the Edward VII Theatre in Paris — is overlaid with baroque both inside and out. With its chandeliers and despite redecorations, it remains much the same as it was. The name was changed to the Globe in 1909.

Light musicals were the staple diet of the early years. Many well-known actors of the day appeared at what became a popular theatre — although there was a riot in 1917 on the first night of *Suzette* when a part of the audience protested at the French music-hall artiste Gaby Deslys. However, the show was a hit. A period followed under the actor/manager Marie Löhr and her husband, with successes by Somerset Maugham, Noël Coward, and, the records say, a sensation in 1927 when Jeanne de Casalis appeared in pyjamas. The '30s saw foreign visits — the Pitoeffs from France in *Saint Joan*, the German actor Moissi playing Hamlet, a Japanese company and a play from the US, Elmer Rice's *Street Scene*. In 1937, H M Tennent took over the management with a revival of Shaw's *Candida*, and made the Globe its headquarters.

Other names associated with the theatre include Ivor Novello, Terence Rattigan, Christopher Fry (*The Lady's Not for Burning* with John Gielgud), Emlyn Williams, Edith Evans, Owen Nares, Yvonne Arnaud, Alec Guinness and Beatrice Lillie. Then came Robert Bolt's *A Man for All Seasons* with Paul Scofield, Anouilh's *The Rehearsal*, *There's a Girl in My Soup*, *Kean*, *The Changing Room*, Edna Everidge and, more recently, *Songbook*.

Underground: Piccadilly Circus (Bakerloo, Piccadilly)
Bus: 14, 19, 22, 38 or 3, 6, 9, 12, 13, 15, 53, 88, 159 to Piccadilly Circus
Map: 154 M3

Greenwich Theatre

Crooms Hill, SE10 8ES
Box Office: **858 7755** (10 00-21 00) Admin: **858 4447/8**
Performance Space: Open stage *Seating:* 426

Bookings: Postal (cheques to Greenwich Theatre Ltd) s.a.e Phone (held 3 days) Subscription (see **Other**) Credit cards — Access, AmEx, Barclaycard/Visa. **Prices:** £1.60-£3.75 **Concessions:** Student & OAPs. Standby 1hr before show £1.60; Parties: Mondays, Saturday mats & previews 70p OAPs & Students £1 **Perf Times:** 20 00 eves & 14 30 Saturday mats **Mailing List:** £1 p.a. **Catering:** Full restaurant (858 1318) 18 30-24 00 **Bars:** Wine bar & pub (18 00-23 00) **Wheelchairs:** No **Cloakrooms:** 1 (Attendant) **Parking:** Greenwich Car Park directly opposite — 10p **Other:** Free art gallery, jazz club, Greenwich Film Society. Subscription scheme: 7 shows for price of 5, etc. Friends of Greenwich Theatre £5 p.a. for 20 per cent discount on seats, free programmes, special events, reciprocal membership with Arts and Hampstead Theatre Clubs.

Policy: A mixture of classics, revivals and new plays in a season from September to June (7 plays). No resident company. Generally small casts.

Perspective: Greenwich Theatre, one of the first in Britain to be built as part of a complex, opened in 1969 after years of local fund-raising. Its modern, intimate auditorium without a proscenium arch was built out of the shell of an old music hall which had been the Greenwich Hippodrome before being used as a cinema and a warehouse. The Hippodrome itself began life before 1869, when the landlord of the Rose and Crown pub next door needed to expand to meet the demand for the entertainment he was providing. (The Rose and Crown is still there today.)

Greenwich's first director, Ewan Hooper, started a campaign for a new theatre in 1962 when the Hippodrome was bought by the council for demolition, and its first production was *Martin Luther King*, a play with music by Ewan Hooper. The support of the local people (including successful money-raising music-hall evenings at the Green Man pub) formed the basis for the subscription booking scheme (one of the first in Britain and now catching on more widely), which helps develop a loyal audience for the theatre. Alan Strachan took over as artistic director in 1978.

Its credits are notable — from the Robin Phillips season to the Jonathan Miller season, from Mia Farrow, Tom Courtenay, Glenda Jackson, Vivien Merchant and Susan Hampshire to Penelope Keith, Max Wall, Leonard Rossiter, Susannah York and Lynn Redgrave. Alan Ayckbourn's three comedies, *The Norman Conquest*, were seen here on their way to the West End. The theatre is relaxed, the food good and the exhibitions worth more than a glance.

British Rail: Greenwich
Bus: 108B, 177, 180, 185, 188
Map: 146 E

Greenwich Young People's Theatre

Burrage Road, Plumstead, SE18 7JZ
Box Office: **855 4911** or **854 1316** (10 00-20 00) Admin: **855 4911**
Performance Space: Back & front hall (flexible) *Seating:* Both seat approx 100

Bookings: Club membership required (incl in ticket) Postal (cheques to Greenwich Young People's Theatre Ltd) s.a.e. Phone (held up to ½ hr before show) No credit cards **Prices:** 75p **Concessions:** 50p students, 30p school & youth club groups **Perf Times:** 19 30 or 20 00 **Catering:** Coffee/sandwich bar for light meals 17 00-21 00 (open to public) **Bars:** No **Wheelchairs:** Yes **Cloakrooms:** No **Parking:** Street

Policy: To provide theatre-in-education and arts workshops in local boroughs, with a programme dealing with themes relevant to the lives of the young people.

Perspective: In 1965, the director of the Greenwich Theatre, Ewan Hooper, started a youth theatre as part of his wish to extend the role of drama in that area of south-east London. By 1969, a professional theatre-in-education team had been set up, which moved to a disused church in Plumstead (the present address).

With a grant from London's education authority, it became one of a group (with the Cockpit and the Curtain) providing plays for schools. Greenwich Youth Theatre existed alongside Bowsprit, which worked among younger children. These names were dropped in 1978 in favour of the all-embracing Greenwich Young People's Theatre (GYPT). It has earned itself a reputation for artistic integrity and high standards, and now offers a range of activity for people aged between 5 and 21, covering drama, photography, silk screen printing, all kinds of music and dance. It has a programme of visiting companies as well as its own work. The Youth Theatre has staged, for example, Peter Weiss's *Marat/Sade* and a rock *Othello*.

The emphasis of the GYPT is on participation and relevance to the local community. It has tackled subjects such as unemployment and racial tension (eg its 13 to 15 year old programme *Race Against Time* which includes workshops as well as a play exploding racist myths). For 10 to 12 year olds, there has been *Role Play*, looking at sex stereotyping, and for 6 to 8 year olds, *Nowhere to Go*, which examined social responsibility. It has also devised projects with schools designated as 'Educationally Sub-Normal', and, as Bowsprit, produced an excellent infants' programme on social behaviour called *Polly the All-Action Dolly*.

British Rail: Woolwich Arsenal
Bus: 51, 53, 192 or 54, 75, 96, 99, 122, 122A, 161, 161A, 177, 180, 198, 269, 272 to Woolwich General Gordon Place
Map: 145 D

Grove Theatre

The Grove Tavern, 83 Hammersmith Grove, W6 0MQ
Box office: **743 2877** (times vary) or **741 3696** (Monday-Friday 09 00-17 00)
Admin: **743 2877** *Performance Space:* Ex-banqueting hall adapted to studio theatre *Seating:* 60

Bookings: Members only (25p p.a. purchaseable at door) + 1 guest. Postal (cheques to Grove Theatre, 3 Roxwell Road, W12) s.a.e. Phone (held 1 week) **Prices:** £1.80 **Concessions:** No **Perf Times:** 20 00 **Mailing List:** Automatic with membership **Catering:** Snacks & pub food downstairs **Bars:** as for pub **Wheelchairs:** No **Cloakrooms:** No **Parking:** Ample in street **Other:** Reciprocal membership with most other fringe theatres

Policy: To produce a provocative mixture of new and unperformed plays and classics especially adapted to suit the space.

Perspective: This was the first new theatre in London to open in 1980 and as such attests to the spirit of our theatres as they enter the much talked-of 'difficult decade for the arts'. In 1979 Paul Caister and John Spierman wrote to 300 publicans in West London, seeking to establish a new pub theatre in the area. The initiative was based on their conviction that West London audiences, put off by ticket prices in the West End, provide one of London's strongest fringe theatre support groups. Only one pub replied to the letter, the Grove Tavern, and here the new theatre was founded, situated a stone's throw from both the Lyric, Hammersmith and the Riverside Studios, making the Grove another addition to the burgeoning number of cultural amenities in Hammersmith.

From July to December 1979 the studio was converted from the shell of an ex-banqueting hall on a shoe-string budget of £1,500. Two former Bush Theatre stage managers are responsible for the results, which include three-quarter raked and cushioned bench seating, full lighting, sound and scaffolding rigs and a dressing room built into the corner of the room.

The Grove opened in February 1980 with an American play *True Facts*, followed in March by a shortened *Romeo and Juliet*. To date the theatre has depended on the enthusiasm of many Equity actors who have been prepared to work for a cut of the box office takings and their expenses.

Underground: Hammersmith (District, Metropolitan, Piccadilly)
Bus: 9, 11, 27, 33, 72, 73, 91, 220, 260, 266, 267, 290, 701, 704, 710, 714, 715, AV300, 311, 320, 322
Map: 145 E

Half Moon Theatre

27 Alie Street, E1 8DA
Box Office: **480 6465** (10 00-18 00) Admin: **480 6726/7**
Performance Space: Open staging, flexible *Seating:* 100-110 (2 levels)

Bookings: Postal (cheques to Half Moon Theatre) s.a.e Phone (held to ½ hr before show) No credit cards. Sterling travellers cheques **Prices:** £2.50-£3
Concessions: Students, OAPs, groups, children **Perf Times:** Variable, some mats
Mailing List: Free **Catering:** No, except snacks for Cabarets **Bars:** No **Wheelchairs:** Yes **Cloakrooms:** No **Parking:** Street after 18 30 **Other:** Writers' workshops, schools tours, young people's workshops, summer school courses

Policy: To produce popular theatre on broad local, national and international issues. New and foreign plays frequently staged, foreign companies welcome. Strong links with East End community.

Perspective: The Half Moon is a name that stands out in the history of the fringe as a venue that has consistently followed a bold policy of exciting drama of a (broadly-defined) left-wing character. Taking its name from the alley that runs into the street the theatre stands on, the Half Moon was set up in a 19th-century synagogue in 1972 at the height of the fringe's first wave of energy by Maurice Colbourne, Guy Sprung and Michael Irving, and immediately established a reputation for challenging productions. Its notable contribution has been to offer a good standard of theatre that draws both a middle-class and a local working-class audience.

The Half Moon became as popular for its influential productions of Bertolt Brecht (eg *In the Jungle of the Cities, The Mother*, which transferred to the Round House, *St Joan of the Stockyards, The Resistible Rise of Arturo Ui*) as for its plays about local issues (eg *Get Off Our Backs*, about the threat to dockland, or *Fall in and Follow Me*, about a school children's strike in 1911 written by a docker from Hull and a local 18-year-old, Billy Colvill, who has become a fixed feature of the Half Moon). Other community plays have dealt with Jack the Ripper (who stalked this part of the east end) and, perhaps the most famous, *George Davis is Innocent, OK?*

About a third of the year, the Half Moon is a venue for touring groups, such as 7:84 or Belt and Braces, which played *Accidental Death of an Anarchist* here before it went into the West End. It has also become associated with some new writers, such as Steve Gooch, and runs a young writer's workshop.

The Half Moon hopes to move into new premises in 1983, not far away in the Mile End Road. A Methodist chapel there is being converted but was christened in 1979 with its first Half Moon production, a walk-about *Hamlet* with Frances de la Tour following a fine tradition as a female Prince of Denmark. Opposite the existing theatre is a cheap Indian restaurant, and round the corner in Whitechapel is the Jewish restaurant Blooms and Tubby Isaac's whelks and cockles stall. You can take drinks into the theatre from the White Swan pub next door.

Underground: Aldgate (Circle, Metropolitan)
Aldgate East (District, Metropolitan)
Bus: 9, 10, 15, 22A, 23, 25, 40, 42, 44, 67, 95, 253, 723
Map: 157 S6

Hampstead Theatre

Swiss Cottage Centre, NW3 3EX
Box Office: **722 9301** (10 00-20 00) Admin: **722 9224**
Performance Space: Open stage *Seating:* 157 (raked)

Bookings: Members only (+ unlimited guests) £1.50 p.a., mailing list, seats any night Postal (cheques to Hampstead Theatre Ltd) s.a.e. Phone (held 3 days) No credit cards or travellers cheques **Prices:** £2-£2.50 **Concessions:** Students, OAPs, Parties **Perf Times:** 20 00 Monday-Saturday, 16 30 Saturday mats **Catering:** Coffee bar, confectionery **Bars:** 19 00-23 00 **Wheelchairs:** Yes **Cloakrooms:** No **Parking:** Swiss Cottage Tube Station **Other:** Honorary membership for all members of Camden Library for bookings any night except Sat. Theatre affiliated to other theatre clubs

Policy: The Club is dedicated to the presentation of new plays and the encouragement of new writers. Productions change every six to eight weeks.

Perspective: The theatre was founded 21 years ago by James Roose-Evans, who became its first artistic director. He was followed in this post by Vivian Matalon, who in turn was succeeded in 1973 by Michael Rudman. David Aukin, who in 1975 became the administrative director, succeeded Michael Rudman in 1978.

Hampstead Theatre has established itself as one of the leading club theatres and in 1978 won the *Evening Standard* Special Award for Outstanding Achievement — the first time that this award had been given to a theatre as distinct from an individual.

The theatre has transferred a number of plays to the West End, and in 1979 three were playing at the same time: *Bodies* by James Saunders, *Clouds* by Michael Frayn and *Gloo Joo* by Michael Hastings. Later in 1979 a fourth play, *Outside Edge* by Richard Harris, also transferred to the West End.

Michael Rudman's productions of Michael Frayn's *Alphabetical Order* and Peter Handke's *Ride Across Lake Constance* both transferred to the May Fair Theatre. Another transfer to the May Fair Theatre was a play which caused some controversy in the women's movement and brought Pam Gems to the public eye, *Dusa, Fish, Stas and Vi*. One of the theatre's most famous productions was *Abigail's Party* by Mike Leigh which was recreated for television and shown twice on the BBC Play For Today slot.

As a matter of policy, Hampstead has invited outside companies once a year to present or co-present a production. One of these visitors, Foco Novo, presented John Berger's play about migrant workers, *A Seventh Man*, and also, in a co-production with Hampstead Theatre, Bernard Pomerance's *The Elephant Man*, which later opened on Broadway. From abroad, Hampstead recently invited the Nimrod Theatre of Australia to present David Williamson's *The Club*, which transferred to the Old Vic, and also staged the British Premiere of the Soviet play *The Ascent of Mount Fuji*.

Underground: Swiss Cottage (Jubilee)
Bus: 2, 2B, 13, 31, 113, 187, 268, C11, 707, 717, 732
Map: 146 **C**

Her Majesty's Theatre

Haymarket, SW1Y 4QR
Box Office: **930 6606** (10 00-20 00) Admin: **930 6435**
Performance Space: Proscenium arch *Seating:* 1,263 (4 levels)

Bookings: Postal (cheques to Her Majesty's) s.a.e. Phone (held 4 days) Credit cards (930 6606) AmEx, Barclaycard/Visa **Price:** £2-£8 **Concessions:** Parties of 20 + Monday-Friday. Student Standby **Perf Times:** Wednesday, Saturday mat, eve **Catering:** Coffee bar in foyer, confectionery, ices **Bars:** 4 **Wheelchairs:** 2 (back stalls) **Cloakrooms:** 1 (Attendant) **Parking:** NCP behind National Gallery

Policy: To provide a venue for shows suited to the large size of the theatre.

Perspective: The name most associated with Her Majesty's is that of actor/manager Beerbohm Tree, who staged spectacular Shakespeare there, started a drama school associated with the theatre, which became the Royal Academy of Dramatic Art (RADA), and is commemorated by a tablet on the corner of Charles II Street. He introduced Afternoon Theatre for plays that would not do well at the box office, and referred to Her Majesty's as 'my beautiful theatre.' Now owned by the New Zealand government, the site was the second stable yard up the Hay-Market before the first theatre was built by architect and playwright Sir John Vanbrugh (and managed by the great Restoration dramatist William Congreve) when there was a row at Drury Lane.

The home of Italian opera, it changed its name from the Queen's (after Anne) to the King's, and had to be rebuilt because of fire as one of the finest opera houses in Europe. Remodelled in 1818, its name was changed again in 1837 to Her Majesty's Theatre, Italian Opera House (the latter phrase being dropped 10 years later).

Burnt down again, it was rebuilt, stripped by auction, demolished and another theatre, the present one, built (1897) in French renaissance style, with an open arcade and a Portland stone exterior, topped off with a dome, and a baroque interior with marble pillars.

Apart from odd bits of history, like music-hall king George Robey playing Falstaff, Her Majesty's, with its large size, excellent stage machinery, and good acoustics and sightlines, has now become best known for its musicals — beginning in 1916 with *Chu Chin Chow*, (2,238 performances), and coming up to date with *West Side Story, Bye Bye Birdie, Fiddler on the Roof, Company, Applause* and *Ipi Tombi*.

Underground: Piccadilly Circus (Bakerloo, Piccadilly)
Bus: 3, 6, 9, 12, 13, 15, 53, 88, 159 or 14, 19, 22, 38 to Piccadilly Circus
Map: 155 N4

Institute of Contemporary Arts (The ICA)

Nash House, The Mall, SW1 5AH
Box Office: **930 3647** (12 00-20 00) Admin: **930 0493**
Performance Space: Flexible staging & seating systems *Seating:* 200

Bookings: Day membership required (+ 1 guest) 35p at door. Postal (cheques to ICA) s.a.e. Phone (held 3 days) No credit cards **Prices:** £1.50-£2.50
Concessions: Parties negotiable, 1 free ticket with 12 **Perf Times:** Tuesday-Sunday 20 00, some lunch & late-night **Mailing List:** For full members (see **Other**)
Catering: Self-service restaurant hot & cold 12 00-21 00 **Bars:** 1 (evening pub hrs)
Wheelchairs: Yes **Cloakrooms:** No **Parking:** NCP Trafalgar Square & meters in Waterloo Place **Other:** Full membership £6 p.a. gives exhibition previews, bookshop offers, 1 guest to all events, 2 tickets for price of 1 for previews & openings. Associate membership £4 p.a. gives free entry to building. Bookshop stocks cover all art forms.

Policy: Primarily a venue for British and foreign touring companies, the ICA also produces some plays itself. Emphasis on imaginative, progressive work not seen elsewhere, and new to London. Special attention to performance rather than script-orientation.

Perspective: Just down the Mall from Buckingham Palace across the road from St James's Park may not seem the most likely spot for an exciting theatre, but, despite ups and downs and a threat to close the venue as an economy measure, the Institute of Contemporary Arts (ICA) has housed many original, imaginative productions as well as bringing to London experimental companies from outside the capital (eg Ken Campbell's Science Fiction Theatre of Liverpool) and from abroad, such as the Project Arts Centre based in Dublin and performance groups from Holland.

As part of the Nash Terrace, the elegant cream exterior was designed by Sir Thomas Nash in the early 19th century. Founded by Herbert Read and Sir Roland Penrose in 1947 in Dover Street, the ICA moved to the Mall in 1968, into what used to be the Nash House stables. The theatre opened in 1973 with Mustapha Matura's *As Time Goes By*. With a large acting space and versatile technology (put in under current artistic director John Ashford, who was one of the first theatre editors of the magazine *Time Out*), the ICA has a lively repertoire, encompassing the best new writers, from Snoo Wilson to Stephen Poliakoff, and challenging new groups, such as Beryl and the Perils, Monstrous Regiment or Crystal Theatre of the Saint.

The bookshop is widely stocked and even if you do not go into the main exhibition area, there is usually something worth looking at in the long white corridors leading down to the healthy restaurant and big box of a theatre.

Underground: Charing Cross (Bakerloo, Jubilee, Northern, British Rail)
Bus: 1, 3, 6, 9, 11, 13, 15, 24, 29, 53, 77, 77A, 77C, 88, 159, 168, 170, 172, 176
Map: 155 N4

Intimate Theatre

Green Lanes, Palmers Green, N13 4DJ
Box Office: **886 3798** (10 00-20 00) Admin: **882 5795**
Performance Space: Proscenium arch *Seating:* 452

Bookings: Postal (cheques to The Intimate Theatre) s.a.e Phone (held for 48 hours) No credit cards **Prices:** Vary according to show, approx £1.50 **Concessions:** OAPs, party bookings **Perf Times:** Monday-Saturday with some Sundays **Mailing List:** Twice yearly 50p p.a. **Catering:** Coffee, light snacks, cake in bar available ½ hr before show & interval **Bars:** 1 **Wheelchairs:** No **Cloakrooms:** No **Parking:** Small car park. Street

Policy: To provide good entertainment in an area that is poorly served culturally.

Perspective: Originally a church hall, the Intimate started as a professional company in 1932, and over the years many latter-day stars have performed there. The inspiration behind the Intimate Theatre Repertory Company was Sir John Clements, who many years later ran the Chichester Festival Theatre. The first 3 months were not easy, with the company playing to nearby empty houses, but then with Noel Coward's *Private Lives* the place took off and successful productions of Shaw, J B Priestley, Barrie and Somerset Maugham followed.

The doors closed in 1970, but were re-opened in 1975 with the pleasant well-appointed theatre a venue for visiting companies, both professional and amateur. It continues with the policy of providing varied entertainment in the outer regions of north London, in an area perhaps better known for the poet Stevie Smith. There are some good and not too expensive restaurants nearby, and the bar has a unique licence to open whenever the theatre is open. No need to look for a pub!

British Rail: Palmers Green
Bus: 29, 123, 734, 735, W4, W9
Map: 146 G

Jackson's Lane Community Theatre

271 Archway Road, N6 5AA
Box Office: **340 5226** (10 00-17 30) Admin: **341 1884**
Performance Space: Studio, no staging *Seating:* 120 (raked & flat)

Bookings: In advance from The Little Shop, 251 Archway Road, N6 (10 00-17 30) or at door 1 hr before show (cheques to Jackson's Lane Community Centre) **Prices:** £1.50 **Concessions:** Students, claimants & under 18s 70p, OAPs 30p **Catering:** Snack bar 12 00-17 30 Tuesday-Friday, 11 00-15 00 Saturdays & during shows **Bars:** Members of Jackson's Lane only **Wheelchairs:** Yes **Cloakrooms:** No **Parking:** Ample, surrounding streets **Other:** Youth clubs, films, music, dance events, concerts, Indian dance & other facilities

Policy: To provide a multi-cultural programme catering for the people of the surrounding area, with an emphasis on good experimental theatre, dance, mime, music and children's entertainment. The Centre has a resident puppet company, and acts as a venue for touring fringe theatre companies.

Perspective: If variety is the spice of life, then anyone living within striking distance of the Jackson's Lane Community Centre, opposite Highgate Tube, can lead a very exciting existence. It was set up in 1975 by a co-operative of enthusiastic young people who converted an imposing late-Victorian Methodist chapel into a theatre and arts centre — a bit like a north London version of the Oval House fringe venue (see separate entry). Although Jackson's Lane covers the range of theatre, dance and mime are particularly popular. The centre also has a resident puppet group, Cap and Bells, which holds workshops as well as performing.

Touring professional fringe companies, such as Monstrous Regiment, appear regularly, and when a group from the North of England, like Red Ladder based in Leeds, comes to London, you are more likely to find them at Jackson's Lane than anywhere else. There is a growing emphasis on experimental drama alongside the range of 'mixed-media' activity, encouraging people — young and old, black and white — to take part and not just to watch. Rock, folk, poetry and Kung Fu classes jostle with disco, tap, ballroom and Indian classical dancing, cookery, film and sports.

With a constantly changing programme, Jackson's Lane is one of the best community centres. It makes up in warmth of character what it loses in heat during the winter. There is almost a village atmosphere, but one which encompasses African drumming and art classes. Those who prefer the local Whole Food Cafe to the nearby Greek restaurants will feel at home, but then the opposite is true as well, because Jackson's Lane thrives on variety.

Underground: Highgate (Northern)
Bus: 43, 104, 134, 263
Map: 148 **D**

Jeannetta Cochrane Theatre

Southampton Row, WC1
Box Office: **242 7040** (10 00-20 00 and see press) Admin: **405 1825**
Performance Space: Proscenium arch *Seating:* 351 (2 levels)

Bookings: Postal (cheques to Jeannetta Cochrane Theatre) s.a.e Phone (held 3 days) No credit cards or travellers cheques **Prices:** 50p-£3, variable with each show **Concessions:** Vary with show **Perf Times:** Vary with show **Catering:** Soft drinks, ices from confectionery counter **Bars:** No **Wheelchairs:** 5 **Parking:** Street after 18 30

Policy: The theatre is used by the Theatre Department of the Central School of Art and Design. It also aims to attract professional groups for any kind of production consistent with educational theatre, including dance, music, drama and revues.

Perspective: The Jeanetta Cochrane is named after a costume designer who was the head of the theatre department at the Central School of Art and Design, for which the theatre was built. She introduced more comfortable and better made costumes for actors, and brought up-to-date the design of costumes in Shakespearian productions. She was noted in particular for her work with John Gielgud (eg his *Hamlet* at the Theatre Royal, Haymarket, during the Second World War).

She always wanted a theatre for the school so that her students could have practical experience, and after her death in 1957 it was decided to name the school's new building in her honour. The local education authority had bought the old Holborn Fire Station and converted it for the school. It was opened in 1964 and soon became a venue for experimental work, as well as being used by the students from Central. The Royal Shakespeare Company wanted to hire it for a season to follow up their success at the Arts in 1962 with small-cast innovative plays, but plans fell through. However, in 1966, American Jim Haynes staged a dry-run for his influential Drury Lane Arts Lab, which opened two years later, when he came here for a season from his pioneering Traverse Theatre in Edinburgh. Charles Marowitz directed Saul Bellow, his infamous cut-up *Hamlet* and the premiere of Joe Orton's *Loot*.

The Jeannetta Cochrane plays host to all kinds of theatrical activity now, from dance or the British premiere of Peter Maxwell Davies' opera for children, *The Two Fiddlers*, to music hall and theatre for the deaf. Its educational bias is still strong, including a lot of shows for children. It was also involved in starting the new Ballet Rambert Company and for many seasons was one of the venues used by the National Youth Theatre (NYT). Peter Terson's football play *Zigger Zagger* was first performed here by the NYT before its journey around Britain, abroad and into the exam syllabus.

The White Hart pub across the road is the nearest, and is used by the actors. Round the corner from the pub is the Milli Pini Italian restaurant and in Southampton Row (going towards Euston) a good Italian self-service restaurant.

Underground: Holborn (Central, Piccadilly)
Bus: 5, 7, 8, 19, 22, 25, 38, 55, 77, 77A, 77C, 170, 172, 188, 239, 501
Map: 155 L5

Kenneth More Theatre and Studio

Oakfield Road, Ilford, Essex I61 1BT
Box Office: **553 4466** (10 30-20 30) Admin: **553 4464**
Performance Space: Proscenium arch *Seating:* 365 (raked) & 50

Bookings: Postal (cheques to Kenneth More Theatre) s.a.e. Phone (held to 1 hr before perf. Monday-Friday; to 13 00 Saturday) No credit cards. Sterling travellers cheques **Prices:** £1.20-£2 **Concessions:** Discounts parties 20+ on cheaper seats only. Students, children & OAPs **Perf Times:** Wednesday-Sunday 20 00. Saturday mats when available. Studio 22 30 **Mailing List:** £1 p.a. for membership of Supporters Club, mailings, priority bookings & reductions **Catering:** Bar snacks, coffees. Restaurant open from 11 00-15 00 coffees & lunches; from 18 30 dinners. Licensed, buffet service **Bar:** Open from 19 15 **Wheelchairs:** 3 **Cloakroom:** Yes **Parking:** Side streets, London Car Park opp. theatre

Policy: To meet local needs with a wide range of entertainment including opera, ballet, musicals, drama, variety and children's theatre. Experimental work is produced in the small Studio Theatre.

Perspective: The Kenneth More Theatre was opened on New Year's Eve, 1974, after the Ilford Amateur Theatre had been bought and closed by the Council under a compulsory purchase order. The amateur element remains very strong, with over 50 per cent of the productions staged by 9 local amateur companies (publicity does not always state which productions are amateur and which professional). The upkeep of the theatre is carried out on a voluntary basis by members of the 2,000-strong Supporters Club.

Named after the famous stage and film actor, the theatre passed its 1,000th performance in under 3 years. It is a modern, light, well-equipped house, with a constant turnover of shows from melodrama, farce and panto to variety, thrillers, Shakespeare, and particularly musicals. The Studio is small and used for rehearsals, late-night shows and visiting groups (eg Gay Sweatshop). Director Vivyan Ellacott is also very keen to encourage plays and projects that can attract the local Indian and West Indian communities. Not much for visitors in the locality (except shopping). Best to eat and drink at the theatre. Trains run past midnight, but allow 40 minutes for travelling from central London.

Rail: Ilford (British Rail)
Bus: 25, 86, 123, 129, 139, 144, 145 147, 148, 150, 167, 169, 179, 193, 199, 247A
Map: 146 D

Keskidee Arts Centre

Gifford Street, Islington, N1 0DF
Box Office: **609 4263** (10 00-22 00) Admin: **609 4263/2**
Performance Space: Hall, raised stage *Seating:* Variable (110-220)

Bookings: Postal (cheques to Keskidee Centre) s.a.e Phone (held to ½ hr before show) No credit cards **Prices:** £1.25 **Concessions:** Students, OAPs, parties 10+ 60p **Catering:** Hot & cold West Indian food, soft drinks, tea & coffee from 1 hr before show **Bars:** Opening shortly **Wheelchairs:** No **Cloakrooms:** No **Parking:** Streets **Other:** Membership £3.50 p.a. for use of all centre's facilities, including library, art gallery, restaurant, workshops, but not a requirement for buying theatre tickets.

Policy: To bring Afro-Caribbean art and theatre to London and through it to encourage an understanding of its richness and variety.

Perspective: Three large workshops in the basement of an old Salvation Army mission hall off the Caledonian Road running north from King's Cross make up the Keskidee Arts Centre along with a ground floor exhibition space and small cinema, three more workshops, a library, a meeting room and the theatre on the first floor.

The Keskidee Educational Trust, which runs the centre, was set up in 1972 to meet the needs of the local black population, but the centre, opened in 1976 by Oscar Abrams, broadened out as a focal point for Afro-Caribbean studies and arts. The theatre work forms an integral part of the centre's activities, which range from karate and sculpture to batik, typing, table tennis and dancing.

There are growing exchanges by the resident company both within Britain and abroad. But, as part of the slowly developing ethnic cultural movement which is undersubsidized nationally and locally, it gets little of the publicity of similar 'white' venues, yet remains a vital if draughty outlet for black actors, designers, directors, and above all, playwrights, with a particular emphasis on youth.

British Rail: Caledonian Road & Barnsbury
Bus: 14, 45, 168A, 221, 239, 259, 263
Map: 147 **D**

Kings Head Theatre Club (Kings Head)

115 Upper Street, Islington, London N1 1QN
Box Office: **226 1916** (10 30-20 30) Admin: **226 8561**
Performance Space: Thrust stage, tables & chairs on 3 sides
Seating: 110 (70 dinner & show, 40 show only)

Bookings: Members only (Ordinary 25p p.a. + 1 guest, Full £1.25 p.a. + 10 guests — either available on the night) Postal (cheques to Kings Head Theatre Club) s.a.e. Phone (held to 20 mins before show) No credit cards. Sterling travellers cheques **Prices:** Combined dinner/show £4.50 Monday-Thursday, £4.75 Friday & Saturday; Show only £1.75 Monday-Thursday, £2 Friday & Saturday; lunchtimes 90p **Concessions:** Students **Perf Times:** Lunchtime 13 15 Monday-Saturday; Eves 19 00 dinner, 20 00 show Monday-Saturday **Mailing List:** Full members only **Catering:** Lunchtime hot/cold bar snacks; dinners three course, wine extra **Bars:** As for pub **Wheelchairs:** Yes **Cloakrooms:** No **Parking:** Streets **Other:** Occasional performance-related bookstall. Full membership entitles reduced price preview tickets.

Policy: To encourage and stage new plays and new writing. Many of the productions have gone on to wider audiences in the West End and New York.

Perspective: Canadians Joan and Dan Crawford took over in 1970 an empty pub in the north London borough of Islington called the Kings Head and turned the back room, which had been used for billiards, boxing and folk, into one of the most successful fringe venues in London. The first club theatre in a pub to make a name for itself, the Kings Head consistently offers good-humoured but thoughtful entertainment in a relaxed (if cramped) atmosphere with reasonably priced food and drink.

Half the year the Kings Head operates as a producing company, hiring its own cast and other staff. The other half it acts as a venue, and at lunchtime always appear outside companies. People like working there, and it has achieved a remarkable record, from its early days with plays by Athol Fugard, David Mercer, and Tom Gallacher's premieres, to the recent international hits, such as Hugh Leonard's *Da* and Stewart Parker's play with music about Ireland, *Spokesong*, both of which transferred.

At first, the Kings Head was known as a more experimental, lunchtime venue, working in conjunction with the homeless Soho Theatre (now Soho Poly — see separate entry). Chris Wilkinson and Snoo Wilson, for example, were given London showings which otherwise might never have happened. The Kings Head was able to keep going because the Crawfords pulled the pints as well as staged the shows. But they made a commercial breakthrough in 1974 with *Kennedy's Children* by American Robert Patrick, which broke fringe records that were surpassed only by *Dirty Linen,* ironically when it also transferred to the Arts (see separate entry).

The Kings Head has a knack of surprising you, as when Stewart Trotter put on Terence Rattigan's *The Winslow Boy* to great acclaim — though, of English writers, the theatre has paid special attention to Joe Orton, who used to live round the corner.

Underground: Highbury & Islington (Victoria, British Rail)
Bus: 4, 19, 30, 43, 104, 279, 279A
Map: 147 F

Little Angel Marionette Theatre

14 Dagmar Passage, Cross Street, N1 2DN
Box Office: **226 1787** (10 00-18 00 Monday-Sunday) Admin: **226 1787**
Performance Space: Miniature proscenium arch *Seating:* 100

Bookings: Postal (cheques to Little Angel Theatre) s.a.e Phone (held to 15 minutes before show) No credit cards or travellers cheques **Prices:** £1.50 adults, £1 children at 15 00 shows. £1 adults, 75p children at 11 00 shows **Concessions:** No **Perf Times:** Daily school hols at 15 00; term-time Saturday & Sunday 15 00; all Saturdays 11 00 for under 6s **Mailing List:** £1 p.a. **Catering:** Tea, coffee & snacks **Bars:** No **Wheelchairs:** 5 **Cloakrooms:** No **Parking:** NCP, Angel Station, side streets **Other:** Souvenirs from box office. Special Friends of Theatre Membership £5 p.a. for mailings, back stage visits, lectures etc.

Policy: To present puppetry of a high standard and to promote appreciation of the art.

Perspective: Sandwiched between Upper Street and Essex Road in the north London borough of Islington, the theatre is housed in a charming old building which was once a Temperance Hall and is now listed as a building of historical interest. It is beautifully decorated and well equipped. As well as a coffee bar in the foyer, there is a workshop where the puppets and settings for the various productions are made. It is often possible to be shown around the workshop and backstage after the show.

The theatre was opened in 1961 and is still the only puppet theatre in London to use a wide variety of techniques. The puppets can be controlled from above by strings as with marionettes; from below by rods or by hands, as with rod and glove puppets; from behind as with shadow puppets or from the stage itself as with black theatre puppets. The variety is enormous and the puppets range from the eight foot high devil figures made for Stravinsky's *Soldiers' Tale* to the humble glove puppets for *Wonder Island*.

Between 200 and 300 performances are given each year from the wide repertoire of over 20 plays, including Oscar Wilde's *The Fisherman and his Soul* and Menotti's *Amahl and the Night Visitors*. When the resident company is on tour visiting companies from England and abroad perform at the Little Angel. The company has been awarded gold medals at the Bucharest Festival in 1960 and the Polish Festival in 1978, and their marionettes have appeared in two major films, *Britannia Mews* and the *Tales of Hoffmann*, and in numerous British and Continental TV performances.

The theatre is open to the public every weekend throughout the year and daily during school holidays. Special seasons of evening performances for adults are advertised from time to time.

Rail: Essex Road (British Rail)
Bus: 4, 19, 30, 38, 43, 73, 104, 171, 277, 279, 279A
Map: 147 F

London Coliseum (Coliseum)

St Martins Lane, WC2N 4ES
Box Office: **836 3161** (10 00-20 00) Admin: **836 0111** Info: **836 7666**
Performance Space: Proscenium arch *Seating:* 2,358 (4 levels, boxes)

Bookings: Postal (cheques to ENO) Phone (held 3 days) Major credit cards (240 5258) Sterling travellers cheques **Prices:** £1.40-£8.70 **Concessions:** Discounts for parties and many others, including Student Standby **Perf Times:** 19 00 or 19 30
Mailing List: Joint with Royal Opera, £1.75 p.a. allows priority booking **Catering:** Full facilities from 1 hr before show **Bars:** 5 (from ½hr before show)
Wheelchairs: Yes **Cloakrooms:** 2 (Attendant) **Parking:** NCP in Bedfordbury at rear
Other: Friends of ENO allows free mailing, dress rehearsal parties, meetings, etc. Bookshop in foyer, records. Tours by arrangement 17 30. Music workshops in school with company.

Policy: English National Opera presents old and new opera in English, and, when a Company is away, provides the venue for foreign dance or opera companies.

Perspective: A famous London landmark just past St Martin-in-the-Fields off Trafalgar Square, the Coliseum has a remarkably inviting feel despite its imposing, grandiose architecture which is reflected in the English National Opera's productions. Apart from being in the native tongue, they are generally more down to earth than at Covent Garden, continuing the popular tradition of Oswald Stoll, who opened the theatre with several startling innovations — a *mobile* lounge, on tracks, to take royal parties to their boxes, lifts to upper levels, post office facilities in the spacious foyer, boxes at rear stalls level, and the first revolving stage in Britain, with three revolves that moved separately. Outside were the columns, arches, lions, chariots and eight cupids holding the iron and glass globe which originally had spun round but had to be fixed by law. Movement was suggested by flashing lights.

The reputation for spectacle, whether reproducing a steamboat, a Tyrolean village or Derby Day (in which a jockey was killed), made it an ironic venue for the first stage demonstration of television (1930). The honours list of what is now the capital's largest working theatre is long, going back through Helpmann's delightful *Peter Pan* to *Annie Get Your Gun* (over 1,000 performances), *King Kong*, Diaghilev's Russian Ballet, Sarah Bernhardt, Ellen Terry and Lillie Langtry — but not Marie Lloyd — to today's marathon *Ring* cycles.

The 'Collie's' founder, in top hat and frock coat, was a 'family' man, and had a notice forbidding swearing pinned up in every dressing room. He even had a bust of his mother erected in the vestibule.

Underground: Charing Cross (Bakerloo, Jubilee, Northern)
Leicester Square (Northern, Piccadilly)
Bus: 1, 3, 6, 9, 11, 12, 13, 15, 24, 29, 53, 77, 77A, 77C, 88, 159, 168, 170, 172, 176
Map: 155 N4

London Palladium (The Palladium)

Argyll Street, W1A 3AB
Box Office: **437 7373 or 437 6813** (10 00-20 30) Admin: **437 6233**
Performance Space: Proscenium arch *Seating:* 2,306 (3 levels, boxes)

Bookings: Postal (cheques to London Palladium) s.a.e. Phone (held 3 days) Credit cards — Access, AmEx, Barclaycard/Visa, Diners. US dollars **Prices:** £2.50-£8.50 **Concessions:** Parties; OAPs when available **Perf Times:** Eves & some mats **Bars:** 5 **Wheelchairs:** 2 **Cloakrooms:** 1 (Attendant) **Parking:** Hanover Square or streets **Other:** Souvenir kiosk for records, etc. before, during & after show. Palladium Cellars daily 10 00-21 00.

Policy: To present top international attractions, particularly in the area of family entertainment.

Perspective: Touring circus manager Charles Hengler built his show a permanent home on a site that had belonged to the Duke of Argyll, a Prime Minister and some wine merchants — the latter having dug out deep cellars which in 1980 were turned into an entertainment world, 'Disneyland'.

Circus gave way to ice skating and, when variety was at its peak with about 60 venues in the London area, to a Walter Gibbons who wanted to beat his rivals in music hall entertainment. The plush Palladium (only officially called 'London' in 1934), with classic exterior and spacious vestibule, had a sweeping dress circle, box-to-box telephones, and a Palm Court at the rear of the stalls made of Norwegian granite in which a Ladies Orchestra would play between performances.

All the popular names appeared as the style changed with the times. To match the success of the 'talkies', the theatre — after a three-month stint as a cinema — developed in 1932 its 'crazy week' which turned into the Crazy Gang Shows. At the same time, each Christmas, Jean Forbes-Robertson, Nova Pilbeam, Elsa Lanchester or Anna Neagle would triumph over Captain Hook. This pattern of variety (with big foreign names after the war), panto, and big star shows has continued since.

To many, though, the theatre is most famous for its *Sunday Night at the London Palladium* television variety series, which made national celebrities of comedian comperes such as Bruce Forsyth, Norman Vaughan and Jimmy Tarbuck. The closing moments, with the guests turning on the revolving stage, passed into the mythology of British humour.

Underground: Oxford Circus (Bakerloo, Central, Victoria)
Bus: 1, 3, 6, 7, 8, 12, 13, 15, 25, 53, 73, 88, 113, 137, 159, 500, 616, 710, 715, 735
Map: 151 E4

Lyric Theatre

Shaftesbury Avenue, W1V 8ES
Box Office: **437 3686** (10 00-20 00) Admin: **437 1231**
Performance Space: Proscenium arch *Seating:* 948

Bookings: Postal (cheques to Lyric Theatre) s.a.e. Phone. Credit cards — Access, Am Ex, Barclaycard/Visa. Sterling travellers cheques **Prices:** £2.50-£6 **Concessions:** Student Standby, OAPs Wednesday mats, very good party rates **Perf times:** 20 00 and Wednesday mats **Catering:** Tea at mats, coffee eves, from ½ hr before show and intervals) **Wheelchairs:** 7, with special street-entrance disabled toilet **Cloakrooms:** 2 (Attendant) **Parking:** Difficult, NCP 10 mins away in Brewer St

Policy: To present straight plays, musicals and comedies that will have wide appeal and will run as long as their popularity allows. Comedies have been prominent in recent years. Plays include both revivals and first productions, generally by well established writers.

Perspective: In a Shaftesbury Avenue block with the Apollo and Windmill Theatres, the Lyric was built on municipal ground with money made out of a comic opera *Dorothy*, originally seen at the Gaiety, transferred to the Prince of Wales, and brought in to open the Lyric. It was opened in 1888, the second theatre (by only 2 months) to be built on the Avenue. Refurbished in 1922, the theatre bears the mark of that decade, except for the shops that now occupy much of its frontage.

Musicals with Marie Tempest got the theatre off to a good start, but its most notable visitor was Eleanora Duse, the Italian tragedienne, who made her first British appearance (1893) in *La Dame aux Camelias* (wrongly called on the programme 'Camille'). She played other roles including Nora in Ibsen's *A Doll's House*. The Lyric boasts a distinguished roll of productions and artists since then, a sample including Tallulah Bankhead in the '20s, several appearances by the Lunts and Yvonne Arnaud, Terence Rattigan's *The Winslow Boy* (476 performances), *The Little Hut* (1,261 performances), the musical version of *The Barretts of Wimpole Street* called *Robert and Elizabeth* (957 performances), a year's run for Neil Simon's *Plaza Suite*, Alan Ayckbourn's *How the Other Half Loves* (2 years) and Alan Bennett's *Habeas Corpus* with Alec Guinness. In the second year of its run, the author took over from Patricia Hayes as Mrs Swabb — such things as dreams are made on!

More recent successes include the Ben Travers comedy *The Bed Before Yesterday*, and Eduardo de Filippo's *Filumena*. *Middle-Aged Spread* has been playing to capacity audiences since opening in October 1979.

Underground: Piccadilly Circus (Bakerloo, Piccadilly)
Bus: 14, 19, 22, 38 or 3, 6, 9, 12, 13, 15, 53, 88, 159 to Piccadilly Circus
Map: 154 N3

Lyric Hammersmith and Studio

King Street, W6 0QL
Box Office: **741 2311** (Monday-Saturday 10 00-20 00, Sundays vary)
Admin: **741 0824** *Performance Space:* Proscenium arch flexible *Seating:* 534 & 128

Bookings: Postal (cheques to Lyric Theatre Hammersmith) s.a.e. Phone (held 3 days) Sterling travellers cheques **Prices:** £1-£8 (box for 2) & £2 in Studio
Concessions: Parties. OAPs **Perf Times:** 19 30 & Thursday and Saturday mats; Studio variable, some mats, some Sundays **Mailing List:** 50p p.a. priority booking
Catering: Buffet Monday-Saturday 10 00-22 30, Sunday 12 00-22 00 **Bars:** 3
Wheelchairs: 3 (main theatre) + disabled toilet **Cloakrooms:** 3 (Paralok)
Parking: NCP Glenthorne Road. Ample in streets after 18 30 **Other:** Patrons £10 p.a. Friends £3 for priority bookings, newsletters, special events, price reductions, etc. Saturday jazz & Sunday folk free. Saturday morning children's show, foyer theatre exhibitions, outdoor terrace (summer)

Policy: To provide a variety of theatrical entertainment in pleasing surroundings which will attract both the local community and audiences from further afield.

Perspective: In 1979, the Queen opened the new Lyric Theatre on a site not far from where the first theatre had stood from 1888. Then known as the Lyric Hall, it staged a marionette show with pantomime and was converted in 1890 into a light opera theatre known as the Lyric Opera House. Melodramas followed until rebuilding in 1895.

It reopened that year with a prologue by Lillie Langtry. This elegant auditorium, designed by Frank Matcham, has been restored with its Victorian plasterwork intact in the current building — a return to the past in the middle of a modern, concrete block that contains the smart studio space, comfortable and spacious foyers, bars and a restaurant (all thanks to the local council).

The first great period of this famous theatre in west London came with John East, who during a 12-year rule produced over 400 shows and acted over 120 parts. After his departure, the Lyric became known as the 'blood and flea pit' until Nigel Playfair took the lease (1918) and made theatre history: *Abraham Lincoln* opened for a fortnight and ran for a year, *The Beggar's Opera*, with designs by Claud Lovat Fraser, ran for 3¼ years, Edith Evans played Millamant in *The Way of the World*, and a tradition of revues was established with A P Herbert's *Riverside Nights*.

H M Tennent took over after the war and brought the stars — Peggy Ashcroft, Dirk Bogarde, Richard Burton, Alec Guinness, Flora Robson, Margaret Rutherford. John Gielgud gave a famous season in 1952, Donald Wolfit played *The Master of Santiago*, Michael Codron introduced John Mortimer (*Dock Brief*) and Harold Pinter (*The Birthday Party*, which scraped only 16 performances), and the 59 Company produced a remarkable *Brand*. The old Lyric closed in 1965 and despite protests was demolished in 1972. Rebuilding began in 1974, and the first production (seen by Her Majesty) was Shaw's *You Never Can Tell*.

Underground: Hammersmith (District, Metropolitan, Piccadilly)
Bus: 9, 11, 27, 33, 72, 73, 91, 220, 260, 266, 267, 290, 701, 704, 710, 715, AV300, 311, 320, 322
Map: 145 E

Mayfair Theatre

Stratton Street, W1A 2AN
Box Office: **629 3036** (10 00-20 00) Admin: **629 7777**
Performance Space: Proscenium arch *Seating:* 310 (stalls, side gallery)

Bookings: Postal (cheques to Mayfair Hotel) s.a.e. Phone (held 3 days) Credit cards — Access, AmEx, Barclaycard/Visa, Diners. Travellers cheques **Prices:** £2-£6 **Concessions:** Discounts parties 20+. Student Standby **Perf Times:** Monday-Thursday 20 00, Friday-Saturday 18 00 & 20 45 **Catering:** Kiosk for soft drinks, confectionery; 2 hotel restaurants & coffee shop **Bars:** 3 (Mayfair Hotel bar serves theatre) **Wheelchairs:** 2 **Cloakrooms:** 2 (Attendant) **Parking:** Around Berkeley Sq after 18 30

Policy: The theatre is a venue for new British plays transferred from small grant-aided provincial theatres to London. The plays tend to be more sophisticated than is general for West End audiences. Two productions, on average, a year.

Perspective: The only London theatre inside a hotel, the Mayfair was converted from a restaurant and ballroom, known as the Candlelight Room, the scene of famous big band broadcasts in the 30s, with Ambrose and Harry Roy, into a theatre by the hotel's owners. The new intimate theatre with stepped seating is capable of providing variable acting spaces, though standard proscenium productions have predominated.

Ralph Richardson opened the smart Mayfair Theatre in 1963, six days before he appeared in the first production, Pirandello's *Six Characters in Search of an Author*, which ran for 295 performances. *Beyond the Fringe* transferred in 1964 and ran for over 2 years, and *The Philanthropist* by Christopher Hampton with Alec McCowen came from the Royal Court for a 3-year run, followed by Peter Handke's *The Ride Across Lake Constance* from the Hampstead Theatre Club, and Roy Dotrice in *Brief Lives*.

Other more recent successful transfers include *Are You Now, or Have You Ever Been?* (about McCarthy's anti-Communist committee in the US), Stephen Spear's *The Elocution of Benjamin Franklin* presented by the Nimrod Theatre of Australia, and one of the favourites at Buckingham Palace, Hinge and Bracket.

Underground: Green Park (Jubilee, Piccadilly, Victoria)
Bus: 9, 14, 19, 22, 25, 38
Map: 154 N2

The Mermaid (projected re-opening Summer 1981)

Puddle Dock, Blackfriars, EC4 4DB
Box Office: **(subject to re-opening)** Admin: **236 9521**
Performance Space: Open plan, open apron *Seating:* 614

Bookings: Postal (cheques to Mermaid Theatre Trust Ltd) s.a.e Phone Credit cards — Access, AmEx, Barclaycard/Visa, Diners. Sterling travellers cheques **Prices:** 50p-£4 (in 1978) **Concessions:** Parties **Perf Times:** Subject to re-opening **Mailing List:** £3 p.a. (The Mermaid Association) **Catering:** Coffee/snack bar; quality fast-food cafeteria; a la carte restaurant **Bars:** 2 **Wheelchairs:** Yes + disabled toilets **Cloakrooms:** Yes **Parking:** NCP adjacent **Other:** Combined dinner & theatre ticket available through box office + separate banqueting facilities by arrangement.

Policy: The theatre presents a wide range of new plays and worthwhile revivals, generally for limited runs and often transferring for longer seasons to the West End.

Perspective: The Mermaid closed in 1978 for the builders to put in an extra 100 seats, a walkway from Blackfriars Station into the theatre foyer, an enlarged riverside restaurant, cafeteria and bars, a stage twice as big as before and a small children's theatre. It started life in 1951 in the former St John's Wood School in north-west London, which had been taken over by Bernard and Josephine Miles. They staged shows for two short seasons here, and were then asked to mount a 13-week season in the central quadrangle of the Royal Exchange in the City in 1953. So successful was this 'going public' that the Corporation of London offered them a 7-year lease on a blitzed warehouse at Puddle Dock by the River Thames.

The Mermaid opened in 1959 with *Lock Up Your Daughters*, adapted from Henry Fielding by Miles with lyrics by Lionel Bart, which transferred to the West End. Famous for his egg and Mackeson television advertisements (spoken in a genuine country accent), Miles made the beautifully designed Mermaid into one of the friendliest theatres in London. It had excellent sightlines as well as first-class entertainment, including 15 productions of Shaw, a season of Sean O'Casey, a wide range of foreign plays from Gerhard Hauptmann, Vladimir Mayakovsky and Molière to Bertolt Brecht and Ibsen. Bernard Miles was knighted in 1969, and created a life peer in 1979.

As well as lunchtime food and drink at the theatre, the Mermaid also launched many plays into West End 'hits' — *Hadrian VII* with Alec McCowen, *Alfie, Spring and Port Wine, Breezeblock Park* (from Liverpool) and Brian Clark's *Whose Life Is It Anyway?*, which took Tom Conti — and Mary Tyler Moore — to Broadway. The Mermaid was also well known for its Christmas and children's shows — *Emile and the Detectives, Treasure Island, The Point* — and for its children's theatre, the Molecule Club, founded in 1968.

Underground: Blackfriars (Circle, District, British Rail)
Bus: 45, 63, 76, 109, 141, 155, 168A, 184
Map: 156 T3

National Theatre (Lyttelton and Olivier)

Upper Ground, South Bank, SE1 9PX
Box Office: **928 2252** (10 00-20 00) **928 2256** (24 hr recorded booking)
Admin: **928 2033** Other information: **633 0880**
Performance Space: Lyttelton, proscenium arch; Olivier, open stage *Seating:* Lyttelton, 890 (2 levels); Olivier, 1,160 (2 levels)

Bookings: Postal (cheques to National Theatre) s.a.e Phone (held 3 days) Credit cards — Access, AmEx, Barclaycard/Visa, Diners. Sterling travellers cheques
Prices: *Lyttelton* £1.80-£6 *Olivier* £1.80-£6 **Concessions:** Standby (for everyone, any unsold seats 45 mins before show sold at maximum £3) Also reduced prices for previews, openings & mid-week mats. Further concessions available for groups, schools and student parties, senior citizens: phone theatre for details
Perf times: *Lyttelton* 19 45 & some mats. *Olivier* 19 30 & some mats
Mailing List: See **Other** below **Catering:** *Lyttelton* Lyttelton Buffet (10 00-23 00) for light meals and snacks. NT Restaurant (see **Other** below); *Olivier* 2 coffee bars, 2 snackbars & NT Restaurant (see **Other** below) **Bars:** *Lyttelton* Normal pub hrs, tickets not required. *Olivier* 2 from 17 30 until end of interval
Wheelchairs: Yes (633 0880) **Cloakrooms:** 2 (Attendant) **Parking:** NCP under theatre **Other:** The Cottesloe, Lyttelton and Olivier Theatres are all housed in the same building on the South bank, and share all of the following facilities and structures: All 3 venues keep a number of tickets for sale on the day of performance from 10 00. This means that even if a show is sold out, the vigorous may still obtain tickets (maximum 2 per person) by arriving at the NT to queue up at about 09 30. In the Olivier and Lyttelton, 75 — more seats are held each day. *NT Restaurant* (928 2033 ext 531 days, 561 eves) Full dinners are served from 17 30-01 00 (last orders 23 00). Meals for under £7 inclusive of service and 15% tax. Also Saturday buffet lunches from 12 15-14 30 £4.25 for all-you-can-eat from cold buffet table. On certain evenings restaurant customers are offered a 10% discount on food. *NT Bookshops* — A bookstall in the Olivier is open from 2 hrs before each performance and the main bookstore, in the Lyttelton foyer, is open 10 00-23 00. The shops have a comprehensive stock of theatre and other arts publications, as well as posters from the NT productions. *Tours of the Building* — Tours are held several times daily (except Sunday) and include the backstage areas. These are bookable at the Lyttelton Information Desk 10 00-23 00 or ring 633 0880. Mailing List — £1.75 p.a. individuals, £2.50 Europe, £4 to anywhere else in the world. Members receive full repertoire details and exclusive priority booking. Write to *NT Mailing List* with s.a.e. Platform performances in the Lyttelton at 18 00, in the Olivier 17 45. Special short performances before main shows at 75p per ticket. *Foyer live music* — There is live music every evening from approximately 18 30, usually in the Lyttelton foyer, and free of charge. *Exhibitions* — Art exhibitions throughout the theatre foyers are open all day, free of charge. *Information Desk* — Details about all NT presentations, etc., are available from the information desk in the main entrance foyer (Lyttelton Theatre) from 10 00-23 00 every day except Sunday, or ring 633 0880. *The live foyer music (free), exhibitions, restaurant, bars (some open full pub hours), bookshops, tours, car park are all open to everyone*

Policy: To present a wide mixture of plays embracing ancient and modern classics revivals and new and experimental work (including foreign plays). Visiting companies from the regions and abroad are invited to use the NT as a London venue. The Olivier's open stage is an expression of modern theatre and the Lyttelton's proscenium theatre offers a clean-cut version of the more traditional form.

Perspective: To some it is a white elephant. To others, the ultimate cultural expression of a civilized industrial society. To many, a curiosity that is not as bad as they had first believed. Britain's National Theatre has been argued about since the first proposal for one was made in 1848. Schemes, and as many committees, came and went during the 125 years or so that it took to actually open the building (while other European countries, with less of a theatre tradition, got on with the job of launching their national theatres). Even the site was shifted several times, and the foundation stone ceremonially laid on four occasions in four different places.

Finally, Britain's first Arts Minister, Jennie Lee, inaugurated the work on the present building in 1969 on a site provided by the Greater London Council. The theatre, unique in having been built under a special Act of Parliament, was not ready on time, and the artistic director Peter Hall decided to move in to each of the three auditoria as they became available for public performance.

Founder of the Royal Shakespeare Company, Hall had taken over in 1973 from Laurence Olivier, the first director of the National Theatre when it was formed at the Old Vic in 1963, and after whom is named the largest of the three theatres, with its fan-shaped auditorium that can accommodate dramatists of every age and style. However, the first to open, in March 1976, was the Lyttelton with a transfer from the Old Vic of *Hamlet* starring Albert Finney and directed by Hall (*Hamlet*, directed by Olivier, with Peter O'Toole, had also been the first production of the National at the Old Vic).

The Olivier opened in October 1976 with Hall's production of *Tamburlaine*, again starring Albert Finney, and in March 1977 the small Cottesloe Theatre finally 'went public' (see separate entry). The official opening of the National Theatre complex came in October 1976 to the sight and sound of a funfair and fireworks set alight by Ralph Richardson.

On a plum site opposite Somerset House with St Paul's to the right and the House of Commons to the left, the theatre offers one of the most beautiful views in London, particularly at night. Completing the South Bank arts concrete complex (three concert halls, a cinema and an art gallery), the National has river walks, terraces (used for outdoor performances) and spacious foyers with high ceilings (also used for a range of artistic activity, covering mainly different types of music, which you can enjoy before the show starts).

At the Olivier, most interest has been kindled by the more challenging productions — *Tales from the Vienna Woods*, *The Madras House*, *The Woman* by Edward Bond (the first new play there) and Peter Shaffer's *Amadeus*, which has divided critics and proved a talking point. At the Lyttelton, the first new play performed was Howard Brenton's *Weapons of Happiness*, Alan Ayckbourn's *Bedroom Farce* transferred to the West End, Robert Bolt wrote about the Russian Revolution, and in *Death of a Salesman* Warren Mitchell showed us at last what we knew already — that there was more to him than TV anti-hero Alf Garnett.

Underground: Waterloo (Bakerloo, Northern, British Rail)
Bus: 1, 4, 55, 68, 70, 76, 149, 168A, 171, 176, 188, 239, 501, 502, 503, 513
Map: 155 N6

New Inn Theatre

New Inn, St Mary's Road, Ealing W5 5EX
Box Office: **567 8352** (18 30-22 00 perf nights only) Admin: **567 8352**
Performance Space: Upstairs pub room *Seating:* Max 50 (benches, stools)

Bookings: Members only (+ unlimited guests) 25p p.a. available in advance or at door. Phone (held to ¼ hr before show) No credit cards or travellers cheques **Prices:** £1, Saturday £1.20 **Concessions:** No **Perf Times:** Friday, Saturday & Sunday, normally 20 15. Occasional weekday perfs when available **Catering:** No **Bars:** As for pub **Wheelchairs:** No **Cloakrooms:** No **Parking:** Ample streets

Policy: The New Inn specializes in one-act plays by established modern dramatists, with emphasis on works that are infrequently performed. The theatre has also put on music hall nights and revues and hopes to attract audiences from outside the locality.

Perspective: Founded in October 1977 in the upstairs room of a popular pub in this western suburb of London, New Inn, both the theatre and the pub, then underwent four months of renovation to re-open again in April 1979. The pub is built on the site of an old coaching inn dating back to the 18th century, though the present building has the Dickensian decor of its origins in 1897 as a sawdust-and-spit hostelry.

The community orientation is based on the commitment to new plays, from the improvised *Abigail's Party* by Mike Leigh to a season on marriage, with plays by writers such as Alan Ayckbourn and Harold Pinter. New Inn staged the first production in London of *The Return of Barnum Chicken James* (played by a US actor) in association with the Foothills Theatre Company from Worcester, Massachusetts.

The tone tends to be light — Shaw's *How He Lied To Her Husband* or Michael Frayn's *Chinamen* — but also sophisticated (eg Peter Shaffer's *Black Comedy* and *The Private Ear*, or Joe Orton's *The Ruffian on the Stair*). New Inn is used by visiting companies, and also sells Watney fined bitter for the real specialists. Though it normally stages one-act or short plays, it has also presented revues and music hall to try and bring in a wider audience. The beer helps this aim as well, of course.

Underground: South Ealing (Piccadilly)
Bus: 65, 734
Map: 148 H

Old Red Lion Theatre Club

St John's Street, Islington, EC1V 4NJ
Box Office: **837 7816** (17 30-23 30) Admin: **837 7816**
Performance Space: Large pub studio *Seating:* 60-80 (flexible rostra)

Bookings: Members only 30p in advance or at door. Phone (held ½ hr before show) In person **Prices:** Normally £1.20 **Concessions:** No **Perf Times:** Tuesday-Sunday eves **Catering:** No **Bars:** As for pub **Wheelchairs:** No **Cloakrooms:** No **Parking:** Ample side streets

Policy: Newly opened pub theatre venue for visiting professional fringe theatre groups, with an emphasis on a flexible programme including original productions of new plays, established modern plays and revues.

Perspective: The Old Red Lion Theatre Club originated from the spontaneous impulse of the pub's landlord in late 1979 when he suggested to the many actors who drank there, 'Why not put on a show?' With Anna Sher's Children's Theatre School just up the road the pub was a natural venue for informal productions. Charlie Hanson (Director of London's Black Theatre Co-op) and actor-playwright Robert Pugh took up the initiative and presented the Red Lion's first show *Prime Slot Front Cloth* by Robert Longden, in November 1979, which transferred to the Institute of Contemporary Arts. The precedent was followed by Andy Smith's *Werewolf Boulevard*, which also went on to the ICA. The success of the venture has resulted in an animated pub theatre which attracts both local and professional audiences, and provides a showcase for energetic out-of-work actors — and while most shows are 'home-grown', the venue's flexible policy also allows for visiting fringe groups to play there. Fran Landesman's highly succesful *Loose Connections* had its world premiere here in March, and put the pub more than firmly on the map.

The pub landlord plays an active part in his theatre, and soon after the opening he purchased church pews for seating with attached bible racks that act as 'tables' for drinks! The first pub on the present site (re-built in 1899) was licensed in 1415, and with its double entrances/exits in parallel streets was for a long time known as the 'in-and-out at the Angel'. This was because when cab-drivers deposited their passengers at one door, the passenger very often ran into the pub and disappeared out of the other door leaving the driver with his fare unpaid. But with the Angel tube station opposite, who needs a taxi?

Underground: Angel (Northern)
Bus: 4, 19, 30, 38, 43, 73, 104, 171, 172, 214, 277, 279, 279A
Map: 156 Q2

Old Vic Theatre

The Cut, Waterloo Road, SE1 8NB
Box Office: **928 7616** (10 00-20 00) Admin: **928 6111**
Performance Space: Proscenium arch, slight thrust *Seating:* 878 (3 levels)

Bookings: Postal (cheques to the Old Vic) s.a.e. Phone (held 3 days) Credit cards (261 1821) Access, Barclaycard/Visa. Sterling travellers cheques **Prices:** £1-£6 **Concessions:** Student, OAPs Standby £2.50 when available; Parties 20 + 1 free in 10; 70 standing if full 50p **Perf Times:** Monday-Saturday 19 30, Wednesday & Saturday mats 14 30 **Mailing List:** £1.50 p.a. gives priority booking **Catering:** Stalls wine bar hot & cold food 10 00-15 00 & 18 00-19 30 Tables bookable **Bars:** 3 **Wheelchairs:** 2 **Cloakrooms:** 1 (Attendant) **Parking:** Ample street after 18 30, NCP Waterloo Rd **Other:** Friends of The Old Vic £7.50 p.a. for Mailing List, priority bookings, lectures, seminars & other facilities.

Policy: The Old Vic is the home base of the Old Vic Company, a touring organization with extensive British and overseas commitments. While in its London home, the Company's repertoire is mainly classical with more emphasis on actor and text than on elaborate productions. When on tour, the theatre is an important venue for major touring companies, including music, dance and opera, both national and foreign. The Old Vic Company also works closely with the Old Vic Youth Theatre (928 8501) which holds year-round workshops and stages two productions per year with the help of local children during the Easter vacation.

Perspective: This friendly theatre, which has an honoured place in the history of the British theatre, opened unfinished in 1818 on a site that used to be known as Lambeth Marsh. Called the Royal Coburg Theatre, it thrived as a home for well-known actors (eg Edmund Kean) and melodrama, changed its name four times (until Old Vic settled) and was taken over in 1880 by social reformer Emma Cons who wanted to rid it of its low reputation.

In 1912 her niece Lilian Baylis took full control and dedicated the rest of her life to the Old Vic and to the cause of good theatre at cheap prices for a wide audience. One of her first experiments, after introducing 'moving pictures', was to stage between 1914 and 1923 the entire canon of Shakespeare's plays.

In 1931, the year Baylis rebuilt Sadler's Wells, the first Vic-Wells Ballet (later the Royal Ballet) was staged with Anton Dolin under Ninette de Valois. Soon drama stayed at the Old Vic while opera and ballet played at the Wells. Bombed in the Second World War, the theatre remained closed until 1950 while its company performed elsewhere (eg The New, now Albery). It was wound up in 1963 when the Old Vic passed into the hands of the National Theatre. In 1976, when the National moved to the South Bank, the touring group Prospect used the Old Vic as its London base and is now a revivified Old Vic Company, now under the artistic direction of Timothy West, with Peter O'Toole and Jack Emery as associate directors.

Underground: Waterloo (Bakerloo, Northern, British Rail)
Bus: 1, 4, 55, 68, 70, 76, 149, 168A, 171, 176, 188, 239, 501, 502, 513
Map: 155 O6

Open Air Theatre (Regent's Park)

Regent's Park, NW1 4NU
Box Office: **486 2431** (10 00-20 00) Admin: **935 5884**
Performance Space: Amphitheatre *Seating:* 1,187 plus 60 on grass
(steeply raked, 2 tiers)

Bookings: Postal (cheques to Open Air Theatre, Regent's Park) s.a.e. Phone (held to 45 mins before show) Credit cards — Access, AmEx, Barclaycard/Visa, Diners. Travellers cheques with identification **Prices:** £1.50-£5 **Concessions:** Parties; Student Standby **Perf Times:** 19 45 June-August **Catering:** Supper & snacks available from 18 45 with choice of barbecue or cold buffet **Bars:** Longest theatre bar, open to 24 00 **Wheelchairs:** Side spaces (use of staff car park by prior arrangement) **Parking:** Ample around Regent's Park Inner Circle **Other:** Pleasant park surroundings.

Policy: To present classical repertoire of the highest quality with emphasis on Shakespearian comedies. The resident company tours annually out of season. Other entertainments on the site include Sunday concerts run by Capital Radio, Victorian Music Hall and lunchtime concerts.

Perspective: Despite Britain's notoriously unpredictable weather, Regent's Park has been used for open-air Shakespeare productions since 1900, when it was known as the Royal Botanical Gardens, and the Woodland Players, under the direction of the hardworking actor/manager Ben Greet, tripped the light fantastic there.

In 1932 permission was gained to try out four matinees of *Twelfth Night*, a black and white production, and Sydney Carroll and Robert Atkins made the theatre an established part of London life. Many star names appeared there in the '30s, including Deborah Kerr, Vivien Leigh, Gladys Cooper, Jack Hawkins and Robert Helpmann, with performances continuing, almost without a break, throughout the war years. In 1962 David Conville formed the New Shakespeare Company which quickly made an impact with both critics and public. Its players have included Robert Stephens, Penelope Keith, Dinsdale Landen, Felicity Kendall, Edward Fox, Gemma Jones, Dennis Quilley and Judi Dench.

Although the repertoire has mainly featured Shakespeare, during the last two Summer Seasons an old association has been revived: Bernard Shaw wrote *The Six of Calais* for the Open Air Theatre, and it had its world premiere there in 1934. Now Shaw's work is again being featured in the summer season. A lunchtime programme has also been added.

In 1974 the whole theatre was reconstructed: a new amphitheatre was built, microphones became unnecessary, the deck chairs and wooden seats were done away with, and an off-stage reputation was earned for barbecues, mulled wine and cocktails. Fancy a Puck's Fizz?

Underground: Baker Street (Bakerloo, Circle, Jubilee, Metropolitan)
Bus: 1, 2, 2B, 13, 18, 18A, 27, 30, 74, 113, 159, 176
Map: 150 C3

Orange Tree Theatre

45 Kew Road, Richmond, Surrey TW9 2NQ
Box Office: **940 3633** (10 00-22 00) Admin: **940 0141**
Performance Space: Upstairs pub room *Seating:* 80 (church pews, 3rd row raised)

Bookings: No postal bookings. Phone (held to ½ hr before show) Cheques to Richmond Fringe. No credit cards. Sterling travellers cheques **Prices:** £1.50 & £2 eves. May-August 75p lunchtimes **Concessions:** Students, OAPs & claimants on 1st Monday-Wednesday of new shows; some discounts Wednesday & Thursday lunchtimes **Perf Times:** Monday-Friday 20 00 Saturday 17 40 & 20 30. Lunchtime Wednesday-Friday 13 15, Saturday & Sunday 12 15 **Mailing List:** £2 p.a.
Catering: Pub restaurant (Good Food Guide) full meals & coffee **Bars:** Pub hours. Real ale **Wheelchairs:** Yes, will carry upstairs **Cloakrooms:** No **Parking:** Richmond Station multi-storey

Policy: The theatre stages all its own productions, hiring actors for each new production. Choice of shows is made by taking into account the needs of the local population, which makes up two-thirds of the audience. There is emphasis on local writers and specially-commissioned works.

Perspective: A small group of actors, writers and directors who lived in the Richmond area, south west of London, decided in 1971 to start a lunchtime fringe theatre, and, the story goes, after a second evening's pub crawl arrived at the Orange Tree. It had a room upstairs full of junk, but in just over a month, on the last day of the year, Evan Jones's *Go Tell It On Table Mountain* opened a new theatre.

So successful was it that its list of credits reads more like those of a well-established West End theatre. As well as playing host to other visiting companies, the Orange Tree has also presented an impressive list of lunchtime shows by a range of the best contemporary writers, from Harold Pinter, Tom Stoppard and Fay Weldon to Howard Barker, David Cregan and David Halliwell, many of them 'firsts'.

In 1975, evening performances were introduced after the pub was renovated (it is comfortable but now crowded, except for the cellar bar, and serves Young's real ale). The policy is under the control of artistic director and founder Sam Walters, who directs about one-third of the shows. Informality and cushioned church pews have been maintained along with a lively programme (eg a revival of Howard Brenton's *Magnificence, The Way of the World* performed in track suits, first productions in Britain of plays by persecuted Czech writer Vaclav Havel, and outdoor productions in the summer with a special children's festival. James Saunders wrote *Bodies* for the Orange Tree, where it was first performed before Hampstead staged the production that went into the West End. Orange Tree had its own West End transfer, though, when Israel Horovitz's *The Primary English Class* opened at Wyndham's.

Underground: Richmond (District, British Rail)
Bus: 15, 27, 65, 71, 90, 90B, 202, 265, 270, 290, P235 or 33, 37, 73, 714 to Richmond Red Lion Street
Map: 148 G

Oval House

52-54 Kennington Oval, SE11 5JW
Box Office: **582 7680** (24hr Ansaphone) Admin: **735 2786**
Performance Space: Large downstairs space, smaller upstairs space
Seating: 120 & 40 (both variable rostra)

Bookings: Members only 50p + 1 guest, obtainable or at door (cheques to Oval House) Phone (held to ½ hr before show) No credit cards **Prices:** Downstairs £1.15, Upstairs 90p **Concessions:** Under 18 s 40p in both theatres **Perf Times:** Downstairs 19 30 Wednesday-Sunday; upstairs 21 30 Friday-Sunday **Mailing List:** See under **Other Catering:** Cafe (18 30 onwards) for home-made soups, salads, main dish, coffee & teas **Bars:** No **Wheelchairs:** Up to 10 Downstairs **Cloakrooms:** No **Parking:** Small car park at rear **Other:** Full membership (£5.00 p.a. or £3 3 mths) entitles ticket purchase, workshops, mailings of advance information. Concessional memberships available for under 18 s. Membership is reciprocal with 14 other fringe venues.

Policy: To provide a venue offering learning experiences for all interested in theatre.

Perspective: There could be few more ironic contrasts than the frenetic Oval House in south London and its famous neighbour across the road, the home of Surrey County Cricket, a 'gentlemen's' club that has played host to countless test matches. Until 1961, the Oval House was run solely as a boys' club by its parent body, Christ Church (Oxford) United Clubs. Then wider youth activities were introduced, and in 1967, under Peter Oliver, Oval House became almost synonymous with the fringe. Oliver provided free rehearsal space for many innovative groups (eg Freehold, Pip Simmons, Portable) and an outlet for many others, like Moving Being, a mixed-media, dance-based company. Oval House also spawned groups, such as Sidewalk, Theatrespiel, Incubus and Sal's Meat Market, all of which relied a lot on improvisational work.

In 1969, it started its annual 'free' festival of experimental theatre. Then came its radical theatre school, followed by *Feast of Fools* (bringing together 4 groups on one project). You could also see there exciting foreign groups, like the Bread and Puppet Theatre from New York — and more recent US visitors have included Spiderwoman and Hot Peaches. After 1974, Oval House became a grant-aided further education establishment and the community side of the work was stressed more. It developed its workshops and classes – you can try your hand (or feet) at clowning, tap, mime, acrobatics, printing, video.

Christmas shows and children's shows are an important part of the calendar and evolve from projects (eg *The Man from Nazareth*) but the commitment to touring companies remains. Oval House is now run without a director and retains the informal atmosphere that makes it such an important catalyst in the development of the fringe.

Underground: Oval (Northern)
Bus: 3, 36, 36A, 36B, 109, 133, 155, 159, 172, 185
Map: 147 G

Overground Theatre Club

19 Ashdown Road, Kingston-on-Thames, Surrey KT1 2PH
Box Office: **549 5893** (10 30-18 00) Admin: **546 6244**
Performance Space: Converted church hall *Seating:* 120 (raked)

Bookings: Members only (+ unlimited guests) 75p p.a. in advance or at door Postal (cheques to Overground Theatre Company) s.a.e Phone (held to ½ hr before show) No credit cards. Sterling travellers cheques **Prices:** £1-£2.25 **Concessions:** Parties 10 + , students & OAPs 25p off **Perf Times:** Tuesday-Saturday 20 00 No mats **Mailing List:** Free to members, 4 p.a. **Catering:** No **Bars:** 1 (19 00-23 00) **Wheelchairs:** Yes (with one month's notice) **Cloakrooms:** No **Other:** Reciprocal membership with most other London fringe theatre clubs.

Policy: The Overground Theatre Club is a producing company hiring actors for its own productions and aiming to provide a balanced programme of contemporary theatre with a mixture of new plays and established modern drama. New productions are staged every three to four weeks and the programme is designed to appeal to an audience drawn from a wide area.

Perspective: Three minutes from the centre of Kingston, south-west of London, you can see an old church hall painted with a blue-and-white bird motif. That is the Overground Theatre Club, started in 1974 by Alan Pryce and Maria Riccio as a lunchtime theatre in the Kingston Hotel (now demolished) to provide work for unemployed actors living nearby.

They moved two years later to the All Saints Parish Church to continue and expand their successful policy of presenting any and every type of play they liked, regardless of its standpoint, the only criterion being that they thought it was good theatre.

When they were playing at lunchtime, they performed plays at a fast rate, including new work by writers such as Leigh Jackson, Lou Stein, and Royce Ryton. As an evening venue the pace and the range has dropped slightly (eg *Butley* by Simon Gray, *Just Between Ourselves* by Alan Ayckbourn), but the standards are still high. The theatre's bolder side was demonstrated in 1980 when it tackled Eugene O'Neill's mammoth *Long Day's Journey into Night*, and 40 per cent of the productions are still premieres, including in 1980 Edward Albee's new play *Seascape*.

British Rail: Kingston
Bus: 57, 65, 71, 85, 111, 131, 201, 211, 213A, 215, 216, 218, 219, 265, 281, 285, 406, 476, 478, 479, 714, 715, 718, 725, 726, 727
Map: 148 E

Palace Theatre

Shaftesbury Avenue, W1A 4AF
Box Office: **437 6834** (10 00-20 00) Admin: **437 4144**
Performance Space: Proscenium arch *Seating:* 1,450 (3 levels, boxes)

Bookings: Postal (cheques to Palace Theatre) s.a.e. Phone (held 3 days) but in person preferred. Credit cards (437 6834) AmEx, Access, Barclaycard/Visa, Diners **Prices:** Normal West End scale **Concessions:** Parties for certain performances; Student Standby when available **Perf Times:** See daily press **Catering:** Coffee, confectionery, ices **Bars:** 4 **Wheelchairs:** By prior arrangement **Cloakrooms:** 2 (Attendant) **Parking:** NCP Newport St **Other:** Souvenirs from attendants

Policy: West End policy of commercial theatre.

Perspective: Planned as the home of English opera by the first manager Richard D'Oyly Carte, doyen of Gilbert and Sullivan productions, this imposing red brick and terracotta theatre took 2 years to build.

Sweeping round one curve of Cambridge Circus (with its arcade windows, balconies and awnings), it had its own water and electricity supply when it opened in 1891. A grand theatre, with columns, arches and a main staircase inside, it fared better as a music hall with such names as Marie Tempest (making her first variety appearance), Maud Allan (creating a scandal with Salome), Mistinguett from the Moulin Rouge, the prima ballerina Pavlova (in her first London appearance) and George V (for his first Royal Command Peformance.)

C B Cochran ran the Palace as a cinema, but it came back into prominence with the musical *No No Nanette*. Cicely Courtneidge and Jack Hulbert moved in for the war years, and later Peter Daubeny made it the home of visiting foreign companies, preceding his World Theatre Seasons at the Aldwych.

Aside from such performances as Laurence Oliver in the Royal Court transfer of *The Entertainer*, the theatre's biggest hits have been with musicals — *The Flower Drum Song* and *The Sound of Music* (from 1961-1967) by Rodgers and Hammerstein, and *Jesus Christ Superstar* by Tim Rice and Andrew Lloyd Webber, Britain's longest-running musical. In the corridors is a superb collection of playbills owned by the theatre's controller Sir Emile Littler.

Underground: Leicester Square (Northern, Piccadilly), Tottenham Court Road (Central, Northern)
Bus: 1, 14, 19, 22, 24, 29, 38, 176 or 7, 8, 25, 73, 134 to Centre Point
Map: 155 M4

Pentameters

The Three Horseshoes, 28 Heath Street, Hampstead, NW3 6TE
Box Office: **435 6757** (times vary) Admin: **435 6757** (49 Frognal, NW3)
Performance Space: Upstairs pub, open stage *Seating:* 80

Bookings: Temporary membership (20p at door) Phone No credit cards **Prices:** £1
Concessions: Parties by prior arrangement **Perf Times:** 20 00 Friday, Saturday, Sunday — possible future Wednesday, Thursday **Catering:** Pub food, including sit-down during show **Bars:** Normal pub **Wheelchairs:** No **Cloakrooms:** No
Parking: Ample after 18 30 **Other:** Monday eve poetry, Tuesday eve Folk Club

Policy: To provide platform for known and unknown poets and to promote the work of new playwrights. Plays performed at lunchtime and/or evenings for two weekends each. Company drawn from a pool of professional and amateur actors and directors.

Perspective: Founded by Leonie Scott Matthews at the Freemasons Arms in 1968 as the Poetry Theatre, Pentameters became established at the Three Horseshoes pub in 1971 where it had developed as a venue for new playwrights as well as for the poets. The original idea was to start a poetry centre (in the wake of a revival in interest in poetry that accompanied the cultural explosion of the '60s). There are few places in London where poets, especially poets in the theatre, can try out their work in a relaxed but supportive atmosphere.

Then its function expanded to give a chance to work, prose and poetry, that might not be seen elsewhere. The first production of Royce Ryton's *The Other Side of the Swamp* was presented here before it went to the Kings Head, and Richard Hoggart's portrait of Lawrence called simply *DHL* was given its first production, before being seen at the Edinburgh Festival, the Theatre at New End and on television. Recently Apollinaire's *The Breasts of Tiresias* was staged. There are occasional amateur performances — but then the venue is let as the Three Horseshoes not as Pentameters (a name taken from a line of verse that has five beats). For three years, Bee & Bustle Music Hall (see Railway) performed at the pub.

The companies also tour (about once a year only) and one of their best spots is the Lace Market Theatre, Nottingham. At the beginning of the week there are poetry reading (Mondays) and a folk club (Tuesdays). An impressive array of names have appeared to read their own work, including Harold Pinter, Ted Hughes, Stephen Spender, R D Laing, Edna O'Brien, and Adrian Mitchell. You can enjoy the village atmosphere of the walk from Hampstead Tube up Heath Street, and you might want to try some of the many (but expensive) restaurants. If you like real ale, the Nag's Head is the place.

Underground: Hampstead (Northern)
Bus: 268 or 210 to Whitestone Pond
Map: 147 **A**

Phoenix Theatre

Charing Cross Road, WC2H 0JP
Box Office: **336 8611** (10 00-20 00) Admin: **836 7431**
Performance Space: Proscenium arch *Seating:* 1,012 (3 levels)

Bookings: Postal (cheques to Phoenix Theatre) s.a.e. Phone (held 3 days) Credit cards (up to 1 hr before show) Access, AmEx, Barclaycard/Visa. Travellers cheques **Prices:** £2.50-£7.50 **Concessions:** Parties 15+ £1 discounts on all but cheapest seats, Student Standby when available **Perf Times:** Monday-Saturday 20 00, Wednesday mats 15 00, Saturday mats 17 00 **Catering:** Coffee available in Noël Coward Bar **Bars:** 4 **Wheelchairs:** 1 **Cloakrooms:** 2 (Attendant) **Parking:** NCP Phoenix car park corner Stacey/New Carpenter streets **Other:** Phoenix Theatreshop, Charing Cross Rd, for souvenirs & tickets — normal shop hours

Policy: Normal commercial West End theatre, drama and musicals.

Perspective: The second theatre to open in 1930, the Phoenix was built on the site of a factory which later became a musical hall of 'ill repute'. At first the entrance was in Charing Cross Road as part of a frontage with shops and offices (now including a theatre bookshop) but it was later moved round the corner to Phoenix Street from which the theatre takes its name (and not from the early 17th-century playhouse in Drury Lane). The unveiling ceremony was recorded to a fanfare of trumpets with a speech from the manager C B Cochran. The opening show was Noël Coward's *Private Lives*, directed by and including the author, Gertrude Lawrence, Adrienne Allen and Laurence Olivier.

Smart in the '30s style, it was considered by Coward and Lawrence to be their theatre. Coward returned with one-act plays in 1936, and in 1969 the 'Master' opened a bar named after him. Just before the war, there was a series of plays presented by Michel Saint-Denis and Bronson Albery (eg Bulgakov's *The White Guard*) in association with the London Theatre Studio, but after that the theatre went over to films.

It had a mixed history during the war (which included John Gielgud's *Love for Love*) and in 1945 staged Thornton Wilder's *The Skin of Our Teeth* and Cicely Courtneidge in *Under the Counter*, which ran for 665 performances. Coward, Gielgud and Terence Rattigan came next until the 1955/56 season that brought Peter Brook and Paul Scofield together. Transfers kept the Phoenix open (eg John Osborne's *Luther* from the Royal Court with Albert Finney) until *Canterbury Tales* (1968) ran for over 2,000 performances. A series of short runs followed, including a transfer of *Godspell*, but more recently Tom Stoppard's *Night and Day* has dug in for a long run. There is an interesting collection of prints and pictures in the Circle bar, and even a photo of a London bus advertising *Canterbury Tales*. The bar is known, of course, as the Chaucer.

Underground: Tottenham Court Road (Central, Northern)
Bus: 1, 14, 19, 22, 24, 29, 38, 176 or 7, 8, 25, 73, 134 to Centre Point
Map: 151 E6

Piccadilly Theatre

Denman Street, W1V 8DY
Box Office: **437 4506** (10 00-20 00) Admin: **437 2124**
Performance Space: Proscenium arch *Seating:* 792 (2 levels, boxes)

Bookings: Postal (cheques to Piccadilly Theatre) s.a.e. Phone (held approx 3 days) Credit cards (379 6565) Access, AmEx, Barclaycard/Visa, Diners. Sterling travellers cheques **Prices:** £3-£7.80 **Concessions:** Parties (836 3962) Student Standby **Perf Times:** 19 30, Thursday mat 14 30, Saturday 16 00 & 20 00 **Catering:** Coffee at mats, confectionery kiosk at intervals **Bars:** 3 from ½ hr before show **Wheelchairs:** 4 (Box, & Royal Circle — street access) **Cloakrooms:** 1 (Attendant) 4 (Paralok) **Parking:** NCP Brewer St. **Other:** Royal Retiring Room available for entertaining.

Policy: West End Commercial Theatre.

Perspective: A corner theatre tucked round the back of Piccadilly Circus in what is in danger of becoming a rip-off area, it was built in 1928 (designed by Bertie Crewe) on a site covered by out-of-use stables. The white Portland stone front has stayed the same but the interior was redecorated in 1955 and again in 1960, when changes included the installation of the first full air-conditioning in a London theatre.

After Evelyn Laye's opening show, Warner Brothers moved in with Vitaphone films, the 'talkies' and Al Jolson. Back as a theatre in 1929, the Windmill's empire expanded to embrace the Piccadilly in the '30s until 1937 when Firth Shepherd introduced *Choose Your Time*, a mixture of newsreel, Donald Duck, 'swingphonic orchestra', and variety acts. Then came a run of transfers at reduced prices, and, after being closed by the war, Noel Coward's *Blithe Spirit* (1941) began its long run. Flying bombs damaged the theatre, which had an up-and-down history until the Albery family won a battle for control in 1960 and transferred *The Amorous Prawn*, which ran for a year.

Marcel Marceau, the great French mime, visited twice, *Who's Afraid of Virginia Woolf?* was a big hit but moved out to make room for a musical, and transfers saved the day — Prospect's *Richard II* and *Edward II* with Ian McKellen playing both leads, *Vivat Vivat Regina!* from Chichester, and, from the Royal Shakespeare Company, *Wild Oats*, *Privates on Parade*, *Piaf*, and *Once in a Lifetime*. *Gypsy* with Angela Lansbury, Claire Bloom in *A Streetcar Named Desire* and Edna Everidge have also done well.

Underground: Piccadilly Circus (Bakerloo, Piccadilly)
Bus: 3, 6, 9, 12, 13, 14, 15, 19, 22, 38, 53, 88, 159
Map: 154 N3

Pindar of Wakefield

328 Grays Inn Road, WC1X 8BZ
Box Office: **722 5395** (10 00-19 00) Admin: **586 2856**
Performance Space: Large room at back of pub *Seating:* 100

Bookings: Postal (cheques to Aba Daba Ltd, 30 Upper Park Rd, NW3) Credit cards — Access, Barclaycard/Visa. Travellers cheques **Prices:** £3
Concessions: Parties negotiable. Student Standby/Equity £2 **Perf Times:** 20 15 or 20 30 **Mailing List:** £1.50 p.a. **Catering:** Hot and cold snacks **Bars:** Pub hours
Wheelchairs: Yes **Cloakrooms:** No **Parking:** Street **Other:** Full meals during show for extra price

Policy: The Aba Daba provides an opportunity for professional actors to perform pantomime, music hall, and off-beat shows in an intimate cabaret setting.

Perspective: The Pindar of Wakefield, now home of Aba Daba Music Hall, has been an inn for 400 years and was named after a legendary Plantagenet folk hero who defied one of King John's tax keepers (a pindar was a pound-keeper or someone who looked after stray cattle when they had been rounded up). The single-minded pindar of Wakefield was called George-a-Green, and a comedy was written about him in 1599. Here, however, he is shown resisting Robin Hood and his merry men as they try to trespass in Wakefield.

Music hall started at the pub in 1970 after the large room had been a restaurant — though the wardrobe and dressing room space has a very different history. It was here that Karl Marx lectured, and Lenin was fond of a pint at the Pindar, too. The group Wakefield Tricycle, which took its name from the pub, began here, performing at lunchtime (see Tricycle). Aba Daba, founded in 1969, made theatrical history two years later by staging the first pub pantomime, and, with bawdy, 'adult' Christmas shows such as *Right Up The Beanstalk* and *Babes in the Wood*, complete with pantomime dame and audience sing-songs, this has become one of the hallmarks of the company. They also tour in Britain and abroad, and not just with music hall. They recently took Harold Pinter's *The Birthday Party* to Denmark, and often present a Dickens programme at one of his favourite pubs in the City of London, the George and Vulture. Another favourite venue is the Cafe Royal, Regent Street.

Hallowe'en was last spent with *Things That Go Bump in the Night* and Easter with a Pierrot party. There is no resident company of actors, though many return time and again in between television, radio and West End shows to enjoy the informality of the settings, whether they are performing cabaret or a full-scale spectacular. For £3 it can't be bad.

Underground: Kings Cross St Pancras (Circle, Metropolitan, Northern, Piccadilly, Victoria, British Rail)
Bus: 14, 18, 30, 45, 46, 63, 73, 77, 77A, 77C, 168A, 214, 221, 239, 259, 263
Map: 156 Q1

Players Theatre Club

Villiers Street, Strand WC2N 6NQ
Box Office: **839 1134** (10 00-24 00) Admin: **839 1676**
Performance Space: Proscenium arch, small auditorium *Seating:* 300 (tables & chairs)

Bookings: Members only (+ unlimited guests Monday-Thursday, + 11 guests Friday & Saturday) £8 entrance fee and £12 p.a. Temporary membership foreign visitors only £4 one week, or £10 quarter Postal (cheques to Players Theatre) s.a.e. Phone (held 4 days) Cancellations accepted up to 2 days. No credit cards or travellers cheques **Prices:** Free to members, £2.30 per guest **Concessions:** No
Perf Times: Monday-Saturday 20 30 **Catering:** Dinners in Supper Room 19 00-23 30
Bars: 2 open to 24 00 **Wheelchairs:** 2 **Cloakrooms:** 1 (Attendant) **Parking:** Charing Cross garage next door to 24 00 **Other:** Souvenir book from box office. Dancing nightly after show to 24 00

Policy: To re-capture the best of Victorian music hall with two-weekly programme changes. Acts are performed by West End professionals with slots for newcomers. The Club stages a Victorian pantomime every Christmas.

Perspective: Underneath the arches behind Charing Cross railway station you can be welcomed by the chairman to an evening of enchanting, enthralling, enticing, expostulatory entertainment in the style of our Victorian forebears. In 1936, the Players Theatre Club leased premises in King Street, Covent Garden, which had been the home of the National Sporting Club and a famous Victorian song and supper rooms called Evans — Late Joys, after the name of the family who had owned it as a hotel (Joy) and the actor (W C Evans) who had opened a music-hall supper room there in the 1820s.

In 1937, the first revival of Victorian cabaret was held there, and in 1940 the theatre passed into the hands of Leonard Sachs, now familiar for his role as the Chairman in the television music-hall series *The Good Old Days*. The blitz forced him to Albemarle Street, where the club stayed until 1946 when it acquired the lease of two arches in Villiers Street, numbered 173 and 174. This area had been known since the 1850s for its music hall, run by the Gatti brothers, whose coffee and ice rooms were a familiar part of the local Hungerford Market.

All the great music-hall names appeared at Arch 174, the largest, with its audience at tables and the chairman overseeing the ceremonies. The experimental Gate Theatre came here in the 1920s and '30s as well. When Sachs and Jean Anderson moved in, old music hall was brought back to life with structural changes to the theatre and a new interior design. But the Players Theatre became really famous in 1953 when it staged Sandy Wilson's musical *The Boy Friend*, which has since gone round the world and onto film. The Players has continued since to entertain the ladies and gentlemen with its Late Joys and burlesque Christmas pantomimes.

Underground: Charing Cross (Bakerloo, Jubilee, Northern, British Rail), Embankment (Bakerloo, Circle, District, Northern)
Bus: 1, 3, 6, 9, 11, 12, 13, 15, 24, 29, 53, 77, 77A, 77C, 88, 159, 168, 170, 172, 176
Map: 155 N5

Polka Children's Theatre

240 The Broadway, Wimbledon, SW19 1SB
Box Office: **543 4888** (Tuesday-Saturday 09 30-16 30) Admin: **542 4258**
Performance Space: End stage, raked auditorium *Seating:* 300

Bookings: Postal (cheques to Polka Children's Theatre) s.a.e Phone (held to 1 week before show) No credit cards **Prices:** £1 children, £2 adults **Concessions:** School parties reductions **Perf Times:** Normally 10 00 & 14 00 during school term, weekends & holidays vary, some Saturday specials 11 00 **Mailing List:** £1 p.a. £2 3 yrs, £5 10 yrs, £25 life **Catering:** Polka Pantry (juice, cakes, etc) 10 00-16 30 Tuesday-Saturday, 12 0-19 00 Saturday **Bars:** No **Wheelchairs:** Full facilities for disabled children, incl toilet **Cloakrooms:** Coat-hanging pegs **Parking:** Street **Other:** Puppet exhibitions, children's and adults workshop courses, Polka 'After School Clubs', 'Quiet Rooms' (for meetings, clubs, rest, etc.), playground

Policy: To stimulate imagination and creative responses through entertainment for children of a very high cultural standard.

Perspective: With cuts and closures, it was heartening in 1979 to welcome a new theatre, especially one that was designed for children. It was, after all, the International Year of the Child. Dedicated to Charlie Chaplin, the Polka can be found to the south west in Wimbledon. It was opened by the Queen Mother after years of hard work by its founders, Richard Gill and Elizabeth Waghorn.

Gill's love of puppets came from his fruit-farmer father, who ran an amateur marionette show. Waghorn was a scenic designer, who had worked a great deal in the West End and regional theatres. They came together after Gill had passed through Bertram Mills Circus, as Croc with his life-sized puppets, various reps, and writing his first play for children in 1962.

In 1967, Polka was born. Its first performance was given at the Swan, Worcester, with *Harliquinade*, a mixture of mime, masks, clowning and puppets that proved a hit. By 1971, having bought a house to serve as workshops, store and rehearsal spaces, Polka's audiences had reached 250,000 a year. With the explosion in theatre for children, Polka continued its touring work, bringing skill, craft and colour to all parts of Britain. But they needed a theatre, which they found when they went to look at the Holy Trinity Halls, built in 1926. Fortunately the house next door fell vacant, and they moved in on 1 May 1977, and opened a splendid, exciting theatre in November 1979 built largely by the Polka's own designers and craftsmen. Its complex offers a wide range of activity involving many arts (music, dance, poetry, painting, mime) and many crafts (sewing, carpentry, modelling, mask making).

Polka (home of the British Toymakers' Guild) has an exhibition of toys and a toyshop, an oriental style auditorium (where the seats have no arms, to help the disabled), a wonderful puppet collection, a playground, a quiet room, an adventure room for the handicapped, and a magic pantry, where the ice cream tastes so good.

Underground: Wimbledon (District, British Rail)
Bus: 57, 77A, 77C, 93, 131, 155, 200, 293
Map: 148 F

Prince Edward Theatre

Old Compton Street, W1V 6HS
Box Office: **437 6877** (10 00-20 00) Admin: **437 2024**
Performance Space: Proscenium arch, large stage *Seating:* 1,666 (3 levels, boxes)

Bookings: Postal (cheques to Prince Edward Theatre) s.a.e Phone (held 3 days)
Credit cards (**439 8499**) Access, AmEx, Barclaycard/Visa, Diners. **Prices:** £3-£8
Concessions: No **Catering:** Foyer kiosk for confectionery; mat coffees from Stalls
Bar; ice creams **Bars:** 4 **Wheelchairs:** 2 (only in Box E with attendants)
Cloakrooms: Paralok (ladies' & gents' toilets) **Parking:** NCP Brewer St
Other: The foyer kiosk sells records and souvenirs

Policy: To provide a venue for major theatrical attractions.

Perspective: Built in Soho on the site of a draper's shop called the Emporium, which boasted royalty among its clients, the theatre was the first of four new theatres to be opened in 1930, the others being the Cambridge, the Whitehall and the Phoenix. It was designed specifically to stage musicals and revues, with a large stage, and the design of the auditorium and front of house facilities were very lavish, giving the impression of a more intimate auditorium than in fact it was.

However, the theatre was not particularly successful, depspite appearances by international stars such as Josephine Baker, and in 1936 it was converted into a cabaret restaurant showing revues. It had a semi-circular dance floor in the auditorium and kitchens under the stage, and was known as the London Casino (which is what many still call it). It continued to operate as a theatre restaurant until 1940, when the 'blitz' closed it down. Later in the war the building was used as the Queensbury All Services Club.

Afterwards, the theatre was kept fully occupied with a number of productions, including seasons of variety, ballet and pantomime. In 1949 Robert Nesbitt's lavish revue *Latin Quarter* was enormously successful and ran to several editions. In 1954 the Casino became the London home of the new film system, Cinerama, and it stayed a cinema for 20 years until May 1974, when it was converted into a dual-purpose theatre presenting films and shows — the films including such novelties as Andy Warhol's first 3-D horror movie, while the stage shows included *Cinderella* starring Twiggy, Danny La Rue in *Queen Danniella, Dean* and *Peter Pan* with Susannah York in the title role.

In 1978 the film facilities were removed, and the building reverted to theatrical use under its original name of the Prince Edward. The smash hit *Evita*, by Tim Rice and Andrew Lloyd-Webber, directed by Harold Prince and presented by the Robert Stigwood Organization and David Land, opened in June 1978.

Underground: Tottenham Court Road (Central, Northern)
Leicester Square (Northern, Piccadilly)
Bus: 1, 14, 19, 22, 24, 38, 176 or 7, 8, 25, 73, 134 to Centre Point
Map: 155 M4

Prince of Wales Theatre

Coventry Street, W1V 8AS
Box Office: **930 8681/2** (10 00-20 00) Admin: **930 1867**
Performance Space: Proscenium arch *Seating:* 1,088 (2 levels)

Bookings: Postal (cheques to Prince of Wales Theatre) s.a.e. Phone (held 4 days) Credit cards (930 0846), Access, AmEx, Barclaycard/Visa. Sterling travellers cheques.
Prices: £3-£6.50 **Concessions:** Parties 20+ Monday-Thursday. Student Standby when available £2 **Perf Times:** eves, 2 perfs Friday & Saturday **Catering:** Coffee in stalls bar, confectionery, ices **Bars:** 2 **Wheelchairs:** 3 (front stalls)
Cloakrooms: Paralok **Parking:** NCP Whitcomb St

Policy: West End commercial productions with a particular emphasis on family entertainments and musicals.

Perspective: The theatre was originally run by actor/manager Edgar Bruce, who took over the Prince of Wales Theatre when it was off Tottenham Court Road (on a site later occupied by the Scala, and after its demolition by The Other Cinema). He moved to Coventry Street, between Leicester Square and Piccadilly Circus, when his theatre was condemned by the Metropolitan Board of Works.

In the current theatre, the foundation stone of which was laid by Gracie Fields, with its high corner tower, larger stage and seating capacity, the circle is only 11 feet above the stalls (now on street level) and 21 feet from the orchestra pit, when in use. This, and the simple style with sweeping curves, partly explains the theatre's association with musicals, musical comedy, and recently, television broadcasts — a link going back to 1892 and a pioneering musical farce called *In Town*. After a run of revues in the '30s, the theatre re-opened in 1937 with *Les Folies de Paris et Londres*. Comedian Sid Field made his first West End appearance there (as well as his last before his early death), Mae West became Diamond Lil, and Charlie Chaplin's film *The Great Dictator* was shown.

In the '50s, variety took over, with stars such as Winifred Atwell, Frankie Howerd, Benny Hill, and Norman Wisdom, until the success in 1959 of *The World of Susie Wong* which was followed by a string of hit musicals (*Funny Girl, Sweet Charity, Promises, Promises*). Maybe one reason why people enjoy themselves can be found in the spacious bars: the one at stalls level boasts a dance floor area in front of a 46-foot counter made of glass blocks and quick service bar units.

Underground: Leicester Square (Northern, Piccadilly), Piccadilly Circus (Bakerloo, Piccadilly)
Bus: 1, 3, 5, 9, 12, 14, 15, 19, 22, 24, 29, 38, 53, 88, 159, 176
Map: 155 N4

Queen's Theatre

Shaftesbury Avenue, W1V 8BA
Box Office: **734 1166** (10 00-20 00) Admin: **734 1348**
Performance Space: Proscenium arch *Seating:* 989

Bookings: Postal (cheques to Queen's Theatre) s.a.e. Phone (tickets held subject to availability) Credit cards — Access, AmEx, Barclaycard/Visa **Prices:** £3-£7
Concessions: Student Standby, Parties, OAPs depending on visiting management
Perf Times: Eves, and mats twice weekly **Catering:** Coffee available in stalls bar, interval only **Bars:** 3 **Wheelchairs:** Limited **Cloakrooms:** 1 (Attendant)
Parking: Difficult, NCP Brewer St, 10 min walk

Policy: Emphasis is on straight plays, running for as long as audience demand continues.

Perspective: Built in 1907 on a corner in Shaftesbury Avenue as a twin to the Hicks (now the Globe) which was also designed by W R Sprague, the Queen's was hit during the war and only opened its glass doors again in 1959, with its smart, modern front but Edwardian interior. In 1913, the patrons went wild at the Tango Teas, where you danced, watched a fashion parade and, of course, sipped tea. It hit a golden period after Barry Jackson took over (1929), especially with productions of Shaw, and this success continued under H M Tennent, with whom John Gielgud returned to the theatre where he had played his renowned Hamlet, bringing Peggy Ashcroft, Michael Redgrave, Alec Guinness, Anthony Quayle, George Devine, Glen Byam Shaw, and Rachel Kempson (to name a few).

Fittingly, Gielgud re-opened the theatre in 1959 (with a Shakespeare anthology). Since Anthony Newley's zany musical *Stop The World — I Want To Get Off* (1961), the Queen's has had several successful runs — a revival of Noel Coward's *Present Laughter,* Neil Simon's *The Odd Couple,* Peter Ustinov's *Halfway Up the Tree,* plus interesting short visits — the National Youth Theatre playing Shakespeare, Marlene Dietrich playing herself. The premiere of Joe Orton's farce *What the Butler Saw* played here with Ralph Richardson, Stanley Baxter and Coral Browne, and when *Hair* was forced out of the Shaftesbury after the roof fell in, the musical reached its 2,000th performance at the Queen's. More recently, Alec Guinness starred in *The Old Country* and Alan Bates in *Otherwise Engaged.* The theatre also has a power generator so that performances may continue in the event of power failure. No need to bring your candles.

Underground: Piccadilly Circus (Bakerloo, Piccadilly)
Bus: 14, 19, 22, 38 or 3, 6, 9, 12, 13, 15, 53, 88, 159 to Piccadilly Circus
Map: 155 M4

Queen's Theatre, Hornchurch

Billet Lane, Hornchurch, Essex RM11 1QT
Box Office: **(49) 433 33** (10 30-20 00) Admin: **(49) 561 18**
Performance Space: Proscenium arch *Seating:* 200

Bookings: Postal (cheques to Queen's Theatre) s.a.e. Phone (held to 1 week before show) Credit cards — Acess, Barclaycard/Visa **Prices:** £2-£3
Concessions: Students £1 weekdays, OAPs 50p mats, Parties **Perf Times:** Weekdays 20 00, Saturday 20 15, mats Thurs 15 00 & Saturday 17 00 **Mailing List:** 60p p.a. for priority booking **Catering:** Hot & cold snack bar 10 00 to end of eve interval (open to public) **Bars:** 1, pub hrs **Wheelchairs:** 4 & disabled toilet
Cloakroom: 2 (Paralok) **Parking:** Free car park in Billet Lane
Other: Free Dixieland Jazz in foyer at Sunday lunchtime.
Tours by arrangement

Policy: To present a mixed programme including some new plays, musicals, classics, revivals, straight drama, etc. Each play is re-cast with a new company.

Perspective: Hornchurch was more used to pigs and farmers than actors and plays, even though Shakespeare passed this way. Until the 1920s, there was a meeting place for public entertainment alongside a music hall, evoking dim memories of brief visits made by famous actors on market days and even of Charles Dickens giving an indoor reading. Plans to turn a cinema into a community centre were cut short by the war: after peace was declared, the Hornchurch Theatre Trust was set up, and it was decided to turn the building into a theatre.

It opened with Philip King's farce *See How They Run* in 1953, the year of the Coronation — hence the name, the Queen's. In 1968, the theatre went up from two-weekly rep to three-weekly, having achieved some notable productions, such as Brewster Mason in *Othello* directed by the theatre's first director Stuart Burge (who once played Charley's Aunt there). The new Queen's Theatre was opened a stone's throw away in 1975, by Peter Hall (taking on the role Ralph Richardson had performed in 1953).

Well-known directors Peter Coe, Clifford Williams and Jane Howell have also run the Queen's, which operates seven days a week as a social centre for jazz, exhibitions, children's theatre, or just a chat. Actors associated with the theatre include Anthony Hopkins, Tony Church, Glenda Jackson, Bernard Cribbins, Prunella Scales, Joan Plowright, Dave King, Richard Briers, Dandy Nicholls, Ian Hendry, and Ronald Frazer.

Under director John Hole, the Queen's has initiated a number of musicals and new plays, discovered young playwright Nigel Baldwin, presented premieres of David Wood's children's shows, and sent The Who's musical *Tommy* to the West End.

Underground: Hornchurch (District), Emerson Park (British Rail)
Bus: 66B, 165, 193, 246, 248, 294, 370, EN226, 02, 04
Map: 147 H

Questors

Mattock Lane, Ealing W5 5BQ
Box Office: **567 5184** (18 45-20 45 1 week prior & during shows) Admin: **567 0011**
Performance Space: Main theatre & studio, flexible stagings *Seating:* 450 & 100

Bookings: Members only (£10.00 p.a., £3.50 students & OAPs, £3.00 Associates from Membership Sec., 567 8736) + unlimited guests. Postal (cheques to Questors Ltd.) Phone (held 5 days) No credit cards **Prices:** Main Theatre £1.10-£1.50 (10 shows p.a. free for full members) Studio £1.00 **Concessions:** Reduced membership fees only **Perf Times:** 14 prods. p.a. Sat-Sat Main Theatre, 8 prods. p.a. Studio **Publicity:** Local press, posters, mailing list **Mailing List:** Free to members **Catering:** First night suppers. Coffee, confectionery counter **Bars:** Foyer bar and Grapevine Club Members Bar, additional £1 p.a. **Wheelchairs:** 6 **Cloakroom:** No **Parking:** Small car park

Policy: An amateur theatre aiming for professional standards with emphasis on experimental work. There are 600 acting members from a total membership of 4,500, enabling the company to produce plays with large casts. Other activities include seminars, schools work, international and British amateur theatre festivals and young people's groups.

Perspective: Typical of the Questors' unique role in British drama was its invitation to amateur companies from Italy, Belgium and Ireland to take part in its 5th International Theatre Week which launched the theatre's own Golden Jubilee celebrations in 1979.

This pioneer amateur theatre club in west London first moved into a permanent building in 1933, using a converted chapel, 4 years after its first constitution had been adopted by a group of 17 founders. Of those only Alfred Emmet remains, and much of Questors history — and that of amateur theatre in Britain and around the world — is associated with him (he thought of the international week, which has been responsible for bringing over groups from as far afield as Canada and Czechoslovakia).

The present purpose-built theatre was opened in 1964. The members built the adjoining studio in 1969/70. Run by an elected management committee, this registered charity, whose president is Michael Redgrave, has over the years kept to a bold policy in its staging and in its programme, always aiming to improve technique.

Several premieres have been presented, particularly of foreign drama (eg from Hungary). Questors also organizes young people's groups, a student training course, tours, a theatre-in-education team called Questabout, a film society and seminars on the theatre. It is a member of the Little Theatre Guild of Britain. Occasionally, the theatre is let out to other companies. This part of London has several cheap restaurants and pubs that are worth trying, but check your travel arrangements first.

Underground: Ealing Broadway (Central, District, British Rail)
Bus: 65, 83, 112, 207, 273, 274, E1, E2, 734, 790
Map: 145 B

The Railway

100 West End Lane, West Hampstead, NW6 2LU
Box Office: **609 5157** (09 30-18 00 Monday-Friday) & **450 0371** (18 00-23 00 eves and 10 00-23 00 Friday-Sunday) Admin: **As box office**
Performance Space: Large upstairs pub room *Seating:* 100 (tables & chairs)

Bookings: Members (20p for permanent membership) Postal to Bee & Bustle, 32 Exeter Road, NW2 (cheques to Bee & Bustle) s.a.e. Phone bookings preferred (held to 20 30) No credit cards or travellers cheques **Prices:** £1.50 **Concessions:** Parties 20+ £1 **Perf Times:** Alternate Sundays 20 30 **Mailing List:** Free to members **Catering:** Cockels, mussels, nuts & raisins free with tickets **Bars:** As for pub (upstairs bar in theatre) **Wheelchairs:** Yes, steps up **Cloakrooms:** No **Parking:** Broadhurst Gardens **Other:** LPs & souvenirs from box office

Policy: The Railway is the home of the Bee and Bustle Music Hall, a professional Company, many of whose members are well-known West End performers attracted by the opportunity to try out new routines in an impromptu atmosphere.

Perspective: The Railway is a 1950s pub that began life as a hotel in the late 1920s but is now the home of the Bee and Bustle Music Hall. The group, which has toured Switzerland, Germany, and Norway, was formed in 1975 for the enjoyment of performing in the old music-hall style which has never completely died, even if it has been surpassed in popularity and changed out of all recognition since its earliest days.

As was the case with Aba Daba Music Hall (see Pindar of Wakefield), professional actors wanted to do new numbers and try out their skills in a relaxed atmosphere away from the pressures and bright lights of the West End. A regular Bee and Bustle performer, for example, is the much-loved Richard Goolden, whose acting career goes back to 1923, comes up to date with his nightly appearance in *Dirty Linen,* but who is best known as Mole in *Toad of Toad Hall,* which he first played in 1930.

The pub's association with entertainment started in the '60s when it was turned into a discotheque, though now it also has folk and rock, including big-name groups such as the Tom Robinson Band, whose show was filmed by the BBC. There are plans to refurbish The Railway and return it to the style of the '20s, but meanwhile music hall rules — and if you don't believe it, you'd better watch out. The Bee himself, big boss Eamon Jones, comes on at the end of every show, and he has a sting in his tail.

Underground: West Hampstead (Jubilee, British Rail)
Bus: 28, 159, C11
Map: 147 C

Richmond Theatre

The Green, Richmond, Surrey TW9 1QJ
Box Office: **940 0088, 948 2001** (10 00-20 00) Admin: **940 0220**
Performance Space: Proscenium arch *Seating:* 920 (3 levels)

Bookings: Postal (cheques to Richmond Theatre Productions) s.a.e. Phone (held 3 days) Credit cards — Access, Barclaycard/Visa. Sterling travellers cheques
Prices: £1.50-£4 **Concessions:** Parties 10+ discounts. OAPs Wednesday mats
Perf Times: Monday-Friday 19 45, Saturday 17 00, Wednesday mats 14 30
Mailing List: £1 p.a. **Catering:** No **Bars:** 3 **Wheelchairs:** No **Cloakrooms:** No
Parking: Around The Green

Policy: To provide a venue for touring companies, pre-West End shows and pantomimes. The emphasis is on family entertainment with varied programmes appealing to all types of audience, some of whom come from well outside the area.

Perspective: Since 1719 the south-west suburb of Richmond, favoured by royalty, rank, and riches, has only been without a professional theatre for 6 years. The first Richmond Theatre was a timber-built structure on Richmond Hill. It lost its licence in 1756 but continued as a snuff warehouse at which the public paid for the snuff and had the entertainment free.

The next theatre was opened in 1765 on the corner of Richmond Green. The most famous of its actors was Edmund Kean, who later lived in the dwelling house attached to the theatre where he died in 1833, a broken man. The only theatreless years came between the pulling down of this theatre and the opening of the next one in 1890 when the question of a new theatre became a big local issue among the dignitaries.

One of the pioneer managers, F C Mouflet, converted part of the old Assembly Rooms and opened the New Theatre, as it was called, on Easter Monday with a prologue spoken by Lillie Langtry. It established itself as a leading 'out-of-town' playhouse to the extent that Mouflet had to build another theatre. The present Richmond Theatre was opened in 1899 within a minute's walk of the railway station, next to the library, opposite an open space known as the Little Green.

It was a red brick and terracotta ornamental front with two towers and a late-Victorian intricate interior designed by Frank Matcham (including, in the foyer, a plaster portrait of Kean). Recent productions include *The Danny La Rue Show, Stage Struck, Reflections,* and *Joking Apart* by Alan Ayckbourn, and *Robinson Crusoe* at Christmas — typical of a pre-West End venue that offers 'family entertainment' for the suburb.

Underground: Richmond (District, British Rail)
Bus: 15, 27, 65, 71, 90, 90B, 202, 265, 270, 290, P235 or 33, 37, 73, 714 to Richmond Red Lion Street
Map: 148 G

Riverside Studios

Crisp Road, Hammersmith W6 9RL
Box Office: **748 3354** (Monday 11 00-18 00, Tuesday-Saturday 11 00-20 30, Sunday 13 00-20 30) *Admin:* 741 2251 *Performance Space:* Two flexible studios (high ceilings, wide acting areas), foyer space *Seating:* 400 & 200

Bookings: Postal (cheques to Riverside Studios) s.a.e Phone (held 3 days or ½ hr before perf) Credit cards — Access, AmEx, Barclaycard/Visa. Tickets also from Hammersmith/Fulham Entertainment Office, 181 King St, W6 (741 3696) **Prices:** £1-£3.75 **Concessions:** Parties by prior arrangement with box office; limited tickets on the day to personal callers — £1 **Mailing List:** £1.50 p.a. for 12 newsletters **Catering:** Restaurant Monday 11 00-18 00, Tuesday-Saturday 11 00-23 00, Sunday 12 00-22 30 Self-service hot & cold home cooking, salads **Bars:** 1 (normal licensing hrs, Fullers real ale, open to non patrons) **Wheelchairs:** Yes + disabled toilet **Cloakrooms:** Yes (unattended) **Parking:** NCP Queen Caroline St, by Odeon, limited in immediate vicinity **Other:** Bookshop outside (741 3513, ring for times) every day, incl records & second hand books.

Policy: To make available a mixed programme of theatre, music, films, children's activities, exhibitions, dance, etc. As a producing company the Trust mounts its own productions as well as encouraging visiting groups and artists.

Perspective: You don't have to be Dr. Who to meet a Spanish poet, a Japanese film maker or a London cabbie turned actor. They have all appeared at Riverside Studios, one of the brightest additions to the capital's cultural scene, which started life as a foundry. It was converted into film studios between the wars and became the largest television centre in Europe — the home of such personalities as Tony Hancock, Eammon Andrews in *This Is Your Life*, Dr Finlay and that other doctor who saved Hammersmith from the Daleks.

When the BBC moved out, the local council moved in, showing a commitment to the arts other boroughs could well copy. Playwright, theatre director and local resident Peter Gill was made director and, apart from his own highly-acclaimed productions of the classics, has been responsible for an imaginative mix of art forms, from local photography to a French magician. The food is good and wholesome, the atmosphere informal, and the space itself quite invigorating.

Underground: Hammersmith (District, Metropolitan, Piccadilly)
Bus: 9, 33, 72, 73, 710, 714, 715 to Hammersmith Bridge or 11, 220, 295 to Hammersmith Fulham Palace Road or 27, 91, 260, 266, 267, 290, 701, 704, AV300, 311, 320, 322 to Hammersmith Broadway
Map: 145 E

The Round House

Chalk Farm Road, NW1 8BG
Box Office: **267 2564** (10 00-20 00) Admin: **267 2541**
Performance Space: Engine shed converted to theatre-in-the-round, arena, or end-stage *Seating:* 600

Bookings: Postal (cheques to Round House Trust Ltd.) s.a.e Phone (held 3-7 days depending on time of booking) No credit cards **Prices:** £2-£5 (with exceptions) **Concessions:** Parties, students, OAPs as available **Perf Times:** Eves & some mats **Mailing List:** £2 p.a. for monthly newsletter **Catering:** Buffet style salads & snacks 17 30-20 00. Drinks to 23 00 (plus pm when mats) **Bars:** 1 (12 00-15 00, 17 30-23 00) **Wheelchairs:** Yes (limited) **Cloakrooms:** No **Parking:** Round House car park adjacent to theatre (free) **Other:** Occasional Sunday concerts, poetry readings, lectures, etc. Also children's workshops & Saturday mats

Policy: With its season of major foreign and British companies, the Round House has become particularly well-known for bringing outstanding British theatre from the regions to London audiences.

Perspective: Listed as a building of architectural and historic importance, this was originally part of the metropolitan terminus of the London and Birmingham Railway. The Round House, with its arched roof supported by iron pillars, had a turntable at its centre which took locomotives between the up and the down lines or to sidings. It became a warehouse from 1869 until 1964.

In 1966, it was taken over by Centre 42, a movement set up six years earlier by playwright Arnold Wesker (taking its name from the number of a resolution on culture at the Trades Union Congress) to return art to the community, which had mounted six People's Festivals in 1962 in co-operation with local trades councils. Money was hard to find to turn the Round House into an arts centre, and, after internal differences, the plan was dropped, only to be taken up by a Round House Trust which had the interior fitted out as a theatre (1967). It quickly became the home of happenings and counter culture, from Pink Floyd and a Dialectics of Liberation Conference to the Living Theatre's tribal drama.

The versatile space, converted in 1979 to theatre-in-the-round, has been used by many imaginative, innovative groups from Britain (often based outside London) and abroad (eg Mnouchkine's Théâtre de Soleil, Jean Louis-Barrault, Poland's Josef Szajna, the Georgian Rustaveli Company). *Godspell* and *Oh! Calcutta!* started here, but excitement can also be found opposite in Marine Ices (if you like Italian ice cream). There are good restaurants locally (towards Camden Town), serving Greek and Turkish food.

Underground: Chalk Farm (Northern)
Bus: 24, 31, 68
Map: 150 A3

Royal Court Theatre

Sloane Square, SW1W 8AS
Box Office: **730 1745** (10 00-19 00) Admin: **730 5174**
Performance Space: Proscenium arch *Seating:* 401

Bookings: Postal (cheques to Royal Court Theatre) s.a.e. Phone (held 3 days) Credit cards — Access, Barclaycard/Visa. Sterling travellers cheques **Prices:** £1.50-£5 **Concessions:** Members Royal Court Theatre Society (£3 p.a.) Previews £1. Student Standby £1 ½ hr before show. Parties **Perf Times:** Normally 20 00, Saturdays 17 00 & 20 30 **Mailing List:** Free to members **Catering:** Cold food & snack bar (opens 19 00) **Bars:** 2 **Wheelchairs:** 1 **Cloakrooms:** 1 (Attendant) **Parking:** Ample after 18 30 **Other:** Bookstall, works pertaining to current production & contemporary scripts

Policy: This is a writer's theatre whose aim is to promote new work in first productions. The theatre also presents some visiting companies. It runs a Young People's Theatre Scheme.

Perspective: The present theatre, which overlooks Sloane Square from its east side, was opened in 1888 after the previous Royal Court (earlier known as the New Chelsea, then the Belgravia) on the south side was demolished. The first theatre was famous for Pinero farces but a more appropriate link with the new building could be found in the origins of its site — a dissenting chapel — though among the first successes at the new venue were more plays by Pinero. The thread that runs through this influential theatre's history really begins with the management of J E Vedrenne and Harley Granville Barker, who in the 4 years up to 1907 staged 32 plays by 17 authors, promoting particularly Bernard Shaw. Shaw's association continued with Barry Jackson's Birmingham Rep, which presented several notable productions of other modern plays, and with the Macdona Players in 3 seasons of GBS. Closed in 1932, and used as a cinema later, it was renovated in 1952 and came to life in 1956 with *The Threepenny Opera* by Brecht and Weill, and more importantly, the beginning of the English Stage Company under George Devine, the focus for new theatre for many years. Playwrights such as Arnold Wesker, John Osborne and John Arden found national prominence through the Court under George Devine's direction, and later, under William Gaskill, so did Edward Bond, David Storey, and Christopher Hampton. A realistic style emerged with a group of actors, directors and designers (at random, for example, Alan Bates, Lindsay Anderson and Jocelyn Herbert). Many of the best experimental companies from abroad have also appeared in Sloane Square (eg La Mama, Bread and Puppet Theatre). Recently a Young People's Theatre Scheme was launched in the best traditions of this imaginative theatre which commands tremendous loyalty even when going through a shaky period. In 1969, the Theatre Upstairs was opened (see separate entry).

Underground: Sloane Square (Circle, District)
Bus: 11, 19, 22, 137
Map: 158 W3

Royal Opera House (The Garden, Covent Garden)

Covent Garden, WC2E 7QA
Box Office: 48 Floral St WC2 7QA **240 1066** (10 00-19 30) Admin: **240 1200**
Performance Space: Proscenium arch *Seating:* 2,141 (incl 43 standing) 4 levels

Bookings: Postal to 48 Floral St. WC2E 7QA (upper limit cheques only to Royal Opera House) s.a.e. Credit Card bookings only on 836 6903 — Access, AmEx, Barclaycard/Visa **Prices:** £1.50-£21 Ballet top prices £11 (65 amphitheatre seats £1.50 after 10 00 on day) **Concessions:** Students — £1 for 45 slips standing room tickets after 10 00 on day; Parties 20+ by arrangement
Perf Times: 19 30 Monday-Saturday, 14 00 Saturday mats (Note — late comers not seated till first break) **Mailing List:** £1.75 p.a. to London Coliseum, St Martin's Lane, WC2N 4ES **Catering:** Cold supper with wine by reservation 836 9453, cold buffet 1 hr before show, coffee, cakes in intervals **Bars:** 8 **Wheelchairs:** Yes (ring 240 1200) **Cloakrooms:** Attendant & Paralok **Parking:** Space for 400 Centre Park under New London Theatre, Drury Lane **Other:** Friends of Covent Garden £12 p.a. (£5 under 26s) for priority bookings, lectures, master classes, magazines.

Policy: The policy of both the Royal Ballet (Sadler's Wells Ballet) and the Royal Opera (Covent Garden) is to present classical opera and ballet, to introduce new works in a repertoire of productions using national and international artists.

Perspective: The first of 3 theatres on the site in the Covent Garden fruit and vegetable market was built in 1732 by John Rich to replace Lincoln's Inn Fields as the second of only 2 royal patent theatres (the other being Drury Lane). Handel's operas alternated with plays at Rich's new Theatre Royal. In the late 1700s came several 'firsts' — the introduction of the piano, and the premieres of Goldsmith's *She Stoops to Conquer* and Sheridan's *The Rivals.*

The theatre was virtually rebuilt in 1784 and burnt down in 1808 when Handel's organ and some scores were lost. A slightly smaller theatre, modelled on the Minerva Temple in the Acropolis, opened in 1809, but an attempt to raise prices led to the Old Prices protests, and a step-down by the manager after 61 nights of unrest. After a reopening in 1847 as the Royal Italian Opera House, fire destroyed the theatre again, and in 1858 the new theatre designed by Edward Barry opened.

It is much the same today, with its sumptuous red, cream and gold auditorium, splendid dome, and cream columned frontage. From then on, the history is much the same as that of English opera. Great names have appeared — Nellie Melba, Caruso, Gobbi, Callas — and the extravagant galas continue. In the first World War it was a government store, in the second a dance hall. Thomas Beecham took over between the wars (he had introduced ballet in 1911). Since 1939, it has been called the Royal Opera House, and when it reopened in 1945 it became the national home of opera and ballet (with names appearing such as Margot Fonteyn, Frederick Ashton, Ninette de Valois, Rudolph Nureyev). Despite high prices, many queue through the night for tickets.

Underground: Covent Garden (Piccadilly), Leicester Square (Northern, Piccadilly)
Bus: 1, 24, 29, 176 to Leicester Square Station or 6, 9, 11, 13, 15, 77, 77A, 77C, 168, 170, 172, to Strand, Aldwych
Map: 155 M5

Royalty Theatre

Portugal Street, off Kingsway, WC2A 2HT
Box Office: **405 8004/5** (10 00-20 00) Admin: **242 9136**
Performance Space: Proscenium arch *Seating:* 1,016 (2 levels, 4 boxes)

Bookings: Postal (cheques to Royalty Theatre) s.a.e Phone (held 3 days) Credit cards — Access, AmEx, Barclaycard/Visa. Sterling travellers cheques **Prices:** £4.50-£8.50 **Concessions:** Student Standby; parties when available **Perf Times:** 20 00 & 2 mats weekly 15 00 **Catering:** Snack bars from 1 hr before show **Bars:** 2 **Wheelchairs:** No **Cloakrooms:** 1 (Attendant) **Parking:** Ample in street

Policy: To provide entertainment for wide audiences, eg musicals, plays.

Perspective: The Royalty is built on the site of the London Opera House — the brainchild of US impresario Oscar Hammerstein, who wanted to rival Covent Garden but came up against the tight hold on the opera world of his prestigious competitor.

Oswald Stoll, who was dabbling in film-making, turned the theatre into a cinema, complete with orchestra and organist. Variety returned in 1941. The theatre closed in 1957 after such hits as Tom Arnold's Ice Spectacles, the transfer of *Oklahoma!*, Anton Dolin's Festival Ballet, Gershwins' *Porgy and Bess*, *Kismet*, and the last production in the old theatre, *Titus Andronicus* with Laurence Olivier and Vivien Leigh.

In 1960, Edith Evans opened the plush new theatre, with its deep, low auditorium. The first show was Durrenmatt's *The Visit* directed by Peter Brook, but by May the following year the Royalty was back as a cinema — until Paul Raymond took it over in 1970 with an all-male revue *Birds of a Feather*.

It is now a leisure theatre, with spacious bars and comfortable auditorium, refurbished in 1980. Its most recent success was the dazzling US musical *Bubbling Brown Sugar*.

Underground: Holborn (Central, Piccadilly), Temple (Circle, District)
Bus: 1, 4, 6, 9, 11, 13, 15, 55, 68, 77, 77A, 77C, 168, 170, 171, 172, 176, 188, 239, 501, 502, 513
Map: 155 M5

Sadler's Wells Theatre (The Wells)

Rosebery Avenue, EC1R 4TN
Box Office: **837 1672** (10 00-20 00 at 369 St. John St EC1 or at theatre foyer from 18 30-19 30) Admin: **278 6563**
Performance Space: Proscenium arch *Seating:* 1,500 (3 levels)

Bookings: Postal (cheques to Sadler's Wells Theatre) s.a.e Phone (held 3 days) Credit cards (837 3856) 10 00-18 00 Access, AmEx, Barclaycard/Visa, Diners. **Prices:** £1.25-£7.50 **Concessions:** Parties, Student/OAP Standby
Perf Times: 19 30, some Saturday mats **Mailing List:** Free **Catering:** Baylis Room Cold Buffet from 1 hr before show; Wells Room & Upper Circle Snackbar **Bars:** 3 (from 1 hr before show) **Wheelchairs:** Yes **Cloakrooms:** 1 (Attendant) 2 (Paralok) **Parking:** Ample **Other:** Friends of the Sadler's Wells subscription offers films, social events & some dress rehearsals. Bookstall in main box office (10 00-20 00) & stall in foyer for books, records, cassettes, etc. Access to archives by appointment.

Policy: Home base of the Sadler's Wells Royal Ballet since 1977. Provides guest seasons for the best of international and British theatre, especially opera and ballet.

Perspective: Sadler's Wells Musick House was set up in 1683. Highways Inspector Richard Sadler enclosed his gardens as people came to drink the waters that had been discovered in a well there, which in the Middle Ages had been known for miraculous powers. (The last person said to have drunk from under a trap door at the rear stalls was Noel Coward.)

Under the Licensing Act of 1737, only Covent Garden and Drury Lane could perform plays without music, so the owner of Sadler's Wells (as it had become known) asked his customers only to pay for the liquor. Declared a place of 'ill-fame' by a grand jury (1744), it was rebuilt in 1765, and the great Grimaldi played there from 1781-1805.

Renovated in 1838, it presented straight plays and pantos after the breaking of the patent monopoly (1843), allowing all but 3 of Shakespeare's plays to be staged there (a record unchallenged until 1923). Roller skating, boxing, tawdry music hall and films signalled its decline at the start of this century until Lilian Baylis (already running popular drama at the Old Vic) expanded north of the river and took over what was then a derelict shell used as a playground.

She opened in 1931 on 12th night with *Twelfth Night,* but operas proved more popular (over 50 were performed in the next six years) and the company eventually moved to the Coliseum. Also popular was ballet, started by Ninette de Valois at the Old Vic with a company that became the Royal Ballet. The world premiere of Benjamin Britten's *Peter Grimes* in 1945 re-opened the theatre, which was renovated in 1959.

The Wells has a fascinating display of playbills and prints. Try the Harlequin pub behind the theatre, the Old Red Lion in St. John's St, various others in Camden Passage (where you will find several restaurants) or Julius' (Upper St) or the friendly Ballerina, on the corner of Rosebery Ave.

Underground: Angel (Northern)
Bus: 19, 38, 171, 172, 279 or 4, 30, 43, 73, 104, 214, 277, 279A to the Angel
Map: 156 Q2

St Georges Theatre (The Elizabethan Theatre)

49 Tufnell Park Road, N7 0PS
Box Office: **607 1128** (10 00-20 00) Admin: **607 2289**
Performance Space: Balconied stage modelled on Elizabethan lines *Seating:* 600 plus 50 standing

Bookings: Postal (cheques to St Georges Theatre Ltd) s.a.e. Phone (held till ½ hr before show) Major credit cards. Travellers cheques, sterling and dollars
Prices: £2.50-£5 **Concessions:** Student Standby. Party bookings. OAPs
Perf Times: Monday-Saturday see press **Mailing List:** Monthly £1 p.a.
Catering: Hot & cold light snacks, open to non patrons 12 00-22 00 Monday-Saturday **Bars:** Open to non patrons regular pub hrs **Wheelchairs:** 6
Cloakrooms: Yes **Parking:** Rear of theatre. Streets **Other:** Bookstall selling texts, tapes, programmes, badges & posters. Facilities for research on Elizabethan theatre. Educational workshops open to the public (609 2427). Classical concerts on Sundays

Policy: To attempt to recreate the atmosphere of Shakespearian times and to present plays of that period in a form as closely resembling the original productions as possible. Emphasis on educational work. Schoolchildren form a large part of audience. Workshops are highly encouraged.

Perspective: Despite offical welcoming noises, St George's has always had to rely on the support of the public and its private sponsors to pursue the noble aim of recreating Shakespeare's plays in the atmosphere of the Bard's own age (you will find live music played on original instruments by musicians in period costume).

Founder and jazz enthusiast George Murcell must take the credit for keeping the project afloat through its many setbacks and crises, including lack of funds, terrible acoustics, and going dark, with occasional visiting companies. Murcell is one of the few remaining actor/managers, though recently he has put more of his energy into directing and administration. After touring with Donald Wolfit and performing with the major classical companies, Murcell set up (in 1968) the St. George's Elizabethan Theatre Ltd with the idea of rebuilding the Elizabethan Globe Theatre. Helped by internationally renowned scholars and directors, like Tyrone Guthrie, the theatre's first chairman, Murcell later moved into a converted north London church, modelled on a 5th-century Crusaders' church.

Here he created a large open stage thrust into the audience with backstage building known as the 'tiring house', complete with balcony, openings for entrances and exits, and curtains for 'discoveries' — the basic elements of the Elizabethan theatres. The St Georges was opened on Shakespeare's birthday, 23 April 1976. Although leading designers and actors, such as Alan Badel, have worked there, the productions often seem museum-like, but teachers have benefited from visits with their classes. St George's also follows another Elizabethan custom — good food and drink.

Underground: Tufnell Park (Northern)
Bus: 4, 19
Map: 145 C

St Martin's Theatre

West Street, Cambridge Circus, WC2H 9NH
Box Office: **836 1443/4** (10 00-20 00) Admin: **836 1086**
Performance Space: Proscenium arch *Seating:* 560 (3 levels, Upper Circle very steep)

Bookings: Postal (cheques to St Martin's Theatre) s.a.e. (held 3 days) Credit cards — AmEx, Barclaycard/Visa, Diner's **Prices:** £2.50-£5.50 **Concessions:** None
Catering: Soft drinks, ices; tea at mats **Bars:** 3 **Wheelchairs:** Yes
Cloakrooms: 1 (Attendant) **Parking:** NCP St Martin's Lane

Policy: *The Mousetrap* by Agatha Christie, the world's longest running play now in its 28th year, was moved from the Ambassadors to St Martin's in 1974. The theatre's policy is to present this show to capacity audiences, providing a friendly and efficient service. The cast changes annually on or around 25 November, the anniversary of the first night. Although the dialogue never alters, frequent changes in direction are made.

Perspective: The St Martin's was designed by W G R Sprague as a companion to his other theatre, the Ambassadors, which is next door. Held up by the First World War, though, it opened in 1916 and stayed much the same until the son of the first owner took over in 1960, and renovated what was seen at the time as a pleasantly modest auditorium.

C B Cochran was the first lessee, but the programme changed all the time. Management passed to Basil Dean and Alec Rea, who formed Reandean which presented a succession of successful shows, including 3 plays by John Galsworthy, Karel Capek's robot play *RUR*, Frederick Lonsdale's *Spring Cleaning* (which raised some eyebrows because of the prostitute in it) and Clemence Dance's *A Bill of Divorcement*, with Meggie Albanesi, who died aged 24 and to whose memory there is a plaque in the foyer.

Hermione Baddeley, aged 17, made an impact in an East End slum play *The Likes of Her*. Arnold Ridley's perennial *The Ghost Train* first blew its whistle here (1925) at a time when the Playbox Theatre experiment of matinee performances was in full swing. Before *The Mousetrap* got into the saddle, this theatre's previous hit was another thriller, Anthony Shaffer's *Sleuth*.

Underground: Covent Garden (Piccadilly), Leicester Square (Northern, Piccadilly)
Bus: 1, 14, 19, 22, 24, 29, 38, 176
Map: 155 M4

Savoy Theatre

Savoy Court, Strand, WC2R 0ET
Box Office: **836 8888/9** (10 00-20 00) Admin: **836 8117**
Performance Space: Proscenium arch *Seating:* 1,123 (3 levels)

Bookings: Postal (cheques to Savoy Theatre) s.a.e. Phone (held 3 days) Major credit cards, Monday-Friday, 10 00-18 00 (836 8118) **Prices:** £2-£6 **Concessions:** Parties (437 3856) Student Standby **Perf Times:** 20 00 or 17 45 & 20 45 **Catering:** No **Bars:** 4 (from ½ hr before show) **Wheelchairs:** 1 **Cloakrooms:** 2 (Attendant) **Parking:** Savoy Hotel Garage, Embankment entrance **Other:** Discount meals at 'Simpsons-in-the-Strand' with ticket.

Policy: The Savoy aims to present entertaining shows whose long runs will make them economically successful.

Perspective: The Savoy was opened in 1881 by Richard D'Oyly Carte, with Gilbert and Sullivan's *Patience*, as a home for their operas, after the three of them had joined forces for *Trial by Jury* at the Royalty Theatre, Soho (not the current Royalty off Kingsway), an association that continued until 1902 when the theatre became a general West End venue. Rebuilt in 1929, with the entrance switched from the Embankment to the Savoy Court set back off the Strand, the opening production was *The Gondoliers*. To celebrate the centenary of the D'Oyly Carte company in 1975, all the G & S operas were performed, and prints of costumes used in different G & S productions can be seen in the bar. The original theatre had also introduced the first theatre use of electric lighting and the beginning of a very British habit, queueing (for the pit and gallery).

In 1911, the first production of *Where the Rainbow Ends* was staged, the pioneering Vedrenne/Granville-Barker management moved here from the Royal Court Theatre, and many successes were produced over the years (other than G & S) — *Nothing but the Truth, Paddy the Next Best Thing, Journey's End, The Man who Came to Dinner,* Noël Coward's *Sail Away, Alibi for a Judge, The Secretary Bird* (which ran for 4 years), *Lloyd George Knew My Father* and Brian Clark's *Whose Life Is It Anyway?* with Tom Conti. The directors include Dame Bridget D'Oyly Carte, grand-daughter of Richard.

Underground: Charing Cross (Bakerloo, Jubilee, Northern, British Rail)
Bus: 1, 6, 9, 11, 13, 15, 77, 77A, 77C, 168, 170, 176 or 4, 55, 68, 171, 188, 239, 501, 502, 513 to Aldwych
Map: 155 N5

Shaftesbury Theatre

Shaftesbury Avenue at Princes Circus, WC2H 8DP
Box Office: **836 6596** (10 00-20 00) Admin: **836 4634**
Performance Space: Proscenium arch *Seating:* 1,300

Bookings: Postal (cheques to Shaftesbury Theatre) s.a.e. Phone (held 3 days or 1 hr before show) Credit cards — Access, AmEx, Barclaycard/Visa, Diners. Travellers cheques in sterling **Prices:** £1-£6.50 **Concessions:** Parties negotiable. OAPs variable. Student Standby when available ½ hr before show **Perf Times:** eves & twice weekly mats **Catering:** Coffee bar & kiosk ½ hr before & during show **Bars:** 4 (as catering) **Wheelchairs:** Yes **Cloakrooms:** 1 (Attendant) **Parking:** NCP behind theatre; reasonable after 18 30 **Other:** Records from show on sale where relevant.

Policy: The management act as landlords staging musicals, comedies and new plays suitable for a large theatre.

Perspective: Not in the main theatre district of Shaftesbury Avenue nearer the Piccadilly Circus end, this theatre, first called The New Princess, was the last to open in the famous street, and was built at the other end on a prominent corner on the site of run down property. The front is modern Renaissance with a graceful tower. Inside is a mixture of mosaics, fluted figures, columns and panels. The 2 levels each have a bar, one Elizabethan, one Jacobean.

Home at first of melodrama, the theatre staged a season of Gilbert and Sullivan in 1919 when all but 3 of the operas were performed. Diaghilev's Russian ballet visited twice, George Robey presented his revue *Bits and Pieces*, and *Funny Face* with the Astaires was interrupted by a gas explosion which closed the theatre.

Fortunes varied with changes of managements, short runs, revivals, more visits of the D'Oyly Carte, until the theatre was shut for reconstruction in 1962, and reopened as the Shaftesbury with the US musical hit *How to Succeed in Business Without Really Trying*. *Big Bad Mouse* with Jimmy Edwards was followed by *Hair* in September 1968, which opened the day after censorship by the Lord Chamberlain was abolished, and ran until it was robbed of its 2,000th performance there by the roof collapsing. A campaign was waged to save the refurbished theatre from office block 'redevelopment', and it was then put on the list of special interest buildings.

Underground: Tottenham Court Road (Central, Northern)
Bus: 1, 7, 8, 14, 19, 22, 24, 25, 29, 38, 73, 134, 176
Map: 151 E6

Shaw Theatre

100 Euston Road, NW1 2AJ
Box Office: 388 1394 Admin: 388 0031
Performance Space: Modern proscenium with stage thrusting beyond it
Seating: 510 (2 levels)

Bookings: Postal (cheques to the Shaw Theatre) s.a.e Phone (held for 3 days) Travellers cheques **Prices:** £3 **Concessions:** Students, young people under 21, OAPs £1.50 **Perf Times:** Eves & mats according to demand **Mailing List:** To schools **Catering:** Snack bar **Bars:** 1 (before & during show) **Wheelchairs:** 4 + disabled toilet **Cloakrooms:** 1 (Attendant) **Parking:** NCP opposite, Euston Rd. Streets after 18 30 **Other:** Lending & reference library in building. Bookshop. Sunday concerts & occasional lunchtime shows in bar

Policy: To provide high quality shows for young people, at prices they can afford. Plays are selected with a young audience in mind, and school syllabuses are taken into account. The NYT and the Shaw company produce revivals as well as encouraging new writers and the NYT is able to perform classics with casts of up to 100.

Perspective: The modern Shaw Theatre is the home of the National Youth Theatre (NYT) and its professional 'wing' the Shaw Theatre Company. Originally intended as a conference centre, the building was turned into a theatre by the local Camden Council, which has a long history of support for the NYT, and was opened in 1971 with the St Pancras Library upstairs.

Founded in 1956 by ex-seaman turned teacher Michael Croft, the NYT has always had a hard time finding the premises for its adventurous summer seasons which developed from performing exam Shakespeare into a seed bed for new young writers and actors. Every year, 120 young people between the ages of 14 and 21 (but excluding those at drama school or full-time students) are chosen out of 4,000 applicants to take part in the NYT's activities. These centre on a London season but include annual trips to Sunderland and regular touring abroad — the NYT was the first amateur company to be invited to the Berlin Festival, and the only one to be asked back again. Its modern-dress *Julius Caesar*, with a cast of 100, is not only the envy of most managements but also a popular standard in the NYT repertoire.

A breakthrough came in 1967 with what became another standard, Peter Terson's football play *Zigger Zagger* which was toured and televised. The association with Terson continued (eg *The Apprentices, Fuzz, Good Lads at Heart*) alongside the encouragement of young writers such as Barrie Keeffe and Paul Thompson. Many actors got their first taste of theatre with the NYT, eg Helen Mirren, Derek Jacobi, Ben Kingsley, Simon Ward, Paula Wilcox, Ian McShane, Hywel Bennett. The professional Shaw Theatre Company has staged some notable revivals, particularly the first full revival of the Wesker trilogy in 1978.

Underground: Euston (Northern, Victoria British Rail) Kings Cross St Pancras (Circle, Metropolitan, Northern, Piccadilly, Victoria, British Rail)
Bus: 14, 18, 30, 68, 73, 77, 77A, 77C, 170, 185, 239 or 45, 46, 63, 168A, 214, 221, 259, 263 to King's Cross
Map: 151 C6

Soho Poly Theatre Club (Soho Poly)

16 Riding House Street, W1P 7PD
Box Office: **636 9050** (10 00-18 00) Admin: **580 6982**
Performance Space: Small basement studio *Seating:* 40-60

Bookings: Members only (+ 2 guests) £1 p.a. or 20p at door. Postal (cheques to Soho Poly Theatre Club) s.a.e Phone (held to 13 00 on the day) No credit cards **Prices:** £1 **Concessions:** Students of Central London Poly automatic members **Perf Times:** Lunchtime (13 15) with occasional 18 15 performances for very popular shows **Mailing List:** With membership **Catering:** Snack lunches 12 30-13 15 **Bars:** No **Wheelchairs:** No **Cloakrooms:** No **Parking:** Very difficult **Other:** Membership to Soho Poly entitles automatic membership to 14 other London fringe theatres.

Policy: Primarily a writers' theatre, one of the few fringe theatres serving this function. Shows are generally 50 minutes in length, with no fixed casting.

Perspective: Springing from the great fringe explosion of the '60s, Soho Poly was started in 1968 by Frederick Proud and Verity Bargate because they wanted to create work for actors and because, although there were many good one-act plays around, they were not likely box-office bets. From the basement of the condemned Chinese restaurant where they began as the Soho Theatre, taking its name from the neighbourhood, they went to the Edinburgh fringe festival with two landmarks in experimental theatre, *The Local Stigmatic* by Heathcote Williams and *Number Three* by John Grillo.

When they were given an oil-soaked basement of a garage for rehearsals during a project with the Polytechnic of Central London which owned the space they asked if they could stay, and converted it into a theatre with a dressing room in the bottom of the lift shaft. The theatre's name changed to Soho Poly, and, run by Verity Bargate alone since 1975, it has presented a notable range of short, lunchtime plays — 20 in her first year but less as the grant failed to match the wages bill.

Some of the best new writers, such as Howard Brenton, have aired contemporary issues here, and several have been given their break, eg Pam Gems and especially Barrie Keeffe. Well established actors (eg David Warner, Colin Blakely) appear alongside newcomers in usually very sharply directed and imaginatively designed productions. Just shows what you can do with a shoe-box. But get there early: it fills up quickly.

Underground: Oxford Circus (Bakerloo, Central, Victoria)
Bus: 1, 3, 6, 7, 8, 12, 13, 15, 25, 53, 73, 88, 113, 137, 159, 500, 616, 710, 715, 735
Map: 151 E4

Strand Theatre

Aldwych, WC2B 4DF
Box Office: **836 2660/4143** (10 00-20 30) Admin: **836 9817**
Performance Space: Proscenium arch *Seating:* 1,076 (3 levels, boxes)

Bookings: Postal (cheques to Strand Theatre) s.a.e. Phone (held 4 days) Credit cards — Access, AmEx, Barclaycard/Visa (836 4143) Sterling travellers cheques **Prices:** £2.50-£5.50 **Concessions:** Parties **Perf Times:** Mondays-Fridays 20 00 & Thursday mat 15 00 Saturday 17 30 & 20 30 **Catering:** No **Bars:** 4 (from ½ hr before show) **Wheelchairs:** 1 (box) **Cloakrooms:** 2 (1 Attendant) **Parking:** NCP Drury Lane

Policy: Light entertainment — small musicals possible, but concentration on family shows, comedies, etc.

Perspective: The Waldorf, as it was known, was the first theatre to open (1905) in the newly-built Aldwych. The block was to include the Waldorf Hotel and the Aldwych Theatre. W G R Sprague designed both theatres and gave them the same exteriors. Redecorated several times, the interior still has an Edwardian feel. The Waldorf became the Strand Theatre in 1909 (there was a Royal Strand Theatre until 1906 where the Aldwych tube now is) changing its name to the Whitney 2 years later and back to the Strand 2 years after that.

The opening production was a season of opera given by the Italian 'tragedienne' Eleanora Duse and her company. Actor/manager Cyril Maude was based here, though the first period of real success was under Arthur Bourchier (eg Eugene O'Neill's *Anna Christie* and a dramatization of *Treasure Island* which ran for five Christmases). Farces made their mark when Firth Shephard and Leslie Henson took over (Henson had made his first appearance here) and continued to flourish under different managements up to the Second World War. They included work by Ben Travers whose comedies were playing on the other corner at the Aldwych as well. Donald Wolfit kept the theatre going during the blitz with lunchtime Shakespeare and in 1942 *Arsenic and Old Lace* began its run of 1,337 performances. After the war, light comedy and farce again won the day — from *Sailor Beware* and *A Funny Thing Happened on the Way to the Forum* to *Not Now Darling* and the record-breaker *No Sex Please — We're British*, now in its tenth year.

Underground: Covent Garden (Piccadilly), Charing Cross (Bakerloo, Jubilee, Northern, British Rail) Temple (Circle, District)
Bus: 1, 4, 6, 9, 11, 13, 15, 55, 68, 77, 77A, 77C, 168, 170, 171, 172, 176, 188, 239, 501, 502, 513
Map: 155 M5

Sugawn Theatre

Duke of Wellington, Balls Pond Road, N1 4BL
Box Office: **254 1454** (10 00-20 00) Admin: **249 3729**
Performance Space: Intimate back room of pub *Seating:* 40 with tables, chairs, stools

Bookings: Phone (held to 40 mins before show) No credit cards **Prices:** £1.25-£1.50 **Perf Times:** Monday-Thursday only **Mailing List:** Free on request **Catering:** Hot & cold bar snacks, regular pub hours **Bars:** As pub **Wheelchairs:** Yes **Cloakrooms:** No **Parking:** Street **Other:** Friday-Sunday, traditional Ceilidh music takes over

Policy: The Sugawn Theatre provides Irish Drama for the local community ranging from the classics of Irish theatre to modern plays by Irish writers. At weekends, traditional folk music is played by local and visiting musicians.

Perspective: Enterprizing and friendly Jerry O'Neill encouraged the Duke of Wellington pub (built in 1820 and a retreat for performers from the local Collins Music Hall) to be used for traditional new Irish folk singing, and then gradually developed the idea of staging Irish folk plays. O'Neill's own play, *God is Dead on the Balls Pond Road*, went down well, and the Sugawn Theatre began to invite a variety of groups, especially those performing Irish work (by writers such as Hugh Leonard), but also Sean O'Casey, W B Yeats and J M Synge.

Despite the Irish being the largest minority in Britain, there is little 'official' support for their culture, and Irish plays are rarely performed unless they are by a famous playwright who is usually dead. The amateur activity grew in popularity and became a professional outlet in a poorly served part of London which has a very mixed community (though more recently the Rio round the corner in Dalston has been turned into a local entertainment centre).

There are several good restaurants serving food of Greek and Turkish origin (in Essex Road, Mildmay Park, Newington Green area) and a few streets away in Allen Road is the oldest fish and chip shop in London, called Robinson's. Down the road — the other way — is another good fish and chip shop, George's (Essex Road) but if you want to try eel and pie, go down the Balls Pond Road, and turn left at Dalston.

British Rail: Dalston Junction
Bus: 30, 38, 67, 76, 141, 149, 171, 243, 243A, 277
Map: 147 E

Talk of the Town

Hippodrome Corner, Cranbourne Street WC2H 7JH
Box Office: **734 5651** (09 30-21 30) Admin: **734 5395**
Performance Space: Theatre restaurant *Seating:* 758 (at tables & chairs)

Bookings: Postal (cheques to Talk of the Town) s.a.e. Phone (held to 21 15 on the night) Credit cards — Access, AmEx, Barclaycard/Visa, Diners **Prices:** Monday-Thursday £14.50 (for dinner & show) + service; Friday-Saturday & Bank Holidays £16.50 + service **Concessions:** Parties **Perf Times:** 20 00-01 00 **Catering:** Silver service catering includes 3-course dinner, coffee & tax **Bars:** Cocktail bar 19 15-23 00 **Wheelchairs:** No **Cloakrooms:** 1 Men (Attendant), 1 Ladies (Attendant) **Parking:** NCP Swiss Centre, Leicester Square

Policy: To provide an international cabaret spot, with acts appealing to an international audience.

Perspective: On the corner of Cranbourne Street and Charing Cross Road is an island of shops, offices, a pub, an entrance to Leicester Square Tube Station and the famous London Hippodrome, now known as the Talk of the Town, complete still with the horses on the dome. With water supplied to a tank by the Cran Bourne, which runs underneath the stage, the original circus arena theatre was designed by music hall specialist Frank Matcham for Edward Moss, founder of the management 'empire' that took his name.

Opening in 1900 the theatre presented circuses and spectacles, including the famous water shows (one of which almost killed Lupino Lane, while another had a one-legged cyclist who plunged 30ft into a torrent, bike and all, having done his tricks at roof level). The variety artistes who have appeared are legends of the time, from Lillie Langtry and Houdini to the silent acrobat Marceline the Clown and Chung Ling Soo, the Chinese magician who was an Englishman from Liverpool.

Variety plus ballet, operas, and one-act plays followed the reconstruction of 1909 when stalls were put in. London's first taste of *Swan Lake* (though only in two acts) and ragtime gave way to happy revues, starring all the greats — George Robey, Harry Tate, Sophie Tucker and even Paul Whiteman with his swinging band. Jack Buchanan, Cicely Courtneidge and others then made musical comedies a hit and Ivor Novello's *Perchance to Dream*, with the World War II success *We'll Gather Lilacs*, ran for 1,020 performances (his longest run).

From then until 1958, a mixture of Folies Bergere, Arthur Askey, plays, revues, ice shows, musicals and Benny Hill played at the theatre. It was then turned into a restaurant with cabaret, harking back to the old music-hall days of the mid 19th century when you ate, drank and watched a show. Top entertainers from around the world now appear, and have included Shirley Bassey, Lena Horne, Frankie Vaughan, Sammy Davis Jnr, Frank Sinatra, Liberace, Tom Jones, and Danny la Rue.

Underground: Leicester Square (Northern Piccadilly)
Bus: 1, 24, 29, 176, or 3, 6, 9, 11, 13, 15, 53, 77, 77A, 77C, 88, 159, 168, 170, 172, to Trafalgar Square or 14, 19, 22, 38 to Cambridge Circus
Map: 155 N4

Theatre at New End (New End)

27 New End, NW3 1JD
Box Office: **794 0238** (10 00-20 00) Admin: **435 6035**
Performance Space: Unraised end stage *Seating:* 100 (steeply raked)

Bookings: Postal (cheques to New End Theatre) s.a.e Phone (held 5 days or 1 hr before show) **Prices:** £2.40 **Concessions:** Students, Equity, party bookings **Perf Times:** 20 00 Tuesday-Sunday eves **Mailing List:** £1 p.a. **Catering:** Light snacks in coffee bar from 1 hr before show **Bars:** 1 **Wheelchairs:** 1 **Cloakrooms:** No **Parking:** Street

Policy: To present new works and to give opportunities to young directors and writers. No resident company. New shows are presented every 6 weeks. The building is also used for art lectures, music and meetings. Some lunchtime and late-night shows.

Perspective: Rather like a chapel, this compact theatre, originally a mortuary, was a welcome addition to the fringe circuit when it was opened in 1974 by Jean Anouilh's *You Were So Sweet When You Were Little* (with Angela Pleasance and Paul Jones). Despite its success in promoting new work, often by artists from the US and elsewhere abroad, the theatre is forever announcing its closure — only to open again with a remarkable production, like Rob Walker's staging of *The Bitter Tears of Petra von Kant* by Fassbinder or Simone Benmussa's production of her own adaptation, *The Singular Life of Albert Nobbs*.

New End takes some of the best work from other fringe venues, from festivals like Edinburgh, and offers an outlet for companies whose work might not otherwise see the light of day (eg Michelene Wandor's attempt to turn Alan Ayckbourn on his head in a feminist comedy about stereotyping, lesbians and artificial insemination). Give yourself time to get there — the walk from the Tube through picturesque Hampstead is worth taking slowly. It is fascinating (as well as uphill), and the cake in the coffee bar (which also shows modern pictures) is very tasty once you get there.

Underground: Hampstead (Northern)
Bus: 268
Map: 147 **A**

Theatre Royal, Drury Lane

Catherine Street, WC2B 5JF
Box Office: **836 8108** (10 00-20 00) Admin: **836 3687** Sun. Concerts: **836 5876**
Performance Space: Classical design proscenium arch *Seating:* 2,245 (4 levels)

Bookings: Postal (cheques to Theatre Royal Drury Lane) s.a.e. Phone (except Sunday concerts) Credit Cards — Access, AmEx, Barclaycard/Visa, **Prices:** £2-£10 **Concessions:** Student Standby subject to availability, Parties usually Wednesday mat **Catering:** Circle snack bar open 1 hr before show **Bars:** 3 **Wheelchairs:** Yes but must be able to move into a seat **Parking:** Difficult **Other:** Party catering in private room or royal box by prior arrangement with manager. Historic tours (up to 25 people, £1 per person) also prior arrangement. Records, cassettes, souvenir programmes for sale after show or at interval.

Policy: To present top musicals with wide appeal and likely to enjoy long runs.

Perspective: Along with Covent Garden, the most famous theatre in London. After the civil war, Charles II issued only two patents for staging plays, one of which went to Thomas Killigrew, who opened the first Drury Lane as the Theatre Royal, Brides Street, in 1663. His King's Company had to swear a loyalty oath. Nell Gwynne appeared in 1665 but could not stop the Great Fire or the Plague, which closed the theatre for 18 months.

Sir Christopher Wren built a second theatre (after another fire burnt down the first) and the foundations can be seen under the present stage. This theatre was almost gutted when footmen to the gentlemen in the theatre rioted in 1737 because their free admission to the gallery had been abolished. Drury Lane was damaged in the Gordon Riots (1780), was rebuilt again in 1794, and until 1896 a company of guards was always posted for its protection. David Garrick had become manager in 1747, being succeeded by Sheridan in 1776 — his *School for Scandal* opening here a year later.

The legendary names roll on — Siddons, Kemble, Kean, Grimaldi, Macready, Irving, Terry — but the theatre also has a lighter tradition that links it with the postwar years: Dan Leno's pantos, spectacular melodrama (eg Ben Hur's chariot race), interwar musicals (eg *Rose Marie, The Desert Song, Show Boat*) and Ivor Novello's shows. During the war, despite damage, it was the headquarters of the services entertainment unit ENSA, and afterwards come the familiar US titles of *Oklahoma!, Carousel, South Pacific, The King and I, My Fair Lady,* (2,282 peformances), *Camelot, Hello Dolly!, Chorus Line,* and, from Britain, would you believe, *Monty Python's Flying Circus.*

Underground: Covent Garden (Piccadilly), Charing Cross (Bakerloo, Jubilee, Northern, British Rail), Temple (Circle, District)
Bus: 1, 4, 6, 9, 11, 13, 15, 55, 68, 77, 77A, 77C, 168, 170, 171, 172, 176, 188, 239, 501, 502, 513
Map: 155 M5

Theatre Royal, Haymarket

Haymarket, SW1 4HT
Box Office: **930 9832** (10 00-20 00) Admin: **930 8890**
Performance Space: Proscenium arch *Seating:* 909 (3 levels + boxes)

Bookings: Postal (cheques to Haymarket Theatre) s.a.e. Phone (held 3 days) Credit cards, no cancellations (**930 9832**) Access, AmEx, Barclaycard/Visa, Diners **Prices:** £2.50-£6. £1.50 Gallery, non reservable **Concessions:** Parties of 10 or more, certain seats only **Catering:** Tea Wednesday mats only. Ice creams **Bars:** 3 **Wheelchairs:** Yes, easy access **Cloakrooms:** 1 (Attendant) **Parking:** NCPs Wickham St, Cockspur St, Waterloo Place

Policy: To provide a venue for a wide range of drama and comedy.

Perspective: In 1720 carpenter John Potter opened a theatre on the site of an old inn in the Hay-Market and a gunsmiths in Suffolk Street despite being refused a patent — the monopoly to run a theatre still being held by Drury Lane and Covent Garden. The Little Theatre in the Hay staged many burlesques, and under the management of Henry Fielding, one of his plays satirizing the Prime Minister Walpole led to the introduction of censorship by the Lord Chamberlain (which did not end until 1968).

The Royal patent was granted in 1766 (and the name changed accordingly), but only for the summer when the other two theatres were closed. In 1805, troops were called to disperse hundreds of tailors who were angry at the revival of a satire about their trade, and in 1880 there was a first night riot because the pit had disappeared in the conversion work. The present theatre, designed by John Nash, was opened in 1821, slightly further south so that its fine Corinthian portico could be seen from St James Square (a view worth seeing, especially at night). The interior has been redecorated but remains suitably royal, with its ornate gilding and painted ceiling.

When the patent monopoly was abolished in 1843, the Haymarket was seen as the equal of its two rivals, with a proud record of productions (Shakespeare, Congreve, Fielding, Sheridan, Goldsmith) and even a female Falstaff, Julia Glover, who had played Hamlet at the Lyceum as well.

Its history also includes first productions of two Oscar Wilde comedies, *A Woman of No Importance* and *An Ideal Husband*, the first licensed performance of Ibsen's *Ghosts*, John Gielgud's repertory season in 1944 (mounted with HM Tennent), Terence Rattigan's *Ross*, and the formation of a Theatre Royal Haymarket Company under Ralph Richardson. Then came Rattigan's *A Bequest to the Nation*, followed by revivals (*Voyage Round My Father, Crown Matrimonial*.) Queen Victoria's favourite manager John Buckstone keeps an eye on the proceedings still, though patrons need not worry — he is a gentle ghost.

Underground: Piccadilly Circus (Bakerloo, Piccadilly)
Bus: 3, 6, 9, 12, 13, 15, 53, 88, 159 or 14, 19, 22, 38 to Piccadilly Circus
Map: 155 N4

Theatre Royal, Stratford East

Gerry Raffles Square, Stratford, E15 1BN
Box Office: **534 0310** (10 00-19 00) Admin: **534 7374**
Performance Space: Old music hall theatre, proscenium arch
Seating: 477 (3 levels)

Bookings: Postal (allow 7 days, cheques to Theatre Royal) s.a.e. Phone (held 7 days) No credit cards or travellers cheques **Prices:** £1-£3 **Concessions:** Students, claimants, parties Monday, Tuesday & Wednesday **Perf Times:** 20 00 Monday-Saturday. Mats when available. Occasional Sunday concerts **Mailing List:** £5 p.a. membership of Supporters Club for mailings & other facilities **Catering:** Snack bar for hot & cold food **Bars:** Yes (normal licensing hours, open to non-patrons) **Wheelchairs:** 6 (easy access) **Cloakrooms:** No **Parking:** NCP Great Eastern Road, surrounding streets **Other:** Occasional bookstalls when appropriate

Policy: A venue for good entertainment serving the locality. The theatre works in the community, particularly with children and young people.

Perspective: There had been a wooden booth theatre near the place where actor W. Charles Dillon built himself a theatre in 1884 when Stratford was a busy part of London's east end. Within 2 years the success of the playhouse with the local dockers, railwaymen and porters encouraged the new owners, the Fredericks family, to build another 2 theatres nearby.

Melodrama and music hall were the staple diet (with exceptions like David Horne's season of plays, 1946-1949) until 1953 when the Theatre Workshop under the firm hand of Joan Littlewood moved in. It took the lease in 1957 and had the theatre redecorated and redesigned in 1959 by John Bury. With roots in Manchester, going back to 1936, the Workshop came out of the agitprop movement and had toured Britain and the continent before coming to rest in Stratford. Its first West End success was Brecht's *The Good Soldier Schweyk* (1955) which played at the Duke of York's. Its ability to draw on the lives of working people to create a more direct and vigorous type of drama was a major influence on the British theatre (through productions such as *A Taste of Honey, The Hostage, Make Me an Offer, Fings Ain't Wot They Used T' Be, Sparrers Can't Sing,* and the best known *Oh! What a Lovely War* — all of which went into the West End.

But each transfer took with it a whole company, which led to the Workshop's collapse. After a period of drag shows and variety when Stratford itself was declining, Littlewood returned with her compaion Gerry Raffles as general manager to change the theatre into a community-based entertainment complex. Since Raffles' death, attempts have failed to restore the Company to its former glory, when it helped launch names such as Shelagh Delaney, Brendan Behan, Lionel Bart, and many well-known actors. It is a snug, Victorian theatre with a good atmosphere, possibly because the bar keeps normal pub hours.

Underground: Stratford (Central, British Rail)
Bus: 10, 25, 69, 86, 108, 173, 230, 238, 241, 262, S1, S3
Map: 146 B

Theatre Space

48 William IV Street, Covent Garden, WC2N 4LS
Box Office: **836 2035** (12 00-20 00) Admin: **836 2035**
Performance Space: Small studio space *Seating:* 50 fixed, 30 cushions when necessary

Bookings: Members only 25p p.a. in advance or at door. Postal (cheques to Theatrespace) Phone (held to ½ hr before show) No credit cards or travellers cheques **Prices:** £1-£1.50 **Concessions:** Vary according to show **Perf Times:** Monday-Sunday 20 00, early & late shows when available **Catering:** Coffee & snacks from 1 hr before show **Bars:** No **Wheelchairs:** 2 **Cloakrooms:** No **Parking:** NCP Bedfordbury **Other:** Bookstalls when available. Reciprocal membership with other London fringe venues.

Policy: Primarily a venue for small-scale touring companies, Theatre Space aims to demonstrate the quality and variety of work existing in independent fringe productions and tries to run a full programme of experimental theatre by groups with great commitment to the idea of making their techniques and ideas more widely known.

Perspective: Run by the energetic Ann Fenn, Theatre Space affects the parts other theatres fail to reach. It exists to provide a venue in the heart of London for small-scale touring companies that it might otherwise be difficult to see in this area. The theatre was opened in King Street, Covent Garden, in the old premises of Rank Strand, the theatre lighting experts, before moving opposite the old Nuffield Theatre in what was Charing Cross Hospital. Down the road is London's 24-hour Post Office. It took as cue for its name the fact that space has always been hard to find for fringe theatre groups in the centre of the capital.

The informal Theatre Space, like the Little, allows anyone to get a start in life in its basement theatre. A cross-section of touring companies is always available, from Gay Sweatshop and Monstrous Regiment to Avon Touring or Lumiere and Son, in a full programme of constantly changing events. As well as being a shop-window for the fringe, it also allows try-outs by lesser-known names. In 1978, for example, translator Helena Kaut-Howson had had the Polish play *Werewolves* turned down by many managements, although it had been voted best play of the year in its homeland. Theatre Space, though, was prepared to give the unknown Actors Soup Kitchen company a chance to put on this surrealistic, lyrical look at the cruel effect of war on a community, with its setting transferred to Ireland. Such an open-door policy means that it is always worth checking what is on at Theatre Space — it is full of surprises.

Underground: Charing Cross (Bakerloo, Jubilee, Northern)
Bus: 1, 3, 6, 9, 11, 12, 13, 15, 24, 29, 53, 77, 77A, 77C, 88, 159, 168, 170, 172, 176
Map: 155 N4

Theatre-in-the-Square (formerly Spice of Life)

The Crown, 64 Brewer Street, W1
Box Office: **349 2262** (temporary) Admin: **349 2262**
Performance Space: Upstairs pub room *Seating:* 30-40

Bookings: Phone (held to ½ hr before show) In person. No credit cards.
Prices: £2.50 **Concessions:** Students, OAPs, Equity, Groups 10+ £1.25
Perf Times: Monday-Saturday 20 00 **Catering:** Pub food **Bars:** As for pub
Wheelchairs: No **Cloakrooms:** No **Parking:** NCP Brewer Street

Policy: To stage classical works or modern works based on classics, with classical staging. Company to be re-cast for each show.

Perspective: Amidst such established West End venues as the Piccadilly and Criterion theatres, a small-scale venture was launched in the heart of Piccadilly Circus in March 1980: the Theatre-in-the-Square. The producing company, known as Counterpoint Productions, is headed by Emmanuel Gounalakis, who is a producer-member of the National Theatre of Greece, and its artistic director is Hovhanness I. Pilikian, an innovative director especially notable for his productions of classical Greek drama at Greenwich, Guildford, and Chichester.

Counterpoint's first London show was the world premiere of an Armenian play *The Weasel*, performed in a chapel in Soho's Dean Street. Later, motivated by the feeling of 'death in the West End', Pilikian sought to develop a strong new fringe venue in the centre of London. With the familiar problems of financial cuts and diminishing audiences, scepticism was considerable but on 31 January 1980 the Theatre of the Spice of Life in Cambridge Circus opened with James Hadley's highly controversial play *The Whore's Revenge*.

In March 1980 the Spice of Life became Theatre-in-the-Square at the Crown, where it hopes to remain on a permanent basis, working in a style referred to as 'Theatre of Emotions'. Here the venue will operate as a co-operative where, in the director's own words, actors will be treated 'as human beings first, and then as actors'.

Underground: Piccadilly Circus (Bakerloo, Piccadilly)
Bus: 3, 6, 9, 12, 13, 14, 15, 19, 22, 38, 53, 88, 159
Map: 154 N3

Theatre Upstairs, Royal Court

Sloane Square, SW1W 8AS
Box Office: **730 2554** (10 00-19 00) Admin: **730 1745**
Performance Space: Flexible studio *Seating:* 100

Bookings: Postal (cheques to Royal Court Theatre) s.a.e. Phone (held 3 days) Credit cards — Access, Barclaycard/Visa. Sterling travellers cheques **Prices:** £1.50-£2.50 **Concessions:** Members Royal Court Theatre Society (£3 p.a.) Previews £1. Parties **Perf Times:** 19 30 **Mailing List:** Free to members **Catering:** Cold food & snack bar opens 19 00 **Bars:** Royal Court Circle Bar **Wheelchairs:** No **Cloakrooms:** No **Parking:** Ample after 18 30 **Other:** Annual Young Writers Festival presents plays by under 18s. The theatre is also home of Royal Court Young People's Theatre Scheme.

Policy: The aim is to promote new writers work in in-house productions, with some visiting shows. The Theatre Upstairs also presents rehearsed play-readings, directed and performed by professionals, which often lead to full productions in the theatre. (Readings free to members.)

Perspective: The emergence of the fringe in the '60s was a shot in the arm for the theatre. Visits in 1967 by two US groups, Cafe La Mama (Mercury, Vaudeville) and the Open Theatre (Royal Court), acted as catalysts, and the following year many experimental companies passed through the Drury Lane Arts Lab to set up a network of centres around Britain. In 1969, the Royal Court (see separate entry), under director William Gaskill, staged a fringe 'festival' called *Come Together* using upstairs and downstairs. It lasted for 20 days and 20 nights and was the first real occupation of a main theatre by the 'alternative'. Downstairs you could be 'entertained' by chickens and a man vomiting, Upstairs by having eggs smeared all over you — but all that has changed. With the first artistic director of the Theatre Upstairs, Nicholas Wright, came a new play policy that provided an outlet for some of the most exciting and imaginative writing of the time — Howard Brenton's first full-length play *Revenge* appeared in this opening year along with one of the few genuine innovations of the fringe, Heathcote Williams' *AC/DC*. With a high turnover, the theatre presented in its early years a startling range of drama, from Pip Simmons and Ken Campbell to Freehold and the work of writers such as Howard Barker, Snoo Wilson and Mustapha Matura. Many of the productions were connected with young people (eg Barry Reckord's *Skyvers*), and now the Young People's Theatre Scheme stages annual festivals of new plays (in 1980 a teenage cast put many professional productions to shame in Edward Bond's *The Worlds*, directed by the author). Though not as hectic as in the days of its birth, the Theatre Upstairs has kept up its record of interesting and challenging work, providing a venue for visiting shows and producing still some of the best new plays around that sometimes transfer downstairs to a larger audience (eg *Class Enemy* by Nigel Williams).

Underground: Sloane Square (Circle, District)
Bus: 11, 19, 22, 137
Map: 158 W3

Theatro Technis

26 Crowndale Road, London NW1 1TT
Box Office: **387 6617** (18 30-20 30) Admin: **387 6617**
Performance Space: old mission hall, no staging *Seating:* 150 (floor level)

Bookings: Postal (cheques to Teatro Technis) s.a.e Phone (held to ½ hr before show) No credit cards **Prices:** £1.50 **Concessions:** Students, OAPs 75p
Perf Times: 20 00 **Mailing List:** Membership at £1 p.a. or 50p students & OAPs for advance information **Catering:** No **Bars:** Members only **Wheelchairs:** Yes
Parking: Side streets **Other:** Teatro Technis also provides a community advisory service for Cypriots & daily luncheon club for OAPs

Policy: A community theatre dedicated to the enhancement and preservation of Cypriot culture in Britain and to forging links with the community at large. Plays are either specially written or adapted from the classics, and are performed in English, Greek and Turkish. Many have themes of social significance to the Cypriot community.

Perspective: Founded in 1957 by George Eugeniou, Theatro Technis has a proud record of service to its Cypriot community which has continued in the face of many hardships, without the funding such a scheme deserves, and in several different premises. The plays at first were in Greek only, and dealt with subjects such as the Greek junta (in a modern *Antigone*).

Eugeniou, though, always wanted to reach beyond the immediate neighbourhood (there are an estimated 15,000 Greek Cypriots living in London alone) and to break out of the ideas of the ghetto. Theatro Technis toured Liverpool, Manchester, Coventry and Margate in 1974, playing to packed houses with a show about the situation in Cyprus since the Turkish invasion. It has also performed plays involving other ethnic groups (eg *The Vandals are Coming*, about the removal of park railings, which included Indians and English as well as Cypriots).

The company had to move out of its home in a derelict shed that local workers had painstakingly converted, and in 1978, it came to an old Church of England mission hall in the same north London borough of Camden (which has a large Cypriot population). Again, friends and neighbours helped to ensure that the building could function as a theatre as well as a vital centre for information, advice, folk dancing, singing, English, Greek and Turkish language lessons.

Theatro Technis is also used occasionally by touring groups sharing the same concerns (eg Bite Theatre's play about Chile), but still mostly presents its own work (6-8 shows a year) formed around a nucleus of long-standing members. With plays in English, Greek and Turkish (and sometimes a mixture) and a friendly welcome, it stands in marked contrast to some of the nearby pubs and restaurants which have hired bouzouki players for an 'authentic' ethnic atmosphere.

Underground: Mornington Crescent (Northern)
Bus: 24, 27, 29, 46, 68, 134, 137, 214, 253
Map: 151 B5

Tower Theatre (The Tower)

Canonbury Place, Canonbury, N1 2NQ
Box Office: **226 5111** (Tuesday-Saturday 14 15-20 00, Sunday & Monday 18 30-20 00 Admin: **226 5111**
Performance Space: Proscenium arch *Seating:* 156 (raked)

Bookings: Postal (Cheques to Tavistock Repertory Company) s.a.e. Phone (held till ½ hr before show) No credit cards **Prices:** £1.25 (Saturday £1.50)
Concessions: Party bookings, OAPs. **Perf Times:** Productions open on Fridays and play until Sunday (1st week) Then Tuesday-Saturday **Mailing List:** 40p p.a.
Catering: Coffee, confectionery on sale in foyer bar (½ hr before show & interval)
Bars: 1 **Wheelchairs:** 3 (12 places for people with seats) **Parking:** On street **Other:** Club membership scheme £2.50 p.a. entitles members to use of private bar & buttery open 19 00-23 00 daily. Guided tours available after Saturday mat

Policy: This is a non-professional company with a high standard of production. Entry is by audition only. The aim is to provide a training for actors, directors and writers. Twenty shows are produced per year, including new shows, West End revivals and lesser known revivals. The theatre is closed for the whole of August.

Perspective: In 1953, the Tavistock Theatre Company opened the doors of a new theatre in the Canonbury Tower, which itself dates back to 1509 and has been the home of, among others, Francis Bacon, Oliver Goldsmith and the Marquis of Northampton. The Tower Theatre is tucked away in a select part of the north London borough of Islington, and can justly be called one of the area's oldest and finest buildings.

The Tavistock Company, a member of the Little Theatre Guild of Britain, converted the hall into a proscenium stage and the rest of the property was equipped as a club with living accommodation for the warden. The company was founded in 1931, 2 years after the Questors (see separate entry) and 5 years before Unity (awaiting reconstruction after a fire), the other important centres in London of amateur activity, most of which takes place outside the capital.

It was first housed in the Mary Ward Settlement but lapsed during the Second World War, to be re-formed in 1952. It has a broad policy which offers good training for aspiring professionals and dedicated amateurs. Generations of London school children know the Tower because of their visits to see Shakespeare — for many, perhaps, their first and possibly only exposure to the Bard. The company has also toured. The archives go back to 1932 and cover other theatres. Pictures and exhibitions are often mounted. Essex Road side has a good kebab restaurant and fish and chip shop; Upper Street side has Compton Arms, Roxy, Kings Head, kebab restaurant, and, towards Angel, cheap Turkish cafe.

Underground: Highbury & Islington (Victoria, British Rail)
Bus: 38, 73, 171, 277, 271 to Canonbury Square, or 4, 19, 30, 43, 104, 279, 279A to Highbury & Islington Station or 38, 73, 171, 277 to Canonbury Street
Map: 147 F

Tramshed

51-53 Woolwich New Road, SE18
Box Office: **855 3371** (09 30-18 00) Admin: **855 3371**
Performance Space: Hall (raised platform or horseshoe) *Seating:* 160

Bookings: Phone (held until 1 hr before show) Credit cards Barclaycard/Visa only. No travellers cheques. **Prices:** £1.00-£1.50 **Concessions:** Friday only: OAPs 75p, Students & army recruits £1. Other reductions parties 20+ **Perf Times:** Monday-Sunday 20 30. Saturday childrens theatre 10 00. Mat when available **Mailing List:** Free on application **Catering:** Hot & Cold lunchtime, eve bar snacks **Bars:** 1, normal licensing hours **Wheelchairs:** 4 **Cloakroom:** No **Parking:** Multi-storey Calderwood St, surrounding side steets

Policy: To present a wide programme of entertainments that will appeal to the local community, including jazz and other live music, cabaret and music hall, plays and revues by fringe and more traditional theatre companies.

Perspective: As the name implies, this is a converted tramshed which has established itself as part of the local south-east London community since it was opened in 1973 (perhaps the pub hours and the Fuller's ale helped as well as the friendly reception). It was started by Greenwich Theatre because it wanted to broaden its programme from its classical and contemporary work and young people's theatre scheme, to try and reach wider sections of the community with a range of popular entertainment.

Just down the road from the local barracks, The Tramshed is now the home of the Woolwich Theatre Ltd, which puts on its own shows (but has no permanent company) and also invites touring groups to perform. A typical week at the Tramshed might be: Sunday jazz, Monday Latin American sounds, Tuesday rock, Wednesday talent contest, Thursday rhythm and blues, Friday a play, Saturday cabaret.

Old time music hall, special children's shows, and productions of plays studied locally at school (eg Shakespeare, *A Taste of Honey, An Inspector Calls*) mix with star performers such as Kenny Ball, Annie Ross, Jake Thackeray, The Boys of the Lough, and fringe groups dong anything from Brecht to a feminist revue. Recently, The Tramshed staged *Macbeth*, set to music by a local young composer. The 'sound and fury' was brought up-to-date with Mods, Rockers and Punks.

Rail: Woolwich Arsenal (British Rail)
Bus: 51, 53, 54, 75, 96, 99, 122, 122A, 161, 161A, 177, 180, 192, 198, 269, 272
Map: 145 D

Tricycle Theatre (projected opening Autumn 1980)

269 Kilburn High Road, NW6 7JR
Box Office: (Use admin number until box office opens, autumn 1980)
Admin: **328 8626** *Performance Space:* Galleried courtyard with stage in well
Seating: 200

Bookings: Specific details as yet undetermined **Prices:** Intend general fringe prices
Concessions: Planning concessions for students, OAPs, groups
Perf Times: Monday-Saturday evenings **Mailing List:** Write to theatre
Catering: Meals will be available **Bars:** 1 for pre-show & intervals **Wheelchairs:** Up to 12 + disabled toilet **Cloakrooms:** 1 **Parking:** Street parking **Other:** Children's theatre workshops & children's shows planned for Saturdays and afternoons. Other plans provisional

Policy: The resident Wakefield Tricycle Company will present new work by new or established writers, aimed at an audience of both children and adults. When the company are touring, the venue will be used by visiting groups with a similar policy.

Perspective: Opening in the autumn of 1980, the new Tricycle Theatre is both a welcome antidote to the more usual bleak news of theatres closing or groups having their grants cut, and a special boost for the fringe. After another scheme fell through, it was Wakefield Tricycle that managed to move in — a just reward for the years of hard and imaginative work put in by the group since it was founded in 1972 by Kenneth Chubb and Shirley Barrie to present new plays.

They started in a pub near King's Cross called the Pindar of Wakefield (see separate entry) — hence the name. As a touring group, they presented evening shows (eg *Kitty Hawk* by Leonard Jenkin with Theatre Machine at the Bush), as well as lunchtime productions (eg three African plays at the Africa Centre). Many were musical and aimed at non-theatregoing audiences (eg Derek Smith's *The End of the World Show*). They developed a wide range of styles, from shows for under-elevens (such as *The Adventures of Super Granny and the Kid*) to serious, sensitive drama (eg Olwen Wymark's *Loved*, at the Bush) and energetic fun-evenings like Adrian Mitchell's celebration at the Kings Head of the origins of jazz, *Hoagy, Bix and Wolfgang Beethoven Bunkhouse*.

The new galleried courtyard, based on a scaffolding structure, is being converted from the Forester's Hall, which was originally a music and dance hall. It has been made available by the local council and will have room for catering facilities as well as a full programme of children's workshops.

Underground: Kilburn (Jubilee), Brondesbury (British Rail)
Bus: 8, 16, 16A, 32, 176, 616, 708, 719 or 28, 31 to Kilburn High Road
Map: 147 B

Unicorn Theatre for Children

Great Newport Street, WC2H 7JB
Box Office: **836 3334/2132** (10 00-20 00 Monday-Saturday, 13 00-16 00 Sunday)
Admin: **240 2076**
Performance Space: Proscenium arch *Seating:* 337 (2 levels)

Bookings: Members only, aged 4-12 (+ 10 guests, including adults: temporary 5p, annual £1.60, or £1.75 for 2 in same family) Postal (cheques to Unicorn Theatre) s.a.e. Phone (held 4 days) No credit cards or travellers cheques **Prices:** 70p-£2
Concessions: School rates **Perf Times:** 14 00 Tuesday-Friday term time, 14 30 Saturday & Sunday &during half-term & school hols **Mailing List:** Full members
Catering: Green Room snack bar from 12 00 — soups, salads, hot meals; birthday teas by prior arrangement **Bars:** No **Wheelchairs:** 1 **Cloakrooms:** No **Parking:** NCP St Martins Lane **Other:** Bookstall at weekends. Theatre workshops for members weekends & school hols

Policy: To open to an audience unfamiliar with the theatre the full range of theatrical experience by commissioning new plays of different styles and content from professional adult playwrights and novelists.

Perspective: Founded by Caryl Jenner in 1948, the Unicorn Theatre for Young People had toured for many years before becoming resident since 1967 at the Arts Theatre. Caryl Jenner, who died in 1973, began her professional career with the experimental Gate Theatre in 1935. The Unicorn is the only fully professional company in London's West End presenting work exclusively for an audience of children between the ages of 4 and 12 and is, therefore, different from groups working in the theatre-in-education movement.

Under an artistic committee, including the present artistic director Nicholas Barter, the Unicorn offers a main season from September to April, and in the summer sends out small teams of actors to perform in parks and playgrounds. The age range is divided into two main groups (4-6, 7-12) and they are catered for during the Unicorn's absence by visiting, often foreign, companies.

Underground: Leicester Square (Piccadilly, Northern)
Bus: 1, 24, 29, 176 or 14, 19, 22, 38 to Cambridge Circus
Map: 155 M4

Upstream Theatre Club

Short Street, Waterloo, SE1 8LJ
Box Office: **928 5394** (09 30-10 00 & ansaphone) Admin: **633 9819**
Performance Space: Converted church hall *Seating:* 120 (rostra)

Bookings: Membership incl in ticket price. Postal (full members only, cheques to Upstream Theatre Club) s.a.e. Phone (held 3 days) No credit cards. **Prices:** £1-£3 **Concessions:** Parties of 20 (1 free) under 16s £1 at door if available **Perf Times:** 19 45 Monday-Saturday, 16 30 Saturday mat when applicable **Mailing List:** £2.50 p.a. (see also full membership facilities under **Other**) **Catering:** Coffee, soft drinks, confectionery, ices **Bars:** No **Wheelchairs** : 10 **Cloakroom:** No **Parking:** NCP Queen's St, streets **Other:** Full membership (£7.50 indiv, £10 couples) for journal, workshop invitations, socials, previews & all advance information.

Policy: The emphasis is on strong, thought-provoking productions supporting the Company's Christian ideals.

Perspective: Founded in 1974, the Upstream Theatre Company toured productions, such as *Lion in Winter* and Peter Shaffer's *Five Finger Exercise*, for three years until it was invited by the Church Council of St. Andrew's, in the south London borough of Lambeth, to start a theatre club within the church complex. Four months of hard work later, the venue was opened in June 1977 in a converted church hall opposite the Young Vic.

The resident company has 15 members and brings in others depending on the needs of the different shows. The opening production was a trilogy by Wolf Mankowitz. Other writers whose work has been produced here range from Dostoevsky, Alexei Arbuzov and Sartre to Strindberg, Peter Terson, Keith Waterhouse and Willis Hall.

The artistic director Richard Everett quite rightly wants audiences to avoid any preconceptions about 'Christian' drama — and the spread of authors backs up his point. Visited by the Archbishop of Canterbury in 1978, Upstream also runs a children's workshop and has a gallery with a change of exhibition (often connected to the show) about once a month.

Underground: Waterloo (Bakerloo, Northern, British Rail)
Bus: 1, 4, 55, 68, 70, 76, 149, 168A, 171, 176, 188, 239, 501, 502, 503, 507, 513
Map: 155 O6

Vaudeville Theatre

Strand, WC2R ON4
Box Office: **936 9988** (10 00-20 00) Admin: **836 3191**
Performance Space: Proscenium arch *Seating:* 659 (3 levels, 4 boxes)

Bookings: Postal (cheques to Vaudeville Theatre) s.a.e. Phone (held to ½ hr before show) Major credit cards Sterling trevellers cheques
Prices: £2.50-£6.50 **Concessions:** Sometimes **Perf Times:** 20 00 and 2 mats weekly
Catering: No **Bars:** 2 (from ½ hr before show) **Wheelchairs:** Yes **Parking:** NCP Trafalgar Square

Policy: Unlike many West End theatres, most of the shows are put on by the owning management, otherwise the theatre is hired to other producing companies in conventional manner. Most productions are premieres (normally 3 a year) and run for planned seasons (again unlike most theatres in the West End).

Perspective: The first theatre on the site was built in 1870. In 1891 it was largely reconstructed with a new frontage which remains to this day. The interior was totally rebuilt in 1925 and the auditorium made oblong instead of horse-shoe as before. The opening years were full of burlesque, comedy and comic revivals, the most notable production being H J Byron's *Our Boys* which broke all previous records with a run of 1,362 performances (and was revived there successfully 20 years later).

The first productions in England of Ibsen's *Hedda Gabler* and *Rosmersholm* were seen at the Vaudeville in 1891. In 1915 the association with revues began, and this continued until the end of the war. In 1954, *Salad Days* opened for a run of 2,329 performances which beat the record set for musicals by *Chu Chin Chow*. Arnold Wesker's RAF play *Chips with Everything* transferred from the Royal Court in 1962, Dorothy Tutin played Queen Victoria, Sybil Thorndike and Athene Seyler starred in *Arsenic and Old Lace* and *The Man Most Likely To* ran for over 2 years while the management changed hands to Peter Saunders, who presents the *The Mousetrap*.

He refurbished the theatre, putting in air cooling and better dressing rooms, and has scored well with Margaret Lockwood in *Lady Frederick*, Alistair Sim in *The Jockey Club Stakes*, the comedy *Move Over Mrs Markham*, *Spokesong* from the Kings Head, Glenda Jackson in *Stevie* and *An Evening with Dave Allen*.

Underground: Charing Cross (Bakerloo, Jubilee, Northern)
Bus: 1, 3, 6, 9, 11, 12, 13, 15, 53, 77, 77A, 77C, 88, 159, 168, 170, 172, 176 or 24, 29 to Trafalgar Square
Map: 155 N5

Victoria Palace Theatre

Victoria Street, SW1 5EA
Box Office: **834 1317** (10 00-20 30) Admin: **834 2781**
Performance Space: Proscenium arch *Seating:* 1,565 (3 levels, boxes)

Bookings: Postal (cheques to Victoria Palace Theatre) s.a.e. Phone (held 2 days) Credit cards — AmEx Access, Barclaycard/Visa, Diners. Sterling travellers cheques. **Prices:** £3-£7.50 **Concessions:** Parties by arrangement **Perf Times:** Monday-Saturday 19 30, Wednesday & Saturday mats 14 45 **Catering:** Sweet kiosk only **Bars:** 5 **Wheelchairs:** 1 (Stalls) **Cloakrooms:** 1 (Attendant) **Parking:** Side streets after 18 30 **Other:** Souvenir kiosk

Policy: To stage good musically-orientated shows attracting a wide audience.

Perspective: Before Victoria Station was built, a Pimlico pub called the Royal Standard was noted for its entertainment, and held the oldest licence in London for a music hall (having been rebuilt to accommodate its success). It was pulled down in 1910, the area having changed over the previous decades since the opening of the railway terminus.

Experienced music hall architect Frank Matcham was responsible for building the new theatre on the site called Victoria Palace, with its classical front looking like the Palladium and its domed tower which once had a statue of the prima ballerina Pavlova, who, being superstitious, would never look at it (it was removed during the 'blitz' and then disappeared). It still retains the period's mixture of elegance and grandeur.

Until 1934 the Victoria Palace was known for revues (one starring Gracie Fields) and it returned to them after a short period of 'straight plays'. This got off to a dubious start with *Young England*, a patriotic melodrama, which became a cult among those who enjoyed it going over the top, and 'bouncers' had to be hired to keep control. *Me and My Girl*, a musical comedy, was interrupted by the war after playing 1,046 performances, but came back in 1944 to finish its long run.

In 1947, the Crazy Gang moved in and stayed until 1962. They were followed by the *Black and White Minstrel Show*, which ran for an incredible 4,344 performances until 1970, obviously helped by the television series. Used then by stars such as Max Bygraves and Barbara *'Carry On'* Windsor, the theatre was refurbished for the hit musical from the US, *Annie*.

Underground: Victoria (Circle, District, Victoria, British Rail)
Bus: 2, 2B, 10, 11, 16, 16A, 24, 25, 29, 36, 36A, 36B, 38, 39, 52, 70, 76, 149, 185, 500, 503, 507, 700, 701, 704, 705, 706, 707, 708, 714, 717, 718, 729, 732, 737, 790, AV300, 310, 311, 320, 322
Map: 154 P3

The Warehouse (Donmar Theatre)

41 Earlham Street, Covent Garden, WC2H 9LD
Box Office: **836 6808** (10 00-20 00) Admin: **240 2766**
Performance Space: Open space, converted warehouse *Seating:* 200
(2 levels, fixed)

Bookings: In advance from Aldwych Theatre, Aldwych WC2B 4DF. Postal marked Warehouse (upper limit cheques only to Aldwych Theatre) s.a.e. Phone (held 3 days, collection by 18 00 from Aldwych or from 19 00 from Warehouse) Recorded info 836 5332. Day of performance bookings in person from Aldwych to 12 30 & Warehouse from 13 30 mats, from Aldwych to 18 30 & Warehouse from 19 00 eves. No credit cards **Prices:** £3.50 **Concessions:** Student tickets in advance £2 **Perf Times:** 19 30 Monday-Saturday, 14 00 Saturday mat (when available)
Mailing List: See Aldwych Theatre **Catering:** Kiosk for soft drinks, ices **Bars:** No
Wheelchairs: Yes **Cloakrooms:** No **Parking:** NCP St Martin's Lane **Other:** Playreadings, bookstall, workshops.

Policy: To commission and perform new plays by British playwrights using actors from the Royal Shakespeare Company. Playreadings and workshops form an important part of The Warehouse programme and are aimed at giving showings to new works that have previously been denied public performances (for example, its season of plays that television would not do).

Perspective: Built in the 1870s as a vat room for a big brewery, the premises were sold in the 1920s to a film company and became the first studio in Britain to use colour. The fruit trade took it over as a warehouse for banana ripening until 1960, when the theatre manager Donald Albery bought it, possibly foreseeing the future of Covent Garden as an arts and crafts neighbourhood instead of a market. He named the theatre Donmar after himself and Margot Fonteyn, and it was often used for ballet because of its size and mirrors. Peter Brook and Charles Marowitz staged scenes from Genet's *The Screens* as part of the Royal Shakespeare Company's 'Theatre of Cruelty' season in 1964, and before the Company opened it as a second London auditorium, they and other managements had used it for rehearsals.

Converted in a hectic three months in early 1977, it opened with Howard Barker's *That Good Between Us* in a season that put it on the map, which included Edward Bond's *The Bundle*, written for The Warehouse, and transfers from the successful 1976 season at its Stratford-upon-Avon counterpart The Other Place. They included Trevor Nunn's celebrated production of *Macbeth* with Ian McKellen and Judi Dench. The Warehouse has quickly established a reputation for challenging productions of radical plays by many of Britain's best new writers. People queue over an hour before the shows start, so get there early for a good seat and wrap up well in winter (you wait outside, and it is not too warm inside). Interval drinks in Crown and Anchor at end of road.

Underground: Covent Garden (Piccadilly), Leicester Square (Northern, Piccadilly)
Bus: 1, 14, 19, 22, 24, 29, 38, 176
Map: 151 E6

Waterside Workshops and Theatre

99 Rotherhithe Street, SE16
Box Office: **237 9443** Admin: **237 9443** Workshops: **237 0017**
Performance Space: 2 small open spaces *Seating:* 70-90 (some raked, some chairs)

Bookings: Members only (+ 1 guest) 50p p.a. in advance or at door. Tickets in advance or at door only, depending on event **Prices:** vary **Concessions:** Children & OAPs half price **Perf Times:** Phone for details **Catering:** Hot & cold snacks or seated meals when available **Bars:** 1 **Wheelchairs:** No **Cloakrooms:** No **Parking:** Surrounding streets **Other:** Craft workshops, live music, rehearsal rooms, films

Policy: The theatre is a venue for visiting fringe groups working in various forms, including puppetry, mime, music, drama and cabaret. The emphasis is on a broad programme appealing to a wide audience from the local community and Greater London.

Perspective: A few minutes walk from Rotherhithe Tube Station, up the river road from the Mayflower pub, is a five-storey warehouse in the St Mary Conservation area. This part of south-east London was once thriving dockland, but until fairly recently has been empty and derelict. Various bodies have now taken leases or bought outright certain properties for conversion into living accommodation, workshops, theatre and entertainment, shops, etc.

Waterside itself was created by a group of individuals needing somewhere to work at their own trades, originally with their own capital and enthusiasm and later with grant-aid for building improvements. Their premises are still in the process of being made cleaner, drier, warmer and more attractive, while continuing to offer a variety of workshops, rehearsal space, and a room which can be hired out occasionally (all of which make a profit, however small), a shop and a youth club (future projects which are expected to cover their own costs) and the theatre (which usually makes a loss).

The original project was started by Crunchy Frog Studios and The Warehouse Theatre, and Waterside was formed a few years later. Films, music and workshops picked up alongside drama, including street theatre and work with the local tenants' associations. The co-operative body that runs Waterside with this mixture of private and public funding, individual and corporate endeavour, houses various self-employed designer/craftspeople, some of whom have included kite-makers, silversmiths, woodcarvers, instrument makers and repairers, potters, etc.

The Waterside Theatre is in the process of expanding into 101 Rotherhithe Street (next door), and until then some of the facilities mentioned above are not available.

Underground: Rotherhithe (Metropolitan)
Bus: 47, 70, 188, P5
Map: 145 F

Watford Palace Theatre

Clarendon Road, Watford, Herts
Box Office: **Watford (92) 25671** (10 00-20 00) Admin: **(92) 35455**
Performance Space: Proscenium arch *Seating:* 490 and 200 in gallery (benches)

Bookings: Postal (cheques or postal orders to Watford Palace Theatre) Phone (held 10 days, collect 45 mins before perf) No credit cards **Prices:** Monday-Friday £2-£2.30; Saturday £2.50-£2.80 **Concessions:** 1st Thursday and Friday of production £1.50 all seats; Monday eve and Saturday mat 2 for price of 1; Tuesday-Saturday students and OAPs 60p Tuesday-Friday groups of 10 for 1 free ticket **Publicity:** Local press, posters, occasional national press **Catering:** Coffee bar, confectionery, ices **Bars:** 1 open 19 15 and intervals **Wheelchairs:** Yes **Cloakrooms:** No **Parking:** In car park **Other:** Theatre dinner scheme, parties of 10 or more.

Policy: As a producing company without a permanent pool of actors, the emphasis is on plays running from 3 to 5 weeks, interspersed with visits from ballet and touring groups. The programme includes new plays, neglected classics, little known plays by well-known authors, a variety of Sunday concerts with emphasis on jazz and school educational work.

Perspective: This beautiful, ornate, though now slightly dusty, Edwardian theatre has an old world flavour with its turquoise and gold carvings and armless benches in the gallery. However, it has a solid local following. The theatre opened on Boxing Day, 1908 on the site of an inn music hall as the Watford Palace of Varieties. The first show was a gala performance of sketches, acrobatic acts and musical interludes. The first full production of 1908 was a traditional pantomime, and this has become a popular annual event ever since. After a long history as a variety venue, the theatre was taken over by the Watford Civic Theatre Trust in 1964.

The earliest recorded activity is at the inn (1803). The next theatre opened as a touring house in the 1850s. Henry Irving played at Watford with Holloway's Portable Theatre, but after the permanent theatre was built, many famous names appeared (though often then little recognized, as, for example, Charlie Chaplin, who shared a dressing room with three others). As well as Marie Lloyd and Stan Laurel, entertainment stars such as Gloria Grahame and Dora Bryan have made more recent visits. Simon Gray's *Molly* first played at Watford before going into the West End, as did two Ken Lee shows, *Leave Him to Heaven* and *Happy as a Sandbag*. Watford pubs close at 22 30, but there is a Greek restaurant next door.

Rail: Watford Junction (Bakerloo, British Rail)
Bus: 142, 258, 301, 302, 306, 311, 312, 319, 321, 322, 327, 336, 347, 348, 352, 834, W1, W2, W3, W4, W5, W6, W7, W8, W9, W10, W11, 708, 719, 724, 727, CC
Map: 148 **A**

Wembley Complex

Wembley Park, Wembley HA9 0DW
Box Office: **902 1234** (10 00-21 00, enquiries only) Admin: **902 8833**
Performance Space: Stadium, Arena & Conference Centre *Seating:* 45,000 + 55,000 standing in Stadium, 8,000 in Arena, 2,500 in Conference Centre

Bookings: Postal (cheques to Wembley Stadium Ltd.) s.a.e Credit cards — Access, Barclaycard/Visa (for conference centre only) **Prices:** Stadium: £3-£15 depending on the event; Arena: £2-£4.50; Conference Centre: £2-£15
Concessions: ½ price for children for some shows, some party rates, all variable according to event **Perf Times:** Daytime, mats & eve events **Mailing List:** £1 p.a. for notice of events; write to Promotion Dept **Catering:** Snack vendors & snack counters (hot dogs, pasties, etc.). Starlight Grill open for lunch and dinner daily
Bars: 10 Stadium, 8 Arena, 2-3 Conference Centre **Wheelchairs:** Stadium: No; Arena: Yes; Conference Centre: Yes (5) **Cloakrooms:** Stadium: No; Arena: No; Conference Centre: 2 (Attended) **Parking:** Massive at the Complex **Other:** Guided tours of Stadium with sensational effects, when available £1.30 adults, 90 children. Shops with souvenirs, books, gifts, etc.

Policy: The Stadium presents regular (3 times weekly) greyhound racing, and a variety of other events calling for a venue of such scale, among them football, rugby, occasional tattoos and pop-concerts. The Arena presents ice shows, gymnastics competitions, Horse of the Year shows and again, pop concerts. The Conference Centre presents a wide range of events, from Bugs Bunny shows to boxing, and from Shirley Bassey in concert to snooker.

Perspective: You may not notice the funny little marks in some of the terraces when confronted by the grandeur of Wembley, but those foot prints left by herons are a reminder that until 1921, this western part of outer London was virtually unknown, except to golfers who tried to avoid hitting their ball into one of the many pools so beloved by the birds.

The 73-acre site with its fortress towers took 300 workings days to build and involved the removal of 250,000 tons of earth. It opened in 1923, appropriately enough with a Cup Final. Since then, Wembley has meant a lot of different things to a lot of different people, mostly to do with sport. Famous moments are many, but two stick out from recent years: Henry Cooper knocking down Cassius Clay before losing in the fifth, and the day England won the World Cup.

George V spoke for the first time on wireless to millions around the world when he opened the British Empire Exhibition here in 1924. The BBC staged the 1977 Eurovision Contest here, the music for *Star Wars* was recorded here, and many pop stars have appeared here, notably The Who and Elton John. As an entertainment centre, it has travelled the distance between rodeos, labour movement pageants, tattoos, and back to Bugs Bunny and Wonder Woman.

Underground: Wembley Park (Jubilee, Metropolitan), Wembley Complex (British Rail)
Bus: 8, 18, 83, 92, 182, 297, 734 or 245 to Wembley Park Bridge Road
Map: 144

Westminster Theatre

Palace Street, Buckingham Palace Road, SW1E 5JB
Box Office: **834 0283/4** (10 00-20 00) Admin: **834 7882**
Performance Space: Proscenium arch *Seating:* 588 (2 levels)

Bookings: Postal (cheques to Westminster Theatre) s.a.e. Phone (held 5 days) Credit cards (834 0283/4) AmEx only. Sterling travellers cheques **Prices:** £2.50-£6 **Concessions:** Parties 10+. School parties larger reductions. Students **Perf Times:** Normally 2 mats a week, eves **Mailing List:** Friends of the Theatre **Catering:** Foyer snack bar, foyer restaurant for lunches (12 00-14 00) Dinners by arrangement. Service **Bars:** No **Wheelchairs:** 2 (boxes to side of stage) **Cloakrooms:** Yes (Attendant) **Parking:** Ample, surrounding streets. NCP off Victoria St. **Other:** Bookshop (09 30-17 00 & before & after shows). Friends of Westminster Theatre £3.50 p.a. (£1.15 under 20s) for advance notice, issues of Westminster Theatre News. Young People's Theatre Forums.

Policy: To provide good family entertainment with productions that emphasize a positive outlook on life against a background of the problems of the age. Some of the productions are specifically presented for children and young people.

Perspective: Four minutes walk or so from Victoria Station is one of the few theatres that offers simultaneous translations — 4 at a time. What you will hear will be wholesome fare in any language, nearer to the theatre's origins as a chapel than to its intervening history (Pirandello, Shaw, Ibsen, O'Neill) when it was known for being 'avant garde' under Anmer Hall. He transformed the St. James' Picture Theatre (1931) into a new theatre named after his school (Westminster) and hired pioneer director Tyrone Guthrie to direct the first production with Flora Robson (mind you, the chapel was originally funded by a bizarre reverend from the lottery winnings of his wife).

The Dublin Gate Theatre, the Group Theatre (presenting Auden, Isherwood, MacNiece) and the London Mask Theatre, under J B Priestley, all appeared here, and Robert Donat broke records with Oscar Wilde's *The Ideal Husband* before Moral Rearmament took over in 1946, either running their own companies or leasing to others. In 1966, the theatre was reconstructed as part of a new arts centre, with film and other facilities, which makes it popular for business conventions. Many of the shows have been toured abroad and made into films.

Underground: Victoria (Circle, District, Victoria, British Rail)
Bus: 2, 2B, 10, 11, 16, 16A, 24, 25, 29, 36, 36A, 36B, 38, 39, 52, 70, 76, 149, 185, 500, 503, 507, 700, 701, 704, 705, 706, 707, 708, 714, 717, 718, 729, 732, 737, 790, AV300, 310, 311, 320, 322
Map: 154 P3

Whitehall Theatre

14 Whitehall, SW1A 2DY
Box Office: **930 7765, 930 6692** (10 00-20 00) Admin: **930 3055**
Performance Space: Proscenium arch *Seating:* 662 (3 levels, boxes)

Bookings: Postal (cheques to Whitehall Theatre) s.a.e. Phone (will hold 3 days) Credit cards — Access, AmEx, Barclaycard/Visa, Diners. Sterling travellers cheques **Prices:** according to attraction **Concessions:** Parties 10 per cent discount **Perf Times:** Variable. Friday-Saturday 2 shows **Catering:** Snack bar in foyer all day **Bars:** 2 from 45 mins before show **Wheelchairs:** 2 **Cloakrooms:** 1 (Attendant) **Parking:** Ample after 18 30

Policy: The theatre is a general West End venue for producing managements.

Perspective: The third theatre to be opened in September 1930, the Whitehall was built just off Trafalgar Square on the site of Ye Old Ship Tavern (which goes back to 1650 and after demolition moved opposite). It has a simple, bare facade for Whitehall. The interior has been redecorated, but retains a used, but comfortable feel. Its tradition of 'modern comedies' gave way during the war to revue and stripper Phyllis Dixey (subject of a recent television programme) who took over the theatre in 1944 for 3 years.

Delderfield's *Worm's Eye View* opened in 1945 and, overall, ran for 2,245 performances — the only hit before the arrival in 1950 of Brian Rix and his farces, which became synonymous with the theatre for the next 20 years, and many of which were translated to television: *Reluctant Heroes, Dry Rot, Simple Spymen, One for the Pot.* Danny La Rue appeared in *Come Spy With Me,* and Rix's last hit was *Uproar in the House* before entrepreneur Paul Raymond took the lease in 1971. His production *Pyjama Tops,* which began its run in 1969, continued for 5 years. However, interesting plays from other managements have also appeared, such as Willy Russell's Liverpool comedy *Breezeblock Park* with Wendy Craig, and the South African revue *Ipi Tombi.*

Underground: Charing Cross (Bakerloo, Jubilee, Northern)
Bus: 1, 3, 6, 9, 11, 12, 13, 15, 24, 29, 53, 77, 77A, 77C, 88, 159, 168, 170, 172, 176
Map: 155 N4

Wimbledon Theatre

The Broadway, Wimbledon SW19 1QG
Box Office: **946 5211** (10 00-20 00) Admin: **946 3319**
Performance Space: Proscenium arch *Seating:* 1,748 (2 levels)

Bookings: Postal (cheques to Wimbledon Theatre) s.a.e Phone (held 4 days) Credit cards — Access, Barclaycard/Visa. Sterling travellers cheques
Prices: £1.50-£3.50 **Concessions:** Parties of 10 + , OAPs & students at 75p off
Perf Times: Monday-Saturday eves 19 30, Thursday & Saturday mats 14 30
Mailing List: 50p p.a. **Catering:** Coffee only from bars **Bars:** 4 **Wheelchairs:** 4
Cloakrooms: No **Parking:** Ample in streets **Other:** Friends of the Wimbledon Theatre £1.50 p.a. for priority bookings, mailings, lectures

Policy: To provide a wide-ranging variety of entertainment that will appeal to the local audience. Pantomime, with which the theatre first opened in 1910, remains the most popular show. Occasional pre-West End runs (eg Stoppard's *Night and Day*) and concerts by popular artists.

Perspective: With its distinctive dome, the Wimbledon Theatre, in the south-west of London, was the last of the suburban theatres to be built by J B Mulholland, who believed that every community should have its own theatre (he also built the Metropole, Camberwell, replaced by a cinema, and the King's Hammersmith, also now demolished).

This corner site had previously been occupied by a large house surrounded by lawns and winding driveways. A glass of whisky cost only 4d at the opening show in 1910, and you could also take a Turkish bath at the back of the theatre if the excitement of *Jack and Jill* proved too much. This panto started a tradition of family Christmas shows which recently have included stars such as Dick Emery, Jimmy Tarbuck, Terry Scott, and Arthur Askey. By the'20s the theatre had become one of the most successful touring venues in Britain and many great names appeared, including Gracie Fields who was so popular that the staff received double wages that week.

A local campaign to save the theatre led to its purchase in 1965 by the local council. Renovations were completed in 1968, since when many notable visits have occurred — the Red Army, Marlene Dietrich (breaking even Gracie Fields' record), the National Theatre, Royal and Festival Ballet, D'Oyly Carte, the Actors' Company (in its first London season, returning three times), and Danny La Rue. There is friendly rivalry with the Richmond Theatre. Wimbledon has several good pubs and restaurants (particularly Indian) but it gets more expensive as you go towards the Village.

Underground: Wimbledon (District, British Rail)
Bus: 57, 77A, 77C, 93, 131, 155, 200, 293
Map: 148 F

Windmill Theatre

Great Windmill Street, W1V 7HE
Box Office: **437 6312** (11 00-22 30) Admin: **734 9190**
Performance Space: Proscenium arch *Seating:* 312 (2 levels)

Bookings: Postal (cheques to Windmill Theatre) s.a.e. Phone (held 3 days) Credit cards (437 6312) AmEx, Barclaycard/Visa, Diners **Prices:** £5-£6.50 **Concessions:** Parties on application **Perf Times:** Monday-Saturday 20 00 & 22 00; Sundays 18 00 & 20 00 **Bars:** 1, also drinks service from trolley in auditorium
Wheelchairs: 1, easy access **Cloakrooms:** 1 (Attendant) **Parking:** NCP Brewer St

Policy: To stage intimate sex revues by the resident company. The present production *Rip Off* opened in 1976; the acts vary as new talent and specialist spots are incorporated into the show.

Perspective: In 1973, there was a campaign to revive the good old days at the Windmill. Paul Raymond, who now owns the freehold, remodelled what had been for a few years a Classic Cinema into a Revuedeville theatre (without the warm humour of old). Many original features were destroyed but the illuminated windmill on the facade was retained. The theatre had been a cinema before, one of the first small West End houses, called the Palais de Luxe (built in 1910 on the corner of a block that includes the Apollo and Lyric theatres).

When Vivian van Damn took over, the exterior was redesigned and the interior became very intimate. He had been given a free hand by the new owner Mrs Henderson to run non-stop variety in a bid to beat the hold of the 'talkies', and on 3 February 1932, the first Paris-style Revuedeville began (lasting from 14 30 to 23 00). At first he lost heavily, but the productions later proved so popular, with names such as Jimmy Edwards, Tony Hancock and Harry Secombe getting their break, that the Windmill became one of the most famous theatres in Britain.

Its boast, 'We Never Closed' (except for 12 obligatory days in September 1939) became a catchphrase, and stories of the performers sleeping at night in the theatre during the blitz became legend. Such spirit has gone from the neighbourhood now, so beware local pubs selling sandwiches at high prices.

Underground: Piccadilly Circus (Bakerloo, Piccadilly)
Bus: 3, 6, 9, 12, 13, 14, 15, 19, 22, 38, 53, 88, 159
Map: 154 N3

Wyndham's Theatre

Charing Cross Road, WC2H 0DA
Box Office: **836 3028** (10 00-20 00) Admin: **836 5650**
Performance Space: Proscenium arch *Seating:* 759 (4 levels)

Bookings: Postal (cheques to Wyndham's Theatre) s.a.e Phone (held 3 days) Credit cards (379 6565, 09 00-20 00) Access, AmEx, Barclaycard/Visa, Diners. Sterling travellers cheques **Prices:** £3-£8 **Concessions:** Student Standby when available. Omega Party Bookings (836 3962) or to The Party Organizer, The Albery Theatre, St Martin's Lane, WC2N 4AH **Perf Times:** Eves 20 00 **Catering:** No. Hire of Royal Retiring Room & catering service by arrangement **Bars:** 3 **Wheelchairs:** 4 (easy access) **Cloakrooms:** 1 (Attendant) 1 (Paralok) **Parking:** NCP Upper St. Martin's Lane

Policy: Normal commercial West End theatre.

Perspective: This ornate theatre with classical exterior was built in 1899 by actor/manager Charles Wyndham with help from friends and actor Mary Moore, whom he later married (the bust over the proscenium is said to look like her). It is on the Charing Cross Road side of a plot that stretches to St Martin's Lane, later also occupied by the New (now Albery) — both designed by W G R Sprague. The pale blue, cream and gold colour scheme, with dark blue seats, makes this one of the loveliest of London's theatres, and it is also one of the cosiest.

Frank Curzon became part of the management in 1902, to be joined by Charles Hawtrey and then Gerald du Maurier. Tallulah Bankhead made her first West End appearance (1923), but this period is remembered more for the run of thrillers written by Edgar Wallace, the last of which was produced in 1932 on the day before his death in Hollywood.

The theatre has had many successes, such as *The Boy Friend* (which ran for 2,078 performances in 1954), *The Prime of Miss Jean Brodie, Abelard and Heloise* and *The Boys in the Band*. Many of the hits were transfers — Theatre Workshop's *A Taste of Honey, The Hostage* and *Oh! What a Lovely War, Godspell, No Man's Land* with John Gielgud and Ralph Richardson, *Side by Side by Sondheim,* Mary O'Malley's *Once a Catholic, Piaf,* and two farces from the fringe, *The Primary English Class* (from the Orange Tree, Richmond) and Belt and Braces' production of *Accidental Death of an Anarchist*.

Underground: Leicester Square (Northern, Piccadilly)
Bus: 1, 24, 29, 176 or 3, 6, 9, 11, 12, 13, 15, 53, 77, 77A, 77C, 88, 159, 168, 170, 172 to Trafalgar Square or 14, 19, 22, 38 to Cambridge Circus
Map: 155 N4

York and Albany

129 Parkway, NW1 7PS
Box Office: **387 2304** (11 00-14 00 & 17 30-23 30) Admin: **723 7482**
Performance Space: Upstairs pub room *Seating:* 50 (flexible rostra)

Bookings: Members only (+ 1 guest) 25p in advance or at door. Postal to 15 Westbourne Terrace, W2 (cheques to Mouth & Trousers Theatre Co) s.a.e. Phone (held to ½hr before show) No credit cards or travellers cheques **Prices:** £1.50 **Concessions:** No **Perf Times:** Wednesday-Saturday 20 00 **Catering:** No **Bars:** Pub hrs **Wheelchairs:** No **Cloakrooms:** No **Parking:** Ample side streets

Policy: Emphasis is on new works and original adaptations of more established pieces. The resident company, Mouth and Trousers, also administers the space as a venue for visiting fringe companies, particularly those who are having difficulty in getting started.

Perspective: A strange meeting of traditions makes the pub theatre at the York and Albany a lively affair. Before becoming a pub hotel, it was built in the latter part of the 18th century as the town house of the Earl of Southampton, whose ancestor had been a patron of none other than William Shakespeare. The upstairs room used for theatre was the noble Earl's ballroom. Now, it is the home of the resident company, Mouth and Trousers — a name taken from Cockney slang, roughly translated as a lot of hot air.

The group was founded in June 1979 to put on new plays and original interpretations. The members wanted to work away from the West End, offering good theatre at cheap prices in a pub somewhere in the north London borough of Camden. They toured and created their own shows (eg *I'm the Original, Death of Harlequin*) and then moved into the York and Albany in November 1979 with a new adaptation of Jean Genet's fantasy *The Maids*. Another old piece given a new treatment has been the Russian story *The Nose* by Nikolai Gogol. The interests of the group and its director, Leslie Ferris, lie in mime, masks and puppets rather than in naturalistic techniques. This preference is reflected in the types of group which perform at the York and Albany along with Mouth and Trousers — eg The Permanent Wave Theatre, Teatr Kozmo Mimzi (with Pierrot).

The small nucleus that runs Mouth and Trousers, which hires actors for each show it mounts, is keen to receive scripts to read because it wants to provide a much-needed service to aspiring playwrights: rehearsed play readings.

Underground: Camden Town (Northern) Camden Road (British Rail)
Bus: 3, 24, 27, 29, 31, 46, 53, 68, 74, 134, 137, 214, 253, 735
Map: 151 B4

Young Vic

66 The Cut, Waterloo, SE1 8LP
Box Office: **928 6363** (10 00-20 00) Admin: **633 0133**
Performance Space: Main house & Studio, both with raked seating on 3 sides
Seating: 456 & 100

Bookings: Postal (cheques to The Young Vic Theatre) s.a.e Phone (held 2 days & collection ½ hr before show) No credit cards. Sterling travellers cheques
Prices: £2.25 **Concessions:** Students, OAPs, schoolchildren £1.40; Parties 10+ £2 per seat **Perf Times:** 19 45 Monday-Saturday; morns and mats for education service productions when applicable **Mailing List:** £1 p.a. advance info, seat reductions **Catering:** Coffee bar, hot & cold food lunchtimes, before & during shows
Bars: 1 **Wheelchairs:** Yes **Parking:** Streets, NCP, Royal Festival Hall **Other:** Box Office bookstall for play scripts; performance-related foyer bookstalls as appropriate

Policy: To provide good theatre for young people with emphasis on the classics and well-established modern plays. When touring, the Young Vic acts as a venue for visiting companies, like the Royal Shakespeare Company and the Ballet Rambert.

Perspective: Architect William Howell designed a square-shaped theatre with an ample acting area thrusting into the audience sitting on hard, red, wooden seating tiered on 3 sides and 2 levels. Well proportioned, it only took a year to build (with the familiar '60s concrete breeze blocks) on a site that had been bombed in the war — the foyer used to be a butcher's shop.

The permanent Young Vic company arrived in 1970 to the sound of a pop group and fireworks as the brainchild of National Theatre director Frank Dunlop, who wanted a lively theatre in intimate surroundings for young people. He had been running theatres, including the Nottingham Playhouse, since the '50s, and brought his jazzy style to classics, such as *Don Juan*, and new works (eg *Joseph and His Amazing Technicolour Dreamcoat*).

Dunlop has now returned from the US after a flashy reign at the Young Vic by Michael Bogdanov which saw a similar policy of modern work (eg *Look Back in Anger*), visiting fringe groups (mainly in the adjacent studio) and foreign companies (eg Peter Brook's Paris production of *Ubu Roi*). The Young Vic Education Service was set up in 1978 to develop workshops for young people and take performances into schools. The food is healthy but try the Windmill pub in the same road, Buggins (opposite), South of the Border (Joan St — left, off Hatfields) or the cheap café opposite.

Underground: Waterloo (Bakerloo, Northern, British Rail)
Bus: 1, 4, 55, 68, 70, 76, 149, 168A, 171, 176, 188, 239, 501, 502, 503, 507, 513
Map: 155 06

A TICKET FOR THE SHOW

It is often claimed that perseverance and patience are required in order to buy your tickets for the theatre. This is an exaggeration but the following guidelines should help to make the process easier.

Advance Booking

It is advisable to book your seats in advance for West End productions, although it is always worth your while to try and purchase seats just before a performance, since it may not be sold out and it is common in this country for people to decide to go to the theatre at the last minute. However, for 'hit' shows, you are strongly advised to book as far in advance as possible. If in doubt, book early.

This does not apply so much to fringe theatre productions. Indeed, in many cases such theatres do not have a permanent box office, since fringe companies often perform in pubs and halls. Generally speaking, it is best to arrive at the venue about half an hour before the show begins, and you will be fairly certain of being able to get in.

Methods of Buying Tickets

It is necessary to draw a distinction between West End theatres and other established permanent theatres and the fringe. In the case of fringe theatres, as already suggested, the usual way is to buy your ticket on arrival at the venue on the day of the performance you want to see. Fringe theatres do not usually have the outlets enjoyed by West End theatres, but there are, of course, exceptions, and in the case of productions on the fringe which have attracted great interest and critical acclaim, it may sometimes be advisable to phone two or three days beforehand to check that seats are not getting sold out. The main outlets for the West End theatre are:

The Theatre Box Office: Probably the easiest method of choosing the seat you want and purchasing the ticket is to go to the theatre itself, where the box office staff will help you. Theatre box offices usually open at about 10 00 and remain open throughout the day until the start of the evening performance. Most theatres have separate windows for 'Advance' sales and 'Tonight's Performance'. You are advised to avoid the midday period, since this is the only time for people working in London to buy their seats. It is usually also very busy in the early evening.

Some theatres have their box offices on a separate site (eg the Royal Opera House, Covent Garden, and Sadler's Wells), but this is made clear in the entry for every theatre in this guide. Others have a centralized booking office for standby tickets, eg the Avenue Box Office in the Queen's Theatre in Shaftesbury Avenue, which services the other theatres in the immediate vicinity and elsewhere. If in doubt, check this guide or go straight to the theatre you wish to visit.

Postal Bookings: You may make your ticket bookings by writing to the theatre box office in advance, enclosing a cheque for the required amount and a *stamped self-addressed envelope*. You are advised to offer alternatives for the date of performance you are prepared to accept, in case the box office is not able to accommodate your first choice.

The Telephone: Tickets can be reserved over the telephone by phoning the box office, but you must check the arrangements for collecting and paying for your tickets. Usually the box office will insist that you collect them within a stated time (noted in the guide), or send a cheque through the post in time to reach the theatre within three days of your call, or (if you are making a reservation on the day of performance) they will give you a time by which the tickets must be collected and paid for. Otherwise, they will offer them for re-sale and you may be disappointed if you are not able to get in.

It is sometimes difficult to get through on the phone, especially if there is a successful production in the theatre and also if you phone at times when the box office staff are dealing with personal callers. This is where patience is often required. However, don't believe all the negative stories you hear about box-office staff. They have a lot to put up with — like the call to the box office of a London theatre from a tourist enquiring whether the theatre was air-conditioned: the theatre was the Open Air, Regents Park!

Credit Cards: Most theatres in London now accept credit cards (the main ones being Access, Barclaycard, American Express and Diners Club) as the means of paying for tickets. You can even complete a purchase over the telephone by quoting your credit card number, which will save you the inconvenience of rushing in to collect your tickets. They will be held for you until just before the performance, but you are advised to arrive at the theatre at least fifteen minutes before the performance starts, since there may be a small delay whilst you are required to sign the relevant documents. However, you should appreciate that once you have given your credit card number on the phone to the box office, this means that the sale has been completed, and your credit card account will be charged even if you do not turn up for the show. Not all theatres accept payment by credit card unless the purchase is done by telephone. Also you can save yourself time and the cost of a phone call by checking whether there is a special phone number for credit card calls, so check the classified advertisements, the London Theatre Guide — and *Theatre London*.

Concessions: There are various concessions which operate at some theatres, the details of which are usually contained in display advertisements or can be provided on request by the box office. The normal concessions are the following:

Reduced Price Previews: Most West End shows open with about one week of previews prior to the official first night, when the critics are invited. The rate of reduction varies from theatre to theatre.

Student Standby: Most West End theatres operate the Student Standby scheme which was devised by the Society of West End Theatre and the Arts Council. Although this varies from theatre to theatre, the scheme means that students who call at the theatre shortly before a performance may be able to purchase tickets at special standby rates. This is subject to availability, and there can be no guarantee that there will be standby seats. The theatres which participate in this scheme include a large 'S' symbol in their advertisements in the London Theatre Guide, and in the *Evening News, Evening Standard, Guardian, Times* and *Time Out*. Students can enquire during the day whether there are likely to be any standby seats, or you can listen to Capital Radio every weekday evening at 17 30 when theatres at which standby seats are likely to be available are listed. With so many theatres close to each other in the West End, you can always try somewhere else if the theatre of your first choice does not have any available seats. Remember, though, that it is essential that you have a Student Union card to confirm your status. Some theatres offer similar standby facilities to senior citizens; check their entries for this.

Group Rates: Most theatres will offer discounts for groups, usually of 12 or more. The rate of reduction varies from theatre to theatre, but it is essential that you arrange this beforehand. Some theatres advertise a separate phone number for group bookings in their classified advertisements or the London Theatre Guide.

Ticket Agencies: There are a large number of ticket agencies in London, both in the West End itself and in hotels throughout the city, where you can purchase theatre tickets. There are also a vast number of agencies throughout the country where West End theatre tickets can be bought. The advantage of this system is that it can save you queueing for your seats or the frustration and delay often involved in telephoning the theatre box office or the uncertainties and delays in booking by post. The disadvantages are that you have to pay extra (as much as £2 on top of the price of the actual ticket), and you may be required to exchange the voucher given to you by the agency for an actual ticket when you arrive at the theatre, which therefore involves you arriving early.

Other Useful Points

Wheelchairs: Some theatres offer special facilities for people confined to wheelchairs (the details are contained in the entries in this guide). It is very important to make a prior arrangement if you wish to avail yourself of this service.

Methods of Payment: Reference has already been made to the use of credit cards. If you are not paying by cash at the box office, you will need a bank card as a means of identification. Some theatres may be willing to accept payment by travellers' cheque, but only in exceptional cases.

Theatre Clubs: Some fringe theatres are officially constituted as clubs, for which a subscription has to be paid in addition to the price of the theatre tickets, though the subscription is usually a one-off payment for a period of a year. If you are already a member of one club, it is as well to check whether this membership entitles you to reciprocal membership of other clubs.

Ticket Touts: Whenever there is a smash hit show, ticket touts will try to sell tickets at vastly inflated prices. Theatre managements do all they can to stop customers being 'scalped' in this way. You should not believe anyone outside a theatre who tells you that the show is sold out since, even when 'House Full' signs are displayed, there may be occasional returns at the box office which you might be able to purchase at normal prices.

VINCENT BURKE
Development Officer of the Society of West End Theatre

WHAT'S PLAYING TONIGHT?

Other pages in this book will allow you to find your way to over a hundred theatres. Some have fascinating historical associations, but only a few (the Royal Opera House, National Theatre, Barbican Arts Centre) are worth seeing for their intrinsic architectural interest. What matters is the shows for which the bricks and mortar offer a shell. As there is a fast turnover in the range of plays, musicals, variety and other theatre available, any list that we published here would be out of date before you caught your tube. So how *do* you find out? Here are some of the ways — which are most suitable for you will depend on your tastes and pattern of theatregoing.

Mailing Lists

If you want to go to several productions at the same theatre in the course of a year (which will generally be the case with those which house a permanent company, or have a policy which especially appeals to you) and you like to plan well in advance, the best source of information will be that theatre's mailing list, which can generally be posted to you for a nominal annual subscription. For this you will receive leaflets giving dates, times, and prices, together with casting details and other information. Some mailing lists also offer priority booking before tickets go on sale to the general public, whilst others are included in the annual membership fees of club theatres. Availability and costs are noted under individual theatre entries earlier in this edition of *Theatre London*.

Press

Most national newspapers and the London evenings (*Evening Standard* and *Evening News*) carry listings of shows playing each evening in their classified entertainment guides. These are not comprehensive, as the advertisements are paid for by the theatres and therefore exclude many of the smaller houses, but are invaluable as a quick up-to-date check on what's on, where and when. The information given is usually minimal — times of performance, with the phone number but not the address of the theatre (but you don't need that — you've a copy of *Theatre London*!). The title of the show and its stars will of course be included — but the name of the playwright probably only if he's a box-office hit.

'Time Out'

The theatre section in this weekly magazine does aim to be comprehensive — listing everything from the latest blockbuster Drury Lane musical to a single performance at a community centre. The amount of information given is also good, with details of ticket prices (and membership where applicable), running times (so that you can book a table for after the show or make sure you catch your last train), and brief reviews of new productions or one-line comments of a frankly subjective nature (you soon learn how far your prejudices match *Time Out*'s).

There are separate listings for dance and opera, and indeed for the many other entertainments the capital offers. Features dealing with the theatre (often covering the latest season by a company of particular interest) frequently appear. *Time Out* is published each Thursday, and its listings cover Friday through Thursday.

Alternative Theatre in 'The Guardian'
Each Saturday on the arts page, *The Guardian* publishes a listing of 'Alternative Theatre', usually giving more information than a normal entertainment guide and covering small-scale theatres. It is not comprehensive, but concentrates on the better-established alternative venues.

'What's On' and 'Where To Go'
These two weekly magazines are aimed at the tourist, unlike *Time Out* which caters more especially for the Londoner. Their theatre sections are not comprehensive as they tend to concentrate on the West End, but they do give brief descriptions of the shows and their listings are classified into musicals, comedies, thrillers, etc.

Specialist Periodicals
The Stage: The weekly newspaper of the profession, *The Stage* carries news items on forthcoming shows with features of interest to the industry and advertisements for casting, theatre staff, and belly-dancing fire-eaters. Published on Thursdays. Good if you want an 'inside' view. (Also thorough coverage of the regions.)

Plays and Players: A monthly glossy magazine reviewing new productions in words and photographs. Not very useful for tonight's performance unless you want to see stills from a long-running show, but often attractive as a souvenir.

Show Biz: As we went to press London was about to see the publication of this new trade paper for the entertainment industry dealing with everything from classical music through theatre to video and circus. It remains an unknown quantity to us — you may be luckier!

Theatre Quarterly: The leading journal for the more serious-minded theatregoer — though 'serious' certainly doesn't mean 'solemn'. The magazine includes lively interviews with major dramatists and detailed studies of plays in performance. Little up-to-the-minute material, but often valuable background.

Broadcasting
News, magazine features, specialist programmes, interviews, reviews, and even gobbets of drama itself are broadcast from time to time by both radio and television. The times and formats of these programmes change rapidly, so please consult the *Radio Times* (for BBC TV 1 & 2, BBC Radio 1, 2, 3, 4, and Radio London) and the *TV Times* (for Thames Television and London Weekend Television), or look in the newspapers. The most regular arts spot is *Kaleidoscope,* generally on Radio 4 around 21 30 on weekdays.

Local Radio: BBC Radio London (206m), LBC (261m), and Capital (194m) are especially good for snippets and topical information and updates.

Reviews
Most daily newspapers, the evenings and Sundays, as well as many magazines and other periodicals carry reviews of shows when they first open.

It is a life-long task to find a theatre critic whose tastes so coincide with your own that you can rely on his judgement when choosing a show. Even when you find a critic whose opinions you value he will often surprise you with a rave for a show you hated or by panning a production that gave you a magic evening.

The alternative to matching tastes is to plough through all the reviews looking for a consensus. This too presents problems. Many a show has opened to universally bad notices only to be re-reviewed favourably later in its run when public opinion (in the form of box office receipts) has led the critics to a different conclusion about the production merits.

London Theatre Guide

Published fortnightly by the Society of West End Theatre, this handy leaflet gives details of all shows in the West End. It may be found throughout London in theatres and hotels, or a complimentary copy will be sent to you if you send a stamped addressed envelope to Dept LTG, Theatre Despatch, P2 Butler's Wharf, Lafone Street, London SE1 2LX. (Overseas readers should send their addressed envelope with an international reply coupon.)

Fringe Mailing List

A sister of the London Theatre Guide, this pocket-sized leaflet gives details of alternative theatre including brief descriptions of the shows. It is sent to subscribers every four weeks. For details, please send a stamped addressed envelope to Dept FML, at the above address.

Ceefax, Oracle, Prestel

These three systems display information on a specially adapted television receiver. They are all in their infancy and their availability at present is limited.

Ceefax, broadcast by the BBC, includes reviews of new shows (indexed on page 280) and news about the arts (indexed on page 230).

Oracle, broadcast by ITV, has classified listings of West End and out-of-town shows, and the repertoire houses (indexed on pages 306-308).

Prestel, which is connected via the GPO telephone network, offers a listing of West End shows with full-page reviews, two line verdicts, and a star rating system (page 350500), together with information supplied by *Time Out* (page 441).

Student Standby

Capital Radio (194 m) provides a daily broadcast of theatres offering the Student Standby scheme (see page 139) at 17 30.

Posters and Leaflets

Posters and leaflets for many shows are to be found in hotels, ticket agents, public libraries, colleges, and the theatres themselves throughout London. In addition, posters for all the West End shows are on display on the side of the Palace Theatre in Cambridge Circus, and between the Wyndham's and Albery Theatres, off Charing Cross Road.

PHILIP ORMOND
Director, Theatre Despatch

HOW-TO-GET-THERE MAPS

The black and white sketch maps at the beginning of this section have been designed to show how easily the outer-London fringe theatres can be reached using the London Underground system. Please refer to the Underground map on page 160 for details of the lines and interchange stations.

The central London theatres are covered by full-colour maps showing a local street plan and giving details of all bus routes and Underground stations. When using the Underground, if in any doubt always consult the 'You are Here' map in the ticket hall of each station.

For further information and help in planning your journey, please phone (01) 222 1234 (any time night or day) or write to:

Travel Enquiries,
London Transport,
55 Broadway,
London SW1H 0BD

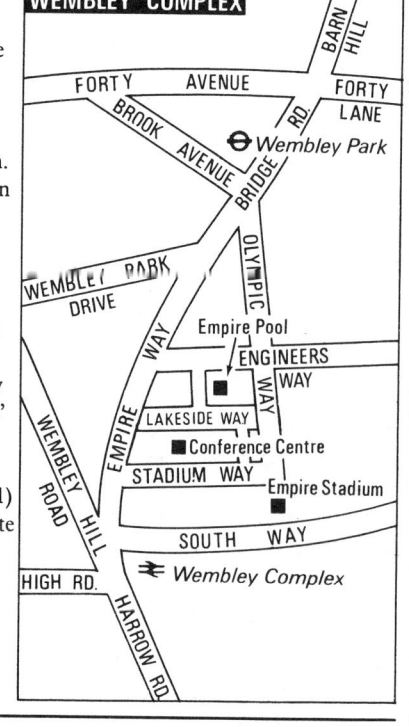

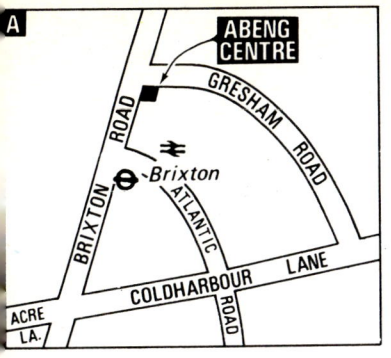
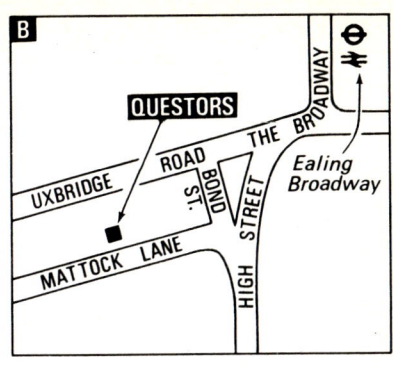
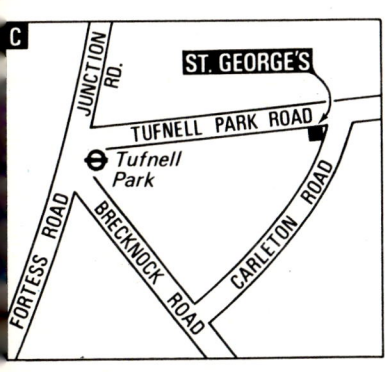
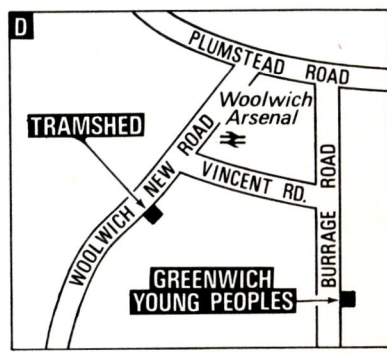
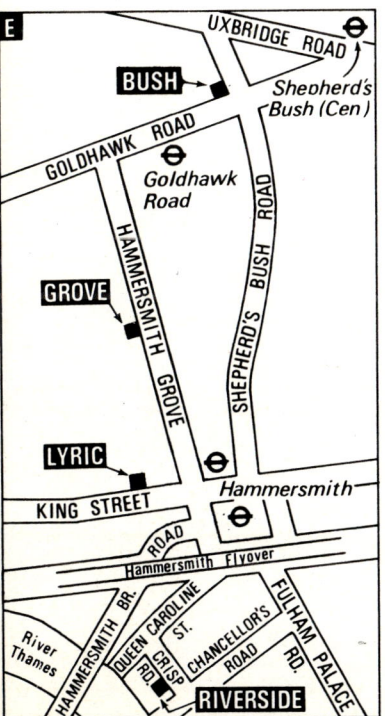
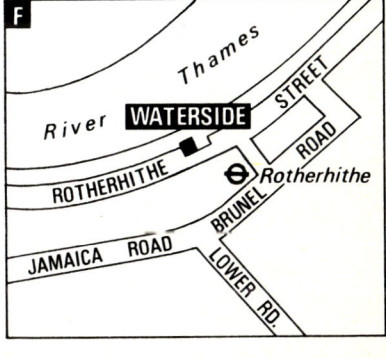
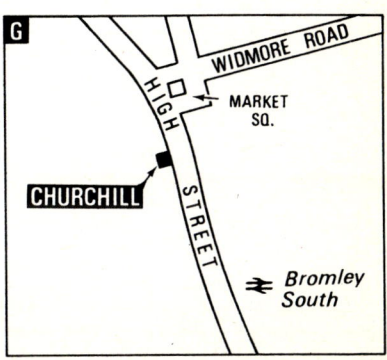

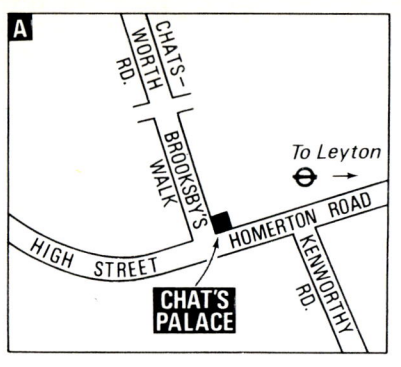
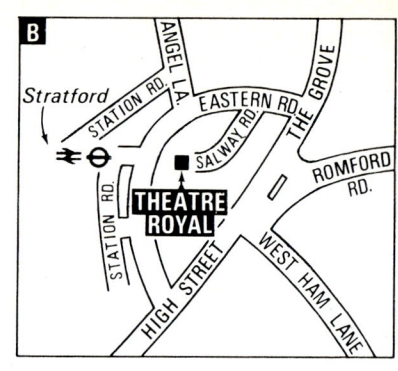
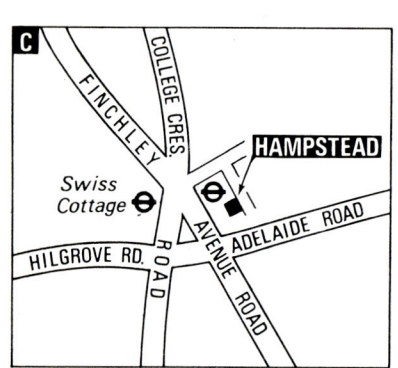
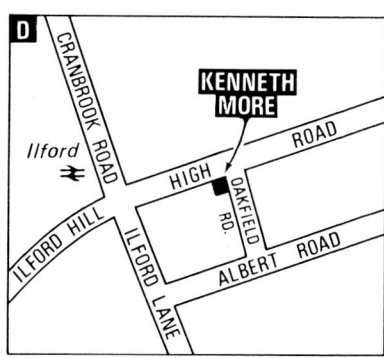
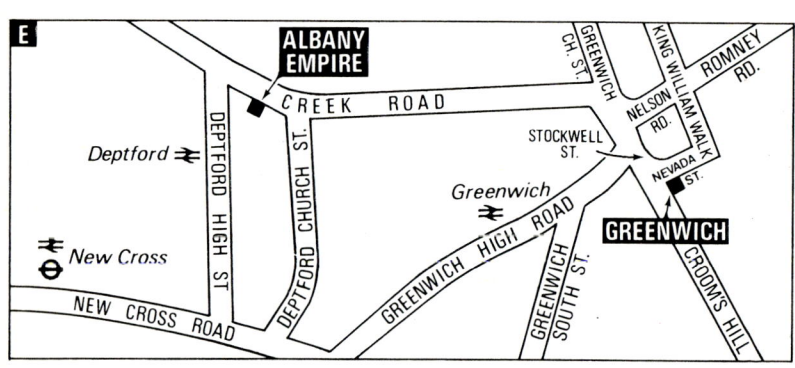
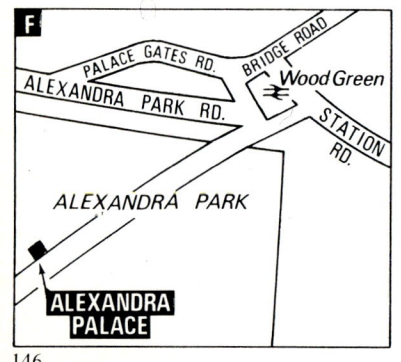
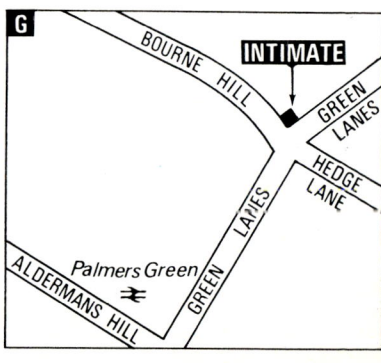

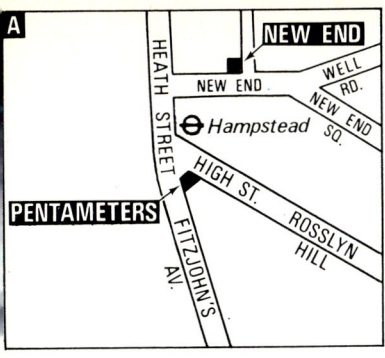
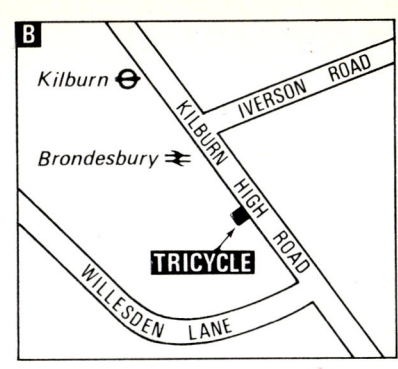
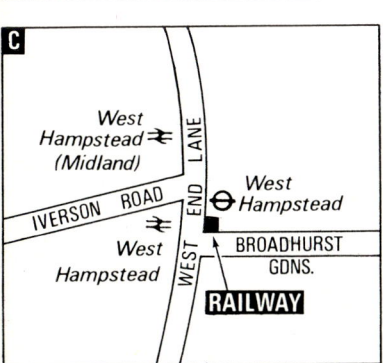
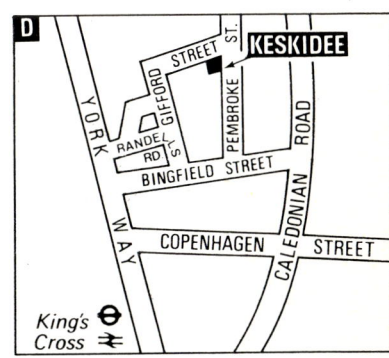
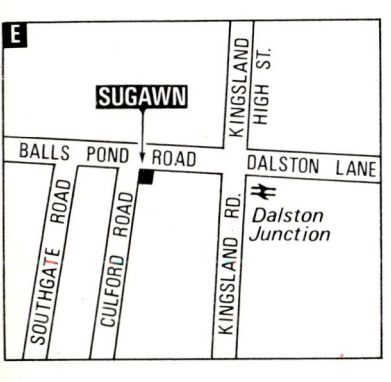
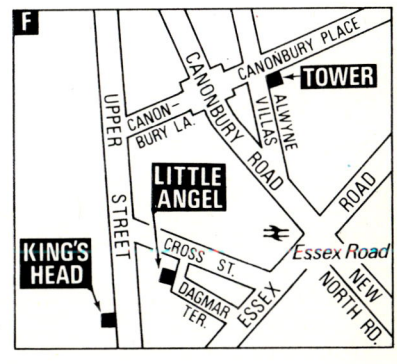
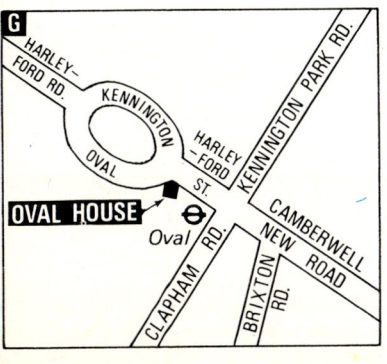
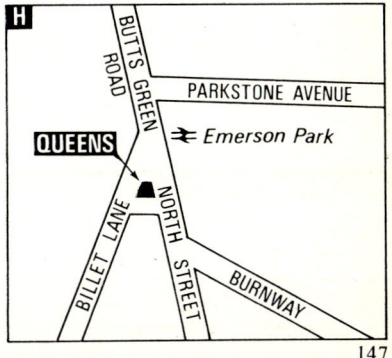

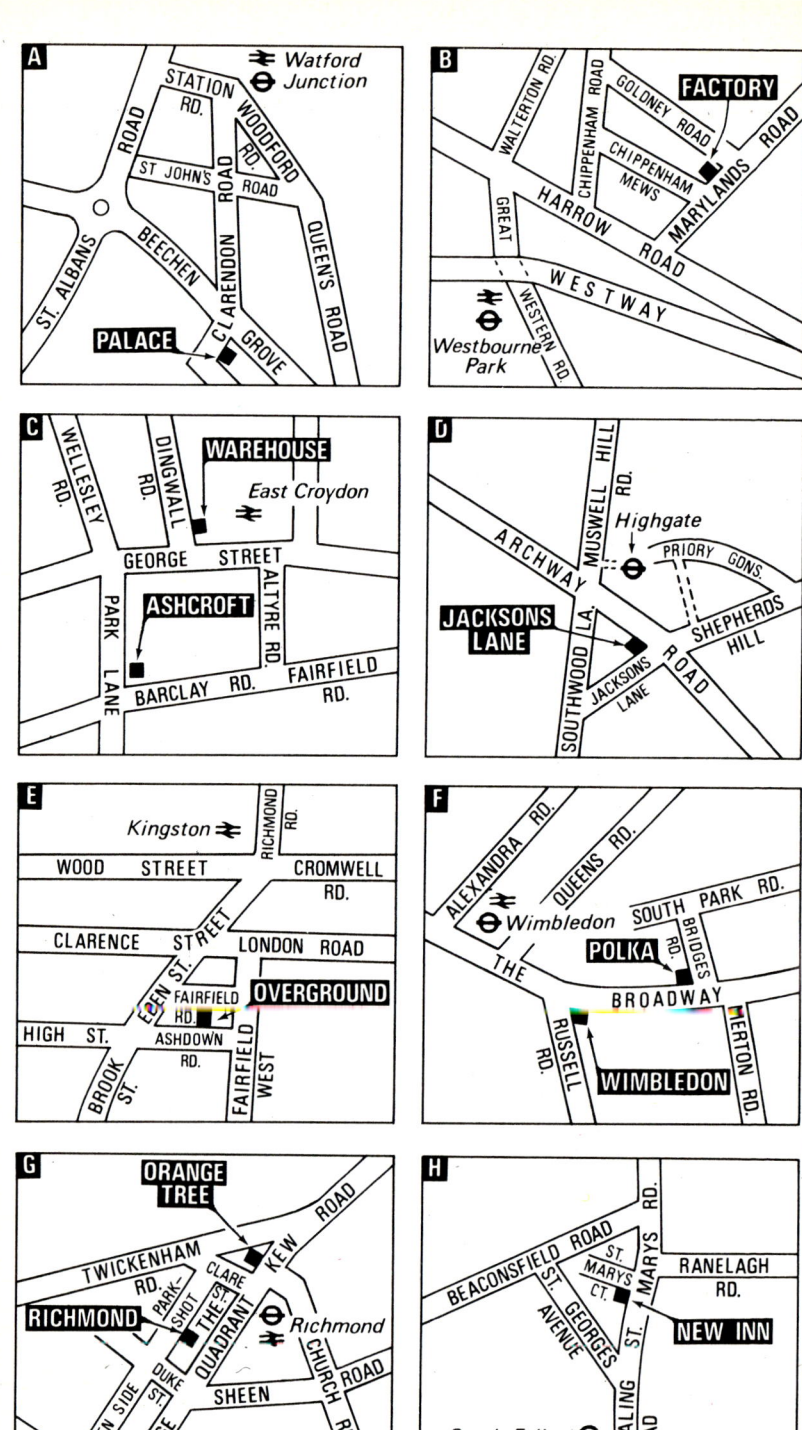

Key

16	Regular Daily Service	●●●	Main Shopping Street
187	Certain Days of the week only (Details shown at bus stops)	M	Street Market
☽	Night Service (Timetable Booklet available from any London Transport Travel Information Centre)	⚲	Monument or Statue
★ 31	Terminus of Route		Children's Playground
☆	Other Terminal Points		Children's Zoo
i	London Transport Travel Information Centre		Refreshments
⊖	Underground Station		Boating Lake
⇌	British Rail Station		River Trip
⇌	Main Line Terminal		Canal Trip
✈	Air Terminal	▲	Entrance to Towing Path Walk
»	Coach Terminal	♪	Open Air Music (Summer)
	Place of Interest - Full details will be found in "Visitor's London" published by London Transport		University or College
i	Information Centre - London Tourist Board/British Tourist Authority/City Information		Hospital
SAVOY	Theatres (see index)	△	Embassy
			Bus Garage

Scale 0   ¼   ½   ¾ Mile

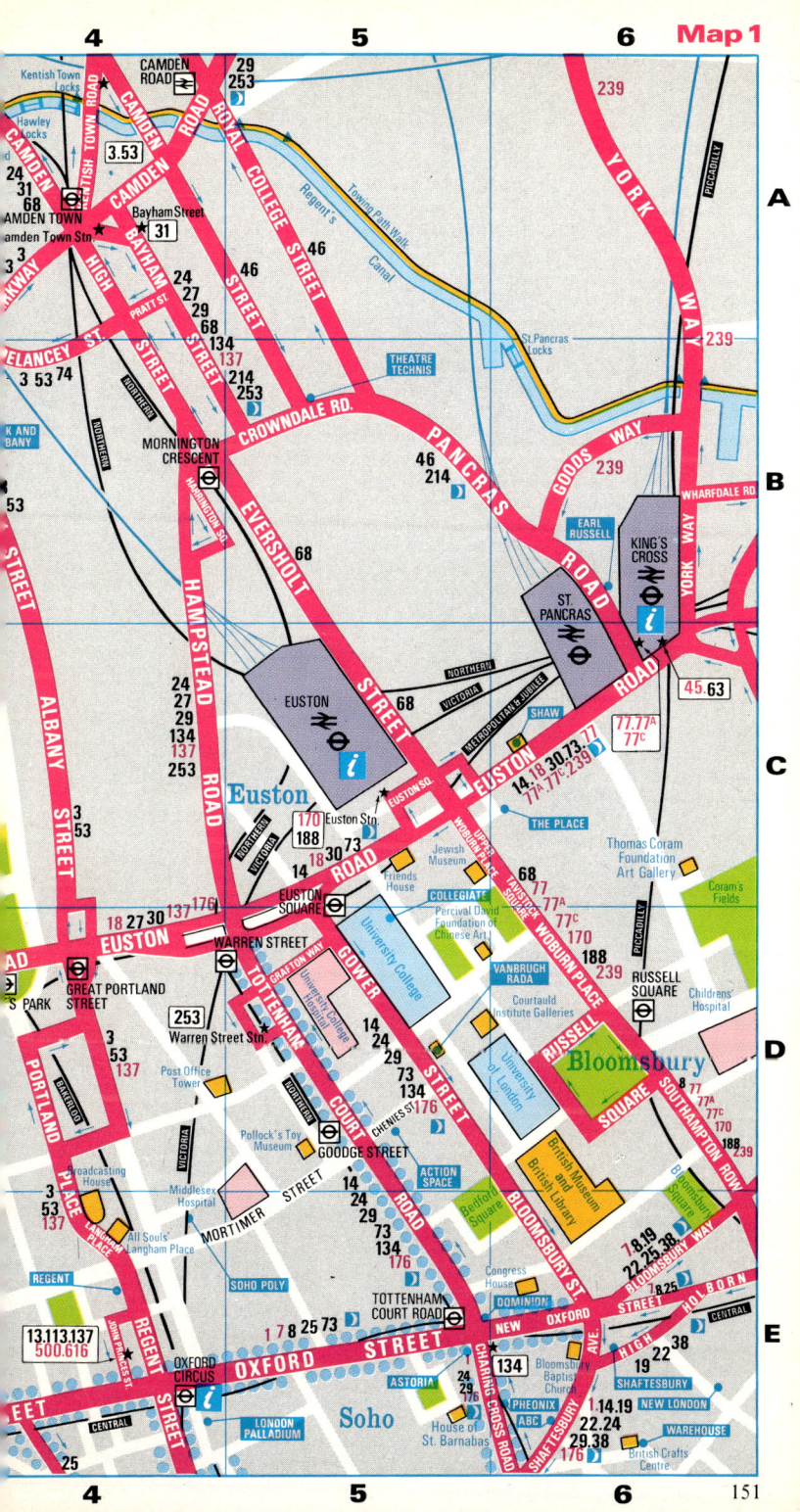

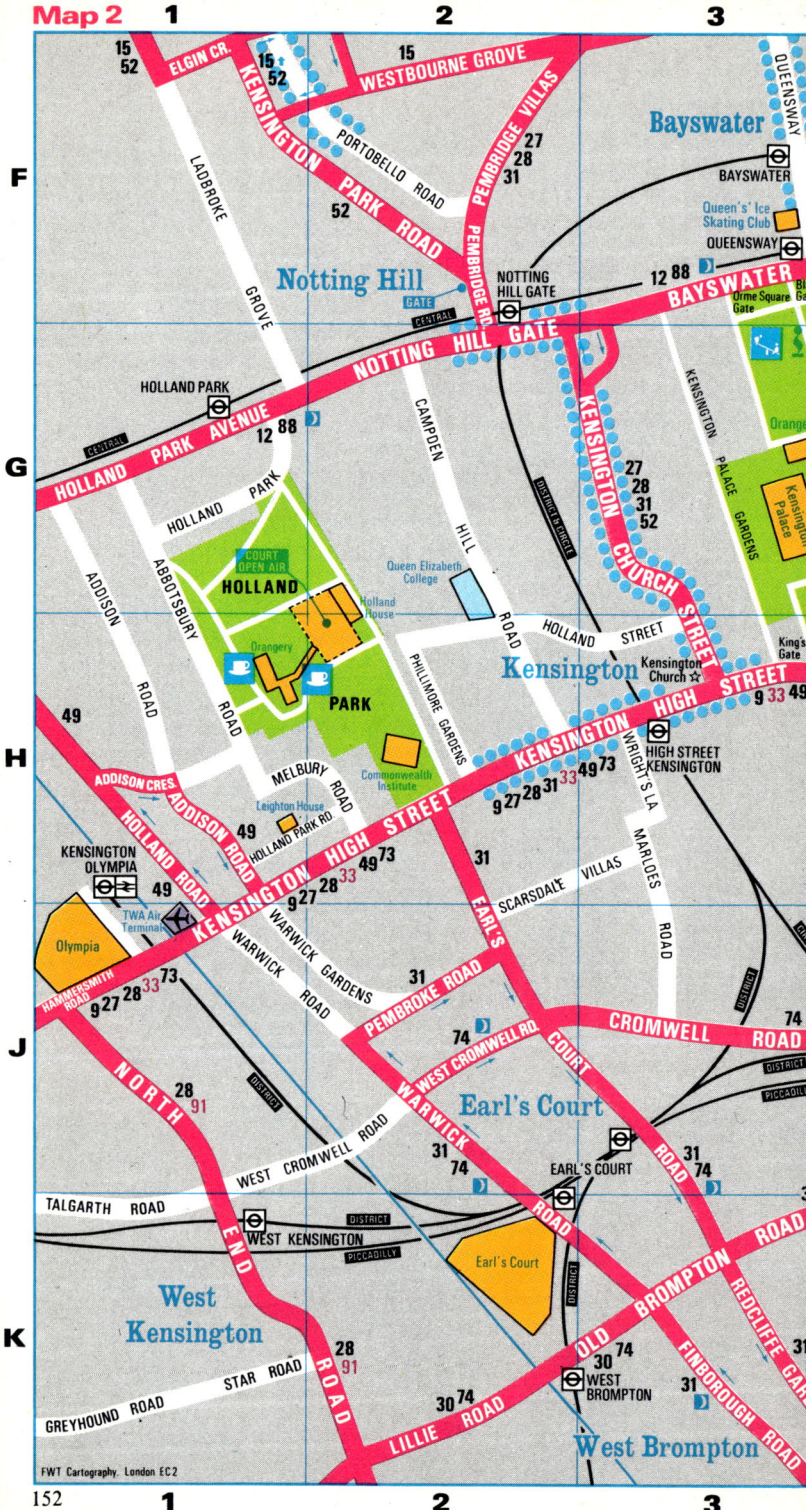

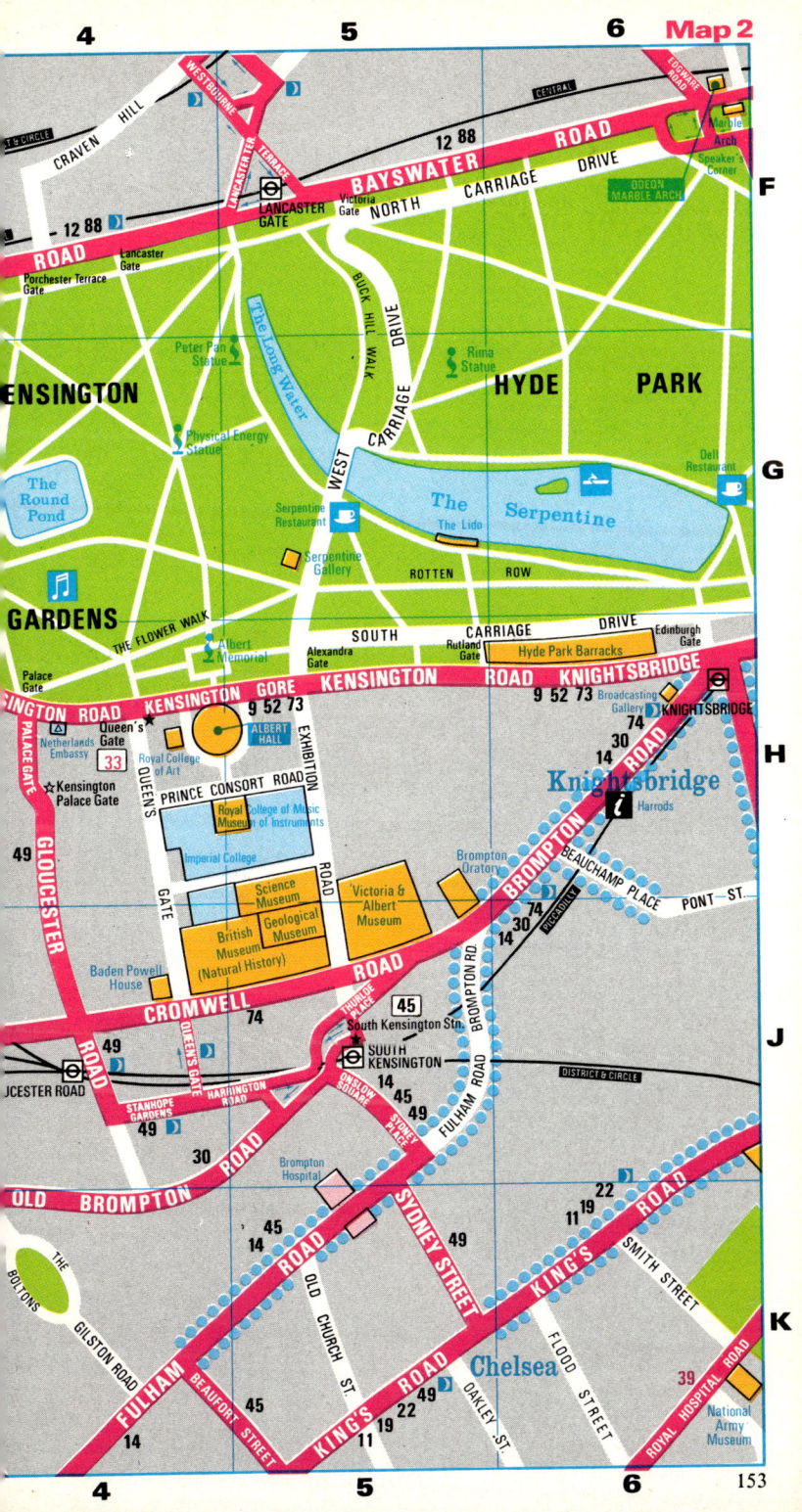

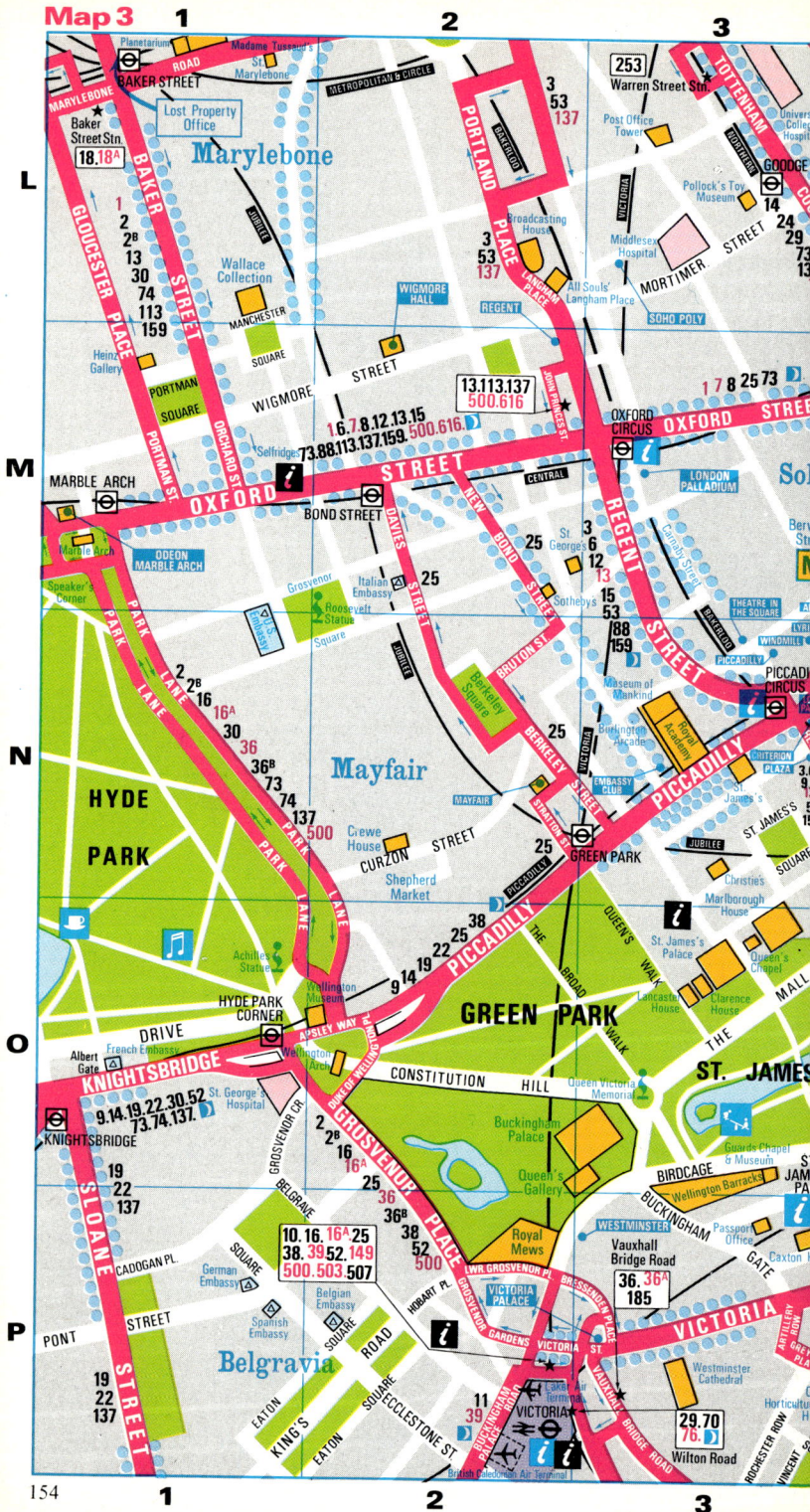

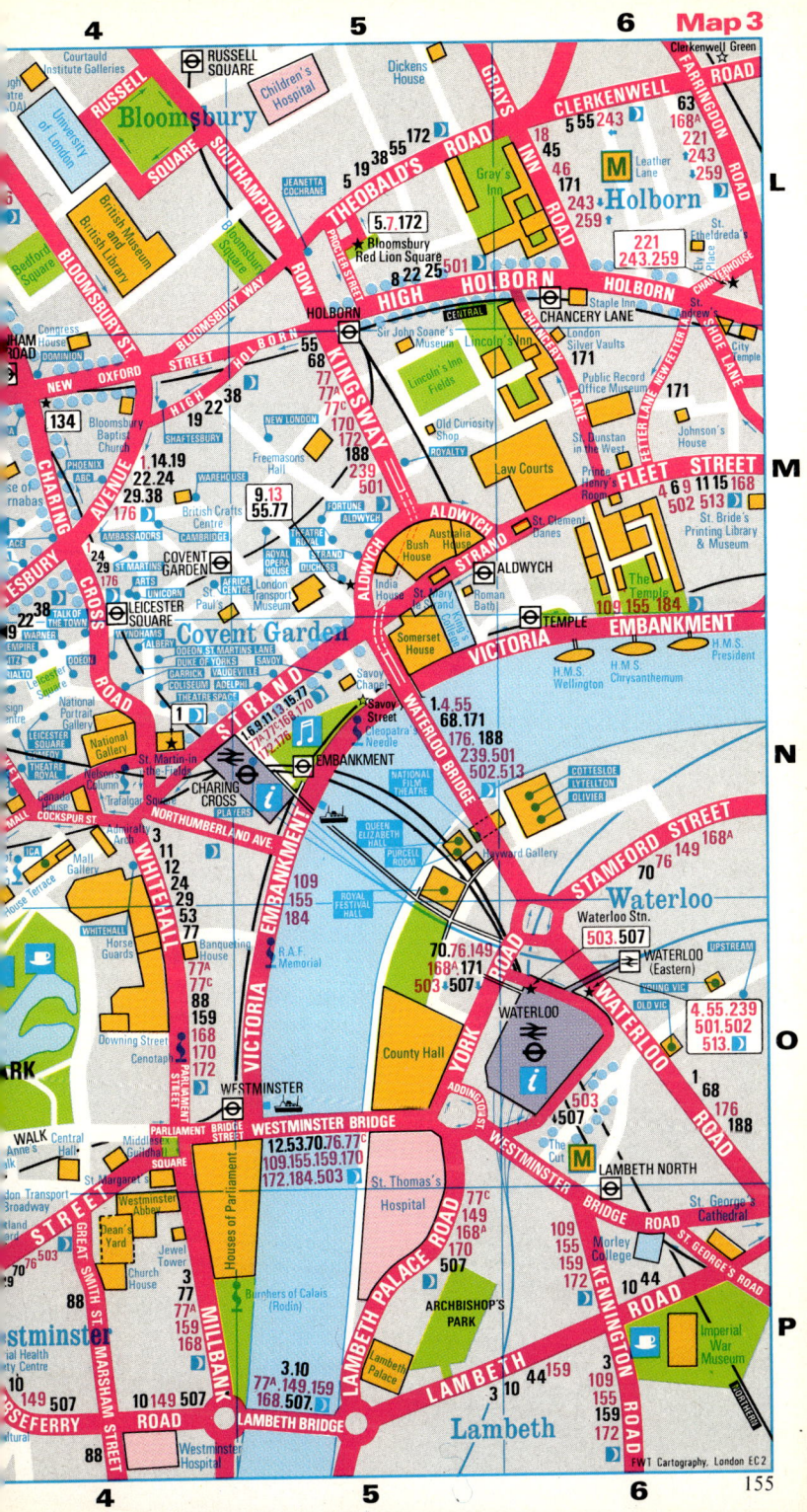

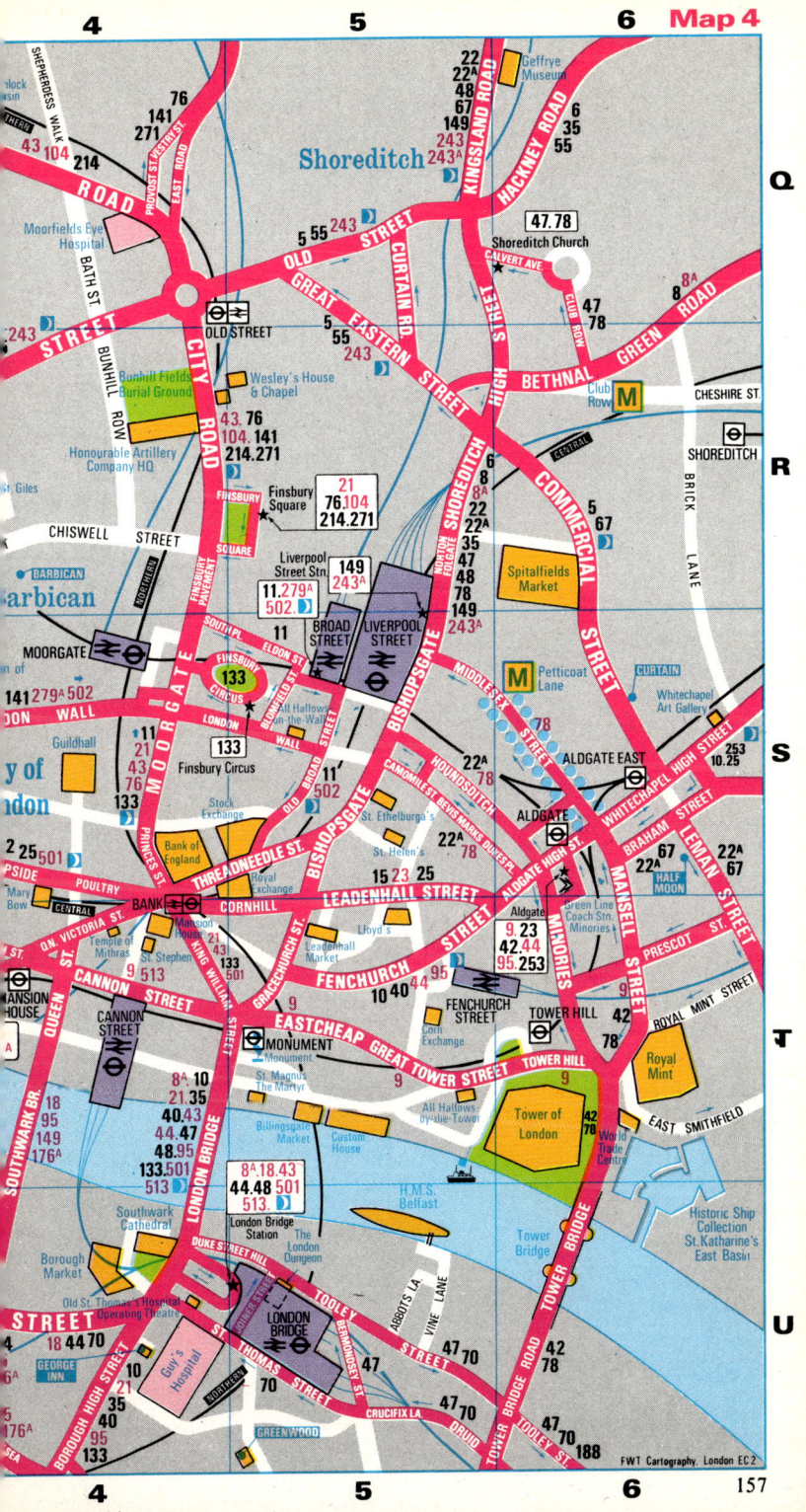

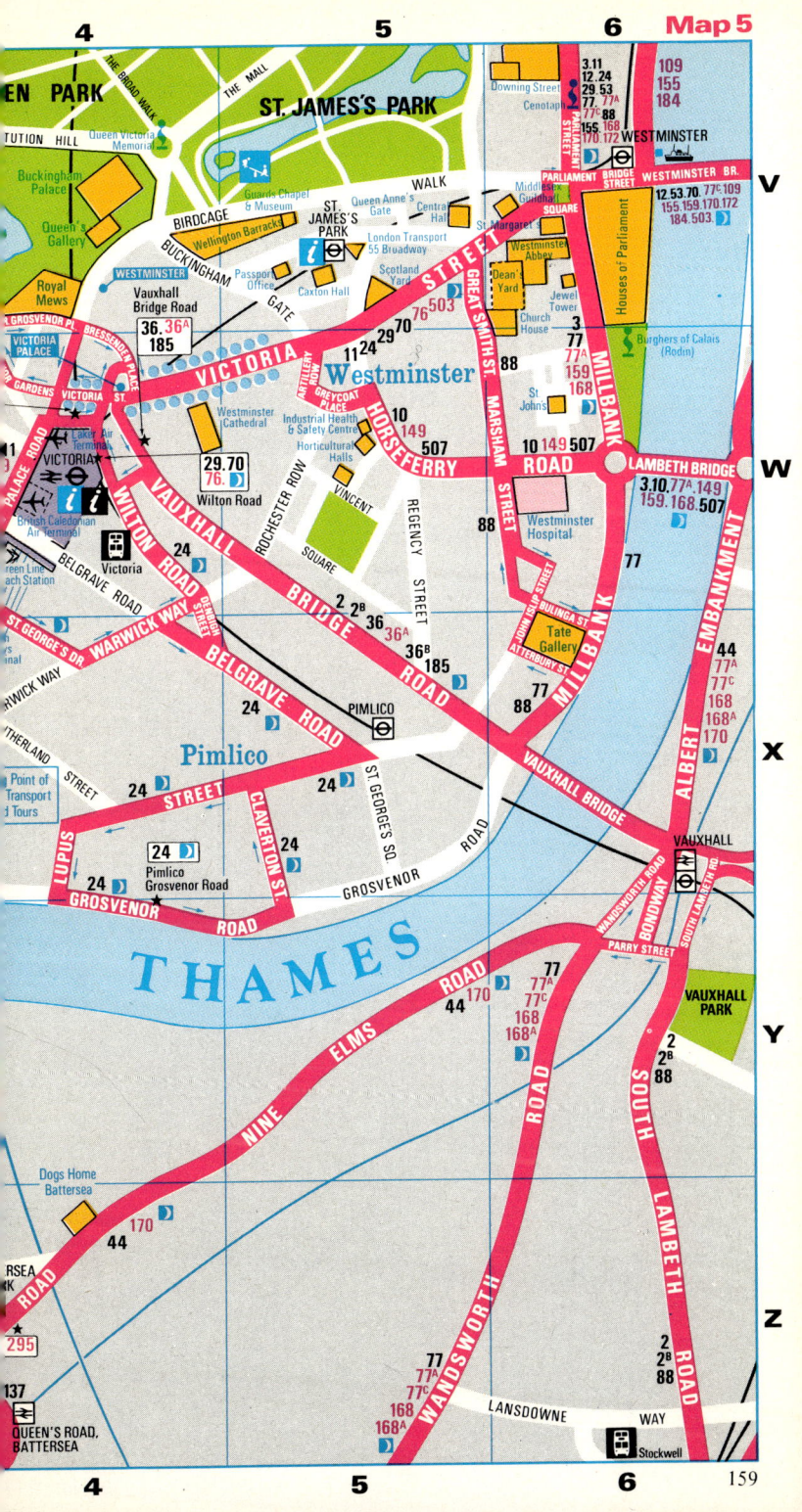

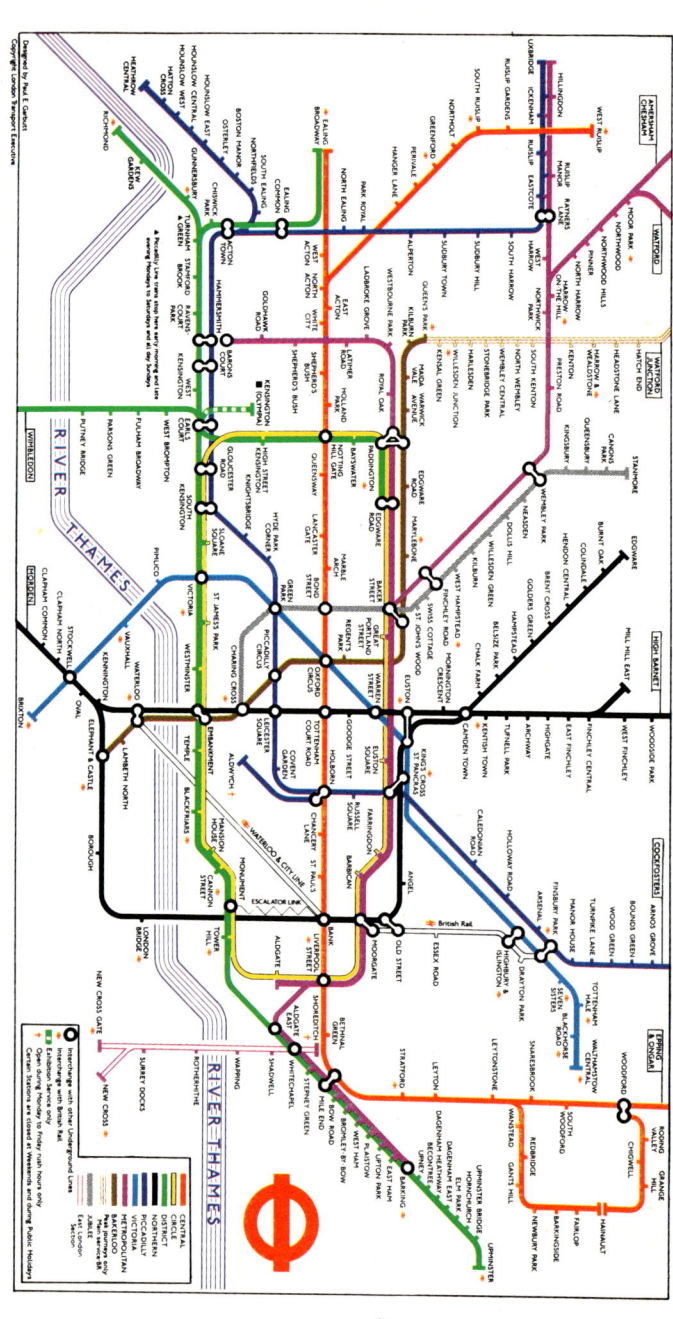

OTHER VENUES

ACADEMIES
COLLEGES
COMMUNITY
MOBILE
LATE-NIGHT
OPEN AIR
CINEMA
MUSIC
IN EXILE

Introductory Note

The following section of *Theatre London* is a selection from the many different kinds of venue in which one can quite often — but by no means regularly — find the performing arts on show.

Thus, each of the several kinds of venue represented in the list opposite can be used for live theatrical performance, though in the case of (say) the musical venues, only rarely will these desert the form for which they were primarily intended. Others — several of the theatres attached to dramatic academies, for example — present regular seasons of plays, at least for parts of each year. When planning a visit, always ensure that there is something playing on the night you have in mind — and that it is indeed 'your kind of show'.

The persevering visitor to London can also check the cultural facilities offered by the various cultural institutes in the capital. Although these are operated mainly as adjuncts to their respectives embassies, one can occasionally find a dramatic jewel on offer, usually in the original language — but inevitably these are limited to only a few evenings a year, or to seasons linked with an anniversary or some other national theme.

Theatres now lost to live performance are not listed here. For example, the Winter Garden Theatre, Drury Lane, was recently replaced by the New London, designed by the late Sean Kenny as Europe's most versatile theatre — only to become a permanent studio for Thames Television. In turn, the purpose-built theatre for Guy's Hospital, the Greenwood, was converted by BBC Television to the same end.

The current planning laws are such that when a place of live entertainment is replaced in the name of progress, provision for a theatre must be made, though the substitute venue is generally a void encased in an office block. A theatre was duly constructed within the concrete mausoleum which replaced the Victorian splendours of the Scala in Charlotte Street — and was duly turned into a cinema.

London between the wars still boasted many fine music halls, and some of the few that survived, having gone through the transitions from cinema to bingo, are now being reappraised as potential theatres. For example, the music hall in Edgware Road which became the Odeon was half-converted back to theatre, and then due to lack of funds returned to cinematic use, in this case as a centre for Indian films. A much older, intimate gem of a music hall — Wilton's in Wellclose Square, Whitechapel — is also currently the focus of various plans for restoration to live performance.

Such are the dead or 'dark' venues *not* listed in this section! But the situation is always changing, and the reader should take the following listings as only a sampling of London's less conventional venues for living theatre.

Index to Other Venues

Alfred Beck Centre   172
Almost Free   189
Barking Drama Centre   173
Blitz   180
Brycbox Arts Workshop   173
Bubble   178
Chanticleer Theatre   164
Charterhouse Ark   173
Comedy Store   181
Corbett Theatre   165
Country Cousin   181
Croft   174
Dominion   184
Drama Centre   165
Elephant Theatre   170
Embassy Theatre   166
Fairfield Hall   186
Fun Art Bus   178
GBS Theatre   168
Golden Lane Theatre   170
Guildhall School   166
Hammersmith Odeon   185
Holland Park   183
Hoxton Hall   174

Kenwood   183
Kilburn Gaumont State   185
LAMDA Theatre   167
Lewisham Odeon   185
Little Theatre, RADA   168
Logan Hall   171
Longhouse   174
Moonshine   175
Mountview Arts Centre   168
Old Bull   175
Open Space   190
Place   167
Polytechnic   171
Poplar Civic   176
Rainbow   186
Rock Garden   182
Royal Albert Hall   187
St John's   187
St Martin's-in-the-Field   187
Sobell   176
Stanley Halls   176
Tube Theatre   179
Vanbrugh Theatre   178

ACADEMIES

Perspective: As the theatre training capital of the world, amongst London's multiplicity of theatrical experiences are its numerous drama school theatres. The following listing including all of London's members of the Conference of Drama Schools, offers a wide selection of venues where young actors undergo the most practical aspect of their professional training: performance before a live and often highly critical audience. Visitors are advised to shed their preconceptions about miserable amateurs — the energy and seriousness of purpose of the pre-professionals to be seen on these stages can on occasions provide more exciting entertainment than that which may be seen in some established, professional theatres.

Chanticleer Theatre

Webber Douglas Academy of Dramatic Art, 30-36 Clareville St, SW7 5AW
Box office: **370 4154** Admin: **370 4154**
Performance Space: Proscenium arch *Seating:* 90

Prices: Free **Perf Times:** 19 30 **Catering:** No **Bars:** 1 (wine & coffee)

The Chanticleer Theatre is the venue for the Webber Douglas Academy, which opened in 1926 for the study of singing and opera. By the early 1950s the academy was firmly established as a school for dramatic training. The Chanticleer has recently been refurbished into a well-equipped theatre, and presents the work of third year finals students. Agents and managements are invited to view these productions and in the not-too-distant past have discovered such talents as Donald Sinden, Penelope Keith and Charlotte Cornwell. The Webber Douglas is noted for its well-deserved reputation for producing versatile musical comedy and television players.

Underground: South Kensington (Circle, District, Piccadilly)
Bus: 14, 30, 45, 49, 74

Corbett Theatre

East 15 Acting School, Rectory Lane, Loughton, Essex
Box office: **508 5983** Admin: **508 5983**
Performance Space: Medieval church tithe barn converted to a fully-equipped theatre *Seating:* 120 (raked)

Bookings: Phone. Postal (addressed to 'Hatfield's', Rectory Lane, Loughton, Essex **Prices:** £1 **Concessions:** Students & OAPs 50p **Perf Times:** 20 00 for school productions **Catering:** Pub-style snacks **Bars:** 1

With the break-up of Joan Littlewood's Theatre Workshop in 1961, Margaret Bury (a member of the company since 1947) set out to establish a school in which Littlewood's work could be implemented and developed. In 1966 the school purchased the medieval tithe barn at Ditchling, Sussex and dismantled and rebuilt it on the premises of East 15 (Theatre Workshop's postal district in Stratford East), thus creating the Corbett Theatre. The conversion to a theatre included the integration of dressing rooms, modern foyer, licensed bar and costume annexe within the barn.

The Corbett Theatre presents the productions of third-year and postgraduate course students, which include musicals, classics, pantomime and modern plays. The theatre also acts as a venue for visiting companies, which in the past have included a variety ranging from marionette theatre for schools to London's experimental fringe group Lumiere and Son.

Underground: Debden (Central)
Bus: 20, 167, 255

Drama Centre, London

176 Prince of Wales Road, NW5
Box office: **267 1177** Admin: **267 1177**
Performance Space: Large hall with open stage *Seating:* 100 (raked)

Bookings: Phone or postal **Prices:** 50p **Catering:** Canteen open from ½ hr before show **Bars:** No **Publicity:** Time Out, Mailing List, leaflets

The Drama Centre was started about 15 years ago in a now-listed building that is approximately 120 years old and until 1940 was a Methodist church. As a theatre venue it presents public performances by final year students at the end of each three terms in their graduating year. The concentration is on classics, and a run is usually four days. During school vacations the space is rented out for rehearsals of visiting companies.

Underground: Chalk Farm (Northern)
Bus: 68 or 31 to Haverstock Hill or 24, 46, to Malden Road

Embassy Theatre

Central School of Speech and Drama, 64 Eton Avenue, NW3 3HY
Box office: **722 8186** Admin: **722 8183**
Performance Space: Fully-equipped proscenium arch theatre and studio
Seating: 310 and 100

Bookings: Phone or post from 1 week before production opens **Prices:** £1 or 80p studio **Concessions:** Students & OAPs 30p **Perf Times:** 19 30 or 16 00 & 20 00 **Catering:** Coffee bar **Bars:** Yes **Publicity:** Mailing list, local press, posters & leaflet distribution

The Central School of Speech and Drama was founded by Elsie Fogerty in 1906 and the Embassy Theatre opened in 1956. The theatre is used for the presentation of student productions which include a wide variety of plays and an end-of-year musical. Productions generally have a run of five performances, and since 1978 Central has also presented small-scale work in its 100-seat studio.

Underground: Swiss Cottage (Jubilee)
Bus: 2, 2B, 13, 31, 113, 187, C11, 707, 717, 732

Guildhall School of Music and Drama

Barbican Arts Centre, EC2Y 8DT
Box office: **628 2571**
Performance Space: Main theatre fully adjustable to proscenium, thrust, traverse and island staging & studio *Seating:* 380 & 120

Bookings: Phone or postal **Prices:** Free **Perf Times:** 19 00 (variable)
Catering: Sandwiches & coffee at bar **Bars:** 1 **Wheelchairs:** Yes **Publicity:** London dailies & Time Out

The Guildhall School of Music and Drama was founded 100 years ago in a disused warehouse. In recent years, however, the school has established itself in the splendid new Barbican Arts Centre, with 2 theatres and a recital room acting as venues for the presentation of Guildhall student productions. With the Royal Shakespeare Company's future London theatre in the same complex, the school has forged links with the RSC, some of whose members give tutorials and direct shows at the school. Besides an opera, there are four plays presented each term by final year students, and though these are aimed mainly at agents, they welcome the public at no charge.

Underground: Barbican (Circle, Metropolitan), Moorgate (Circle, Metropolitan, Northern, British Rail), St Paul's (Central)
Bus: 4, 141, 279A, 502 or 8, 22, 25, 501 to St Paul's Station

London Academy of Music and Dramatic Art

LAMDA Theatre, Logan Place, Earl's Court Road, W8
Box office: **373 7017** Admin: **373 9883/4337**
Performance Space: Flexible theatre allowing for proscenium, in-the-round, open & arena staging *Seating:* 40

Bookings: Phone. Postal (Membership of £1, available on the night + guests) **Prices:** From free up to £1 **Perf Times:** Vary **Catering:** Hot & Cold snacks at bar **Bars:** 1 from 1 hr before show **Publicity:** Time Out, posters, leaflets

The LAMDA Theatre was founded in 1963 to provide an experimental space for the students of the 119-year-old Academy. The three productions per term range in character from the classics to musicals, in order to give students as varied a performance experience as possible. When not in use for student productions, lunchtime concerts and revues, the venue may be used by visiting companies which have included Stephen Berkoff's company, Peter Brook's *Theatre of Cruelty* season and the occasional foreign import.

Underground: Earl's Court (District, Piccadilly)
Bus: 31, 74

The Place

London School of Contemporary Dance, 17 Duke's Road, WC1H 9AB
Box office: **387 0031** Admin: **387 0161**
Performance Space: Converted army drill hall with proscenium arch and stage that may be extended by rostra *Seating:* 255 (raked)

Bookings: Postal. Phone. Membership £2 p.a. or free to Camden Library members, NUS and ICA card holders. **Prices:** Variable **Perf Times:** Variable **Catering:** Restaurant (members only on receipt of tokens purchaseable at box office) **Bars:** 1 **Publicity:** Depends mainly on visiting company

The Place together with London Contemporary Dance Theatre (a top-notch professional dance company) and the London School of Contemporary Dance, are all activities of the Contemporary Dance Trust whose policy is based on the promotion of modern dance. The Place emphasizes presentation of dance and has hosted visits by such major companies as Scottish Theatre Ballet, Toronto Dance Theatre and Ballet Modernes de Paris, as well as smaller experimental groups. This is not to the exclusion of other theatre forms, however, and past seasons have also included visits from the Royal Shakespeare Company, Moving Being, Groupe TSE from Paris and New York's La Mama company. The Place offers some lunchtime concerts and film shows, as well as showers, changing rooms and office facilities for visiting companies.

Underground: Euston (Northern, Victoria, British Rail)
Bus: 14, 18, 30, 68, 73, 77, 77A, 77C, 170, 188, 239

Mountview Arts Centre

Mountview Theatre School, 104 Crouch Hill, N8
Box office: 340 0097 Admin: 340 5885
Performance Space: Mountview Theatre: proscenium stage; Judi Dench Theatre: an 'experimental' theatre-in-the-round *Seating:* 120 & 65

Bookings: Phone. Postal **Prices:** Admission free (donations encouraged towards the school's scholarship fund) **Perf Times:** 19 30 **Bars:** 1 **Publicity:** Handbills, etc

The Mountview Arts Centre's two venues, one a flexible studio, the other a proscenium arch theatre, function mainly for the presentation of student productions. The school, which has offered full-time acting and stage management/technical courses for the past ten years, stages forty productions annually in its two theatres. The public is welcome to attend these performances, and the venues may be rented by visiting groups when they are not in use by the school.

Underground: Finsbury Park (Piccadilly, Victoria, British Rail), or Crouch Hill (British Rail) then bus W2, W7
Bus: 41 to Crouch End Broadway

Vanbrugh, GBS and Little Theatres

Royal Academy of Dramatic Art, 62 Gower Street, WC1E 6ED
Box office: 580 7982 Admin: 636 7076
Performance Space: Vanbrugh: proscenium stage; GBS: flexible staging for in-the-round or in-the-square; Little: Open stage studio for workshops *Seating:* Vanbrugh 342; GBS: 112; GBS: variable

Bookings: Members only (£1.05 p.a.) + 9 guests to Vanbrugh & 1 guest to Little & GBS: Concessionary members may bring 1 guest to each. Postal (to RADA, 62 Gower Street) s.a.e (Phone (held to ½ hr before show) **Prices:** Vanbrugh eve 70p, 50p; mats 30p. GBS 70p. Little 50p **Concessions:** Reduced membership for OAPs, students **Perf Times:** Variable **Catering:** Light snacks **Bars:** 1 in Vanbrugh **Mailing List:** Brochures sent 3 times yearly to all members **Publicity:** Mailing list, local press, posters

The Royal Academy of Dramatic Art was founded in 1904 by Sir Herbert Beerbohm Tree, and enjoys the tradition of being regarded as London's most prestigious drama school. With three separate venues on the premises of the Academy, RADA presents three seasons of plays each year, with four or five main productions per season in addition to a number of smaller-scale works. The venues are used exclusively by students of the Academy, presenting a full spectrum of plays from classical to contemporary. Vanbrugh Theatre productions generate an intensely professional atmosphere and many stars have begun their career treading its boards, among them Laurence Olivier, Glenda Jackson, Alan Bates, and Flora Robson. The entrance to the Vanbrugh is in Malet Street, while the Little and GBS Studios are in the RADA building in Gower Street.

Underground: Euston Square (Circle, Metropolitan), Goodge Street (Northern)
Bus: 14, 24, 29, 73, 176

COLLEGES

Perspective: Most colleges have space for live performances. Some are fortunate in having well-designed, purpose-built theatres with excellent equipment of a standard well above the average; others have empty spaces adaptable with a bit of hard work and enthusiasm into quite adequate performance areas. Normally these spaces have been intended for productions by students, and for the whole range of student activities from union meetings, lectures, live music performances and social functions. A few colleges, however, have embarked on a policy of attracting outside performers to use their facilities, both as a means of utilizing the space available more fully, and in a deliberate attempt to introduce theatre in its widest sense to a student audience.

Where the venue does not have a public licence, the custom is to open shows to members of the student body and their guests (see, for example, The Elephant lunchtime theatre, below). In other cases, where the policy is largely to hire the facility to outside organizations, as in the case of the University of London's Logan Hall, public licences are obtained for each performance and there are no membership rules for ticket purchases.

The four venues described in this section form a small sample of college-based theatres. Student theatre productions can be extremely good, and are usually very cheap. Even where outside professional companies are brought in, prices are kept low to cater for the mainly student audiences. Keep an eye open for advertisements in the London weeklies and don't be put off by the thought of finding your way through the labyrinthine corridors of large educational institutions. The theatres are usually well-marked, and you will generally find plenty of willing guides along the way.

Elephant Theatre

Students Union Building, South Bank Polytechnic, Thomas Doyle Street, SE1
Box Office: **261 1525** (10 00-17 00) Admin: **261 1525**
Performance Space: Specially adapted room, flexible staging *Seating:* 60-120

Bookings: NUS members and guests. Postal (cheques to South Bank Polytechnic Students Union) s.a.e Phone (held to 5 mins. before show) In person. No credit cards **Prices:** NUS members 50p, guests 75p **Concessions:** No
Perf Times: Lunchtimes Monday-Friday 12 45 term-time only. Irregular evening shows **Catering:** Hot & cold food 12 00-14 00 **Bars:** Students Union bar for NUS members only + guests **Wheelchairs:** 6 **Cloakrooms:** No **Parking:** NCP, Elephant & Castle, side streets.

Policy: The lunchtime theatre is run voluntarily by an actor, with assistance from the students union. Where possible the theatre acts as a producing company, using Equity actors, and aims to build up a regular student audience with good one- or two-act plays by new playwrights. Each plays lasts for two weeks, with a total of eighteen produced over the three terms. The space is also let to outside companies for the cost of overheads only, and has been used by well-known touring fringe theatre groups.

Underground: Elephant & Castle (Bakerloo, Northern, British Rail)
Bus: 1, 10, 12, 35, 40, 44, 45, 53, 63, 68, 95, 109, 133, 141, 155, 171, 176, 176A, 177, 184, 188, 705, 706, 729

Golden Lane Theatre

Golden Lane, EC1Y 0RR
Box office: **638 0640** (Variable with show) Admin: **638 0640**
Performance Space: Proscenium arch *Seating:* 410

Bookings: Postal (cheques to Golden Lane Theatre) s.a.e Phone (held 7 days) In person. No credit cards **Prices:** 50p & variable depending on show
Concessions: Students, OAPs 25p **Perf Times:** Eves. Monday-Sunday 19 30 depending on show **Catering:** Buffet for cold snacks **Bars:** 1 **Wheelchairs:** 3 **Cloakrooms:** No **Parking:** Streets.

Policy: The theatre is administered by Arts Educational Schools, whose aim is to present some dozen performances annually by adult drama or ballet students. Between these performances the theatre is hired to amateur societies, normally for short lettings on Thursdays to Saturdays. Longer amateur productions may be staged during school holidays when the theatre is not used so intensively for student productions.

Underground: Barbican (Circle, Metropolitan), Moorgate (Circle, Metropolitan, Northern)
Bus: 5, 55, 243 or 4, 279A to Beech Street or 141, 502 to London Wall

Logan Hall

University of London, Logan Hall, 20 Bedford Way, WC1H 0AL
Box office: **636 1600 x 256** (Enquiries only 09 30-17 00) Admin: **636 1500 x 256**
Performance Space: No proscenium, thrust stage *Seating:* 934 (raked)

Bookings: Hirers make own booking arrangements **Prices:** £1.50-£3.50 depending on show **Concessions:** Variable **Perf Times:** Variable **Catering:** Facilities for cold food if the hirer makes individual arrangements with an outside caterer **Bars:** Up to hirer to make special arrangements **Wheelchairs:** 9 **Cloakrooms:** 1 (Attendant) **Parking:** NCPs, Brunswick Square, Bernard Street, streets

Policy: This large purpose-built hall is used by a wide variety of organizations for public performances, which include jazz, classical music, cultural shows, lectures, conferences, folk dancing and opera. It is also used by student drama societies for their public performances, usually one per term. The Logan Hall is the largest of a complex of halls available for hire to outside organizations and is becoming increasingly widely used by ethnic minority groups for cultural presentations.

Underground: Russell Square (Piccadilly)
Bus: 68, 77, 77A, 77C, 170, 188, 239

Polytechnic of North London

Holloway Road, Islington, N7 8DS
Box office: **607 2789 x 2300** (09 00-17 00) Admin: **607 2789 x 2300**
Performance Space: Large proscenium arch *Seating:* 320

Bookings: Postal (cheques to Polytechnic of North London) s.a.e Phone (held to ¼ hr before show) In person. No credit cards **Prices:** 60p-£1.60 depending on show **Concessions:** NUS members, OAPs daily except Saturdays **Perf Times:** 19 30 Wednesday-Saturday except summer vacation **Catering:** Tea & coffee during interval **Bars:** 1 **Wheelchairs:** 11 **Cloakrooms:** No **Parking:** Streets after 18 30

Policy: The administrator of this purpose-built theatre aims to promote theatre in north London and works closely with the Islington Entertainments Committee, which sponsors fringe touring theatre companies and other events at the venue. The theatre is also used by four student groups based at the Polytechnic — the Shakespeare Players, an operatic group, a repertory theatre group and a Modern Symphony Orchestra.

Underground: Holloway Road (Piccadilly)
Bus: 43, 104, 172, 271, 279, 279A

COMMUNITY

Perspective: In many areas of Greater London the only venues available for public performance are run by the local authority or heavily sponsored by it. The venue may be a purpose-built concert hall or theatre; it may be a civic hall doubling as a dance hall and performance space; it may be a sports centre, or a community centre with a lively programme of events and clubs for all sections of the local community; it may be a centre run by the local education authority and specializing in youth work and educational drama; or it may be a community arts association receiving financial help from the local authority.

What all these venues have in common is the aim of bringing live entertainment to areas which may otherwise be poorly served with amenities. Most venues sponsored by local authorities try to cater for as wide an audience as possible, with a very mixed programme of events ranging from music hall, dance, children's theatre, musical performances and drama. A great deal of interesting work goes on, particularly by touring fringe theatre companies, but it may be difficult to find out what is happening where and when as many of the venues rely on internal advertising and on the local press for publicity, or are for members only. So if from the sample of centres given below there are some whose policy sounds interesting, phone for details. Few will have box offices in the normal sense and some are unable to take advance bookings, but all have expressed their willingness to supply information. In many cases, tickets for shows will be available on the door only. The following list is not exhaustive. It is given alphabetically and no attempt has been made to categorize the venues: simply, in some way or another all are supported by their local authorities.

Alfred Beck Centre

Grange Road, Hayes, Middlesex UB3 2RD
Box office: **561 8371** (10 30-20 00 Monday-Saturday) Admin: **561 7506/7**
Performance Space: Proscenium arch, originally concert hall *Seating:* 598

Bookings: Postal (cheques to Alfred Beck Centre) s.a.e. Phone (held 3 days) In person. No credit cards **Prices:** Variable £1-£5 **Concessions:** OAPs, children, groups **Perf Times:** 19 30 Monday-Saturday, 17 00 Saturday mats when available
Catering: Green Room Restaurant Tuesday-Saturday from 18 00, confectionery kiosk
Bars: 1 open for shows only **Wheelchairs:** 10 **Cloakrooms:** Yes **Parking:** For 300 at rear **Other:** Surrounded by pleasant gardens, bandstand used summers

Policy: A mixed programme of entertainments aimed at the local population, including orchestral evenings, musicals, operatic shows, light drama, variety and films. While a proportion of performances are by amateur groups, a larger number are professional shows in line with the management's policy of giving people first-class entertainment on their own doorstep.

British Rail: Hayes & Harlington then bus 90B, 98, 145
Bus: 207, 790

Barking Drama Centre

Old Bentry School, Heathway, Dagenham, Essex
Box office: **593 7886** (10 00-20 00 3 weeks prior to show) Admin: **593 7886**
Performance Space: 2 large studios *Seating:* 200 (rostra & flat)

Bookings: Members only (by programme at door) Phone (held to ½ hr before show) In person **Prices:** Variable **Perf Times:** 1 show approx. every 6 weeks **Catering:** Coffee, soft drinks **Wheelchairs:** Yes **Cloakrooms:** No **Parking:** Ample, streets **Other:** Shows advertised through education media & internally only

Policy: The Centre is used during the day by theatre-in-education companies performing for school audiences, and in the evenings by youth and adult groups. Occasional performances by touring fringe theatre groups and ballet companies.

Underground: Dagenham Heathway (District)
Bus: 139, 173, 174, 175 or 23, 87 to Heathway or 148 to Dagenham Heathway Station

Brycbox Arts Workshop

Cocks Crescent, New Malden, Surrey KT3 4TA
Box office: **949 4258** (09 00-22 00 Monday-Friday, 09 00-13 00 Saturday) Admin: **949 4258** *Performance Space:* 2 flexible studios *Seating:* 84 (raked)

Bookings: Members only (20p, available at door) Phone, enquiries only. In person at door from 19 30 **Prices:** 80p **Concessions:** None **Perf Times:** Friday eves (not always open to public) **Catering:** Snacks from 19 30 perf. days only **Bars:** No **Wheelchairs:** Yes **Cloakrooms:** No **Parking:** Ample, streets

Policy: Multi-purpose building with day-time services for schools, evening youth projects. A mixed-performance policy catering for the community as a whole, and ranging from local groups to top fringe touring companies.

British Rail: New Malden
Bus: 72, 131, 152, 189, 213A, 285, 725, 726

Charterhouse Ark

39 Crosby Row, off Long Lane, SE1
Box office: **407 5666** (10 00-14 30 prior to perfs only) Admin: **407 1123**
Performance Space: Large hall, staging *Seating:* 200

Bookings: Phone (held to ½ hr before show) In person. No credit cards or travellers cheques **Prices:** 50p **Concessions:** OAPs **Perf Times:** Approx. 1 show every 2 months, Friday 19 30 **Catering:** Snacks & cold drinks **Bars:** No **Wheelchairs:** Yes **Cloakrooms:** No **Parking:** NCP, Kipling Street

Policy: To bring theatre to those who would nor normally see it, including women's theatre groups, touring fringe companies, Young Vic pantomime.

Underground: Borough (Northern)
Bus: 10, 21, 35, 40, 95, 133, 176A

Croft Theatre

Tolworth Recreation Centre, Fullers Way, North Tolworth, Surbiton, Surrey
Box office: **391 1882** (09 00-22 00) Admin: **391 0684** (& enquiries)
Performance Space: Studio theatre, flexible performance area *Seating:* 250

Bookings: Phone (held to ½ hr before show) In person **Prices:** £1.50-£4 **Concessions:** Recreation Centre members 50p, students, children & OAPs half price **Perf Times:** One-night stands only, irregular intervals **Catering:** Light meals, snacks, coffee from 18 30 **Bars:** 1, normal licensing hours **Wheelchairs:** Yes, special facilities **Cloakrooms:** No **Parking:** On site & surrounding streets

Policy: To promote a balanced and varied programme catering for all interests in the local community. Shows have included folk music, fringe theatre groups, dance companies, mime, puppetry, cabaret, jazz and classical music.

British Rail: Tolworth then bus 72, 189
Bus: 152, 710

Hoxton Hall

128a Hoxton Street, N1 6SH
Box Office: **739 5431** (10 00-20 00) Admin: **739 5431**
Performance Space: Old music hall, thrust stage, galleries *Seating:* 140

Bookings: Postal (s.a.e.) Phone (held ¼ hr before show) In person **Prices:** £1 **Concessions:** Students 50p, children 30p, OAPs 20p **Perf Times:** Friday & Saturday eves **Catering:** Coffee bar **Bars:** No **Wheelchairs:** No **Other:** A neighbourhood community centre

Policy: A community arts group with its own permanent theatre-in-education team. As a venue the centre aims to provide regular and varied entertainment for the local community with emphasis on music hall and shows by touring fringe theatre companies.

Underground: Old Street (Northern, British Rail)
Bus: 5, 22, 22A, 48, 55, 67, 149, 243, 243A

The Longhouse

Charlecote Road, Dagenham, Essex RM8 3LD
Box office: **592 1803** (10 00-20 00) Admin: **592 1803**
Performance Space: Large hall, stage blocks *Seating:* 150 (rostra)

Bookings: Members only (guest membership incl. in ticket price) Postal (cheques to The Longhouse) s.a.e. Phone (held to ½ hr before show) In person **Prices:** 50p **Concessions:** No **Perf Times:** Variable **Catering:** Canteen for coffee, tea, cold snacks **Bars:** 1, 20 00-22 30 weekdays **Wheelchairs:** Yes **Cloakrooms:** No **Parking:** Streets **Other:** No outside advertising

Policy: A youth and community centre with an arts policy. A varied programme mainly geared to young people and women, including mime, musical events, touring fringe theatre and women's theatre groups.

Underground: Becontree (District) then bus 62
Bus: 23, 87 or 145, 148 to Wood Lane

Moonshine Community Arts Workshop

Victor Road, NW10 5XQ
Box office: **969 7959** (10 00-20 00 enquiries only) Admin: **969 7959**
Performance Space: Converted church hall, small stage *Seating:* 200

Bookings: Members only (+ guests) £1 p.a. or 25p temporary at door. Advance booking, groups only. Phone (held to ¼ hr before show) In person **Prices:** 60p
Concessions: OAPs, students, children 40p **Perf Times:** Approx. 13 00
Catering: Coffee bar, hot & cold drinks, confectionery **Bars:** No
Wheelchairs: Yes **Cloakrooms:** No **Parking:** Ample, streets

Policy: A community arts centre aiming to involve the local people in arts activities. As a venue for visiting fringe companies and local resident community entertainment groups, the policy is to reflect the multi-racial character of the area through culturally diverse shows.

Underground: Kensal Green (Bakerloo, British Rail)
Bus: 18, 18A, 220

Old Bull Gallery

68 High Street, Barnet, Herts
Box office: **449 0048** (10 00-18 00) Admin: **449 0048**
Performance Space: Small upstairs room, staging *Seating:* 50 (on the flat)

Bookings: Phone (held to ½ hr before show) In person **Prices:** £1
Concessions: Students, OAPs 80p **Perf Times:** Friday or Saturday every 2 weeks 19 30, nightly during 4 week summer festival **Catering:** Coffee & tea **Bars:** No
Wheelchairs: No **Cloakrooms:** No **Parking:** Side streets

Policy: Sponsored by the Barnet Centre Association, the Old Bull aims to encourage new theatre groups and new plays by new playwrights. It also provides a venue for established fringe groups whose productions are not too ambitious for the space.

Underground: High Barnet (Northern)
Bus: 26, 34, 84, 107, 134, 261, 263, 707, 732

Poplar Civic Theatre

Fairfield Road/Bow Road, E3 2SE
Box office: **980 4414** (09 00-17 00, enquiries only) Admin: **980 4414**
Performance Space: Hall, large stage *Seating:* 1,200 (convertible to dance floor)

Bookings: Arrangements vary according to hall hirer **Prices:** Variable **Concessions:** Variable **Perf Times:** Irregular **Catering:** Some shows only **Bars:** 1 (if promoter secures licence) **Wheelchairs:** 12 **Cloakrooms:** No **Parking:** Streets

Policy: The theatre is administered by the London Borough of Tower Hamlets and, in addition to use for the Council's own events, is available for hire by anyone wanting to use its facilities for live shows, dances or films.

Underground: Bow Road (District)
Bus: 10, 25, S2 or 86 to Bow Seven Stars

Sobell Sports Centre

Hornsey Road, Islington N7 7NY
Box office: **607 1632** (08 45-22 00) Admin: **607 1632**
Performance Space: Several small halls, portable staging *Seating:* 100 (variable)

Bookings: In person only **Prices:** 5p-£1.50 **Concessions:** Children **Perf Times:** Approx. 13 00 Friday or Sunday **Catering:** Hot & cold pub snacks, canteen to 18 30 **Bars:** 1 **Wheelchairs:** Yes **Cloakrooms:** No **Parking:** Large car park

Policy: Primarily a sports centre, but aiming to attract a wider community through an expanding theatre programme of shows by touring fringe companies and groups specializing in theatre for the under-fives.

Underground: Finsbury Park (Piccadilly, Victoria, British Rail) then bus 4, 19, 29, 221, 253, 279, 279A, 735
Bus: 14, 168A or 43, 104, 172, 271, 279, 279A to Camden Road

The Stanley Halls

South Norwood Hill, SE25 6AB
Box office: **653 3640** (10 00-17 00, information only) Admin: **653 3630**
Performance Space: Proscenium arch, large auditorium *Seating:* 400 (flexible)

Bookings: Not through box office (promoters make their own arrangements) **Prices:** Variable **Concessions:** Variable **Perf Times:** Wednesday-Saturday eves and Saturday mats, approx. 60 per cent of year **Catering:** Refreshment area can be used by promoter to make own arrangements **Bars:** 1 **Wheelchairs:** 5 **Cloakrooms:** No **Parking:** 3 car parks in vicinity

Policy: The Stanley Halls are owned by Croydon Council, and are for public hire. A wide range of shows are put on, including amateur dramatics and opera, old time music hall, drama festivals and musicals.

British Rail: Norwood Junction
Bus: 12, 12A, 68, 75, 154, 157, 196, 197

MOBILE

Perspective: An exciting part of London's varied theatre life is its 'drama on the move'. Over two-thirds of Britain's touring groups, the backbone of the fringe, is based in the capital. Abrakadabra-Fools Theatre Company, Aesop Emporium and East End Abbreviated Soap Box Company can be seen along with Itinerant Theatre Ltd, Kaboodle, Jail Warehouse and Stirabout, as well as the more nationally established companies such as Monstrous Regiment, 7:84 (England), Belt and Braces and Pip Simmons. Their productions are designed to take place anywhere, and you will be surprised just where they do end up. About 100 such groups can be found in London, travelling from trade union halls to pensioners' clubs, from pub rooms to community centres. But among this number is a special group of mobile *venues* — theatres that move from site to site, whether it is a common or a playground, a car park or in one case, a tube station.

While many take to the streets to perform, these 'groups — such as Bubble, Fun Art Bus and Tube Theatre — take their theatre with them. Details can usually be found in *Time Out* of exactly where they will be in any week, when they will be there, and what sort of show they will be offering.

Bubble
9 Kingsford Street, NW5
Admin: **485 3420**
Performance Space: An inflatable tent
Seating: Variable, according to venue, but usually about 200

Policy: To take the Bubble tent around London, particularly the outer boroughs, and to provide theatre for those who normally do not see live shows.

Perspective: Bubble was founded in 1971 by the Greater London Arts Association as a permanent touring company using its own portable performance space. The company is backed by individual London boroughs, which are responsible for providing additional facilities, advertising, and fixing seat prices. The cast rehearses at the Kingsford Road address, usually from March to May, and performs on tour from June to September. Its repertoire mixes popular entertainment, from the classical (*A Midsummer Night's Dream* or *The Beggar's Opera*) to cabaret and children's shows (eg *Gary Doggerty and the Devil's Circus* or *The Minstrel, the Witch and the Wicked Duke*). Workshops on specific issues and street performances are also included in the Bubble programme. The company has worked with mentally handicapped children, and encourages visits 'back tent' as well as giving talks to clubs.

Fun Art Bus

15 Wilkin Street, NW5
Admin: **485 0881**
Performance Space: Converted London double-decker bus

Policy: To involve people in non-theatre environments, for the enjoyment and development of their creativity. It links up with other Inter-Action projects aimed at all sections of the community from the very young to the very old.

Perspective: Fun Art Bus is part of Ed Berman's Inter-Action empire, founded in 1968 to improve life in London's urban communities. It soon became the model for community projects, spreading its net from advisory work and a permanent base for experimental theatre (Ambiance Lunch-Hour Theatre club at the Almost Free) to playgroups and a city farm, complete with barnyard, riding school and animals. The Fun Bus, a converted London double-decker, houses a cinema, human puppet shows, a theatre and other entertainments. It also carries on its travels Prof Dogg's Troup, Inter-Action's street and children's ensemble. They have a reputation for game playing and spontaneous creation in all kinds of situations as long as it is outside a theatre — for example, christening the National Theatres terraces with Tom Stoppard's *Fifteen-Minute Hamlet*. The Fun Art Bus was started in 1972 with shows such as *The Yellow Submarine Disaster* and *The Big Banana Show*, combining intimate theatre inside the bus with larger-scale work outside.

Tube Theatre

39 Tanza Road, NW3 2UA
Admin: **794 7296**
Performance Space: Any tube train, usually Piccadilly Line
Price: Return tube fare plus £1

Policy: To make tube travel more entertaining without shocking by using the unexpected and the bizarre.

Perspective: Tube Theatre was started in 1972 by actor Ken Ellis, who is a stand-up comic, ventriloquist, and children's entertainer, specializing in Punch and Judy and magic. He had an audience but no venue. With 'stooges' and hand props only, he entertains in one tube carriage preferably on a line that carries theatre audiences and tourists, which usually means the Piccadilly. The reperotire has doubled since Ellis began, some shows developing from improvisations, some from scripts. He mixes new shows with 'classics' such as *The Cut Tie* and *The Seated Strap-Hanger*. Performances are irregular — consult *Time Out*, buy your underground return ticket, plus £1, be a normal passenger and watch the reactions of others as they confront the mishaps of the odd commuter. It is still a very cheap show, and can last you an hour and a half. There are even platform performances during train changes.

LATE NIGHT

Perspective: Contrary to popular belief, all of London does not close down at 23 00 every night, and for those who wish to extend their evening's entertainment beyond pub closing time, there are a number of possibilities available. Many of these also offer the opportunity to eat, drink — and in some cases, talk — during the show. Some music, comedy and cabaret venues have built up a strong following, and, hardly needing to advertise, they are not so easy to learn about for the newcomer. Here are a few suggestions for where to go when your show's curtain has come down, and you're still raring to go.

Blitz

4 Great Queen Street, Holborn, WC2
Box office: **405 6598** Admin: **405 6598**
Performance Space: Spacious ground floor restaurant *Seating:* 100

Bookings: Phone (with booked table there's no cover charge) No credit cards
Prices: £2 cover charge for live shows. Reasonable meal prices (burgers, etc.)
Catering: Full meals with service to 01 00 **Bars:** Cocktails, beer, etc. to 03 00
Publicity: Time Out & Ritz **Parking:** Ample in street **Perf Times:** Show begins 23 00 or 23 30 **Concessions:** £25 p.a. membership gives entry with no cover charge + guests. Monday & Wednesday, parties over 20, no cover

Blitz is an informal, comfortable bar and restaurant with '40s decor, offering late-night live entertainment or discos nightly (including Sunday). As a live-entertainment venue Blitz has a reputation for booking visually-oriented shows ranging from comedy acts to dancers, etc. Many young performers use Blitz as a showcase and the venue prides itself on attracting a wide cross-section of people to its relaxed and accessible setting. Many Australian and American acts have been put on, and the management are happy to use good work from anywhere in the world, but their policy emphasizes the unconventional. Note that you may go to Blitz without dining, but Thursday, Friday and Saturday often sell out so it's best to book in advance or arrive before 22 00.

 Underground: Holborn (Central, Piccadilly)
Bus: 8, 19, 22, 25, 38, 55, 68, 77, 77A, 77C, 170, 172, 188, 239, 501

The Comedy Store

69 Dean Street, W1
Box office: **437 3278** Admin: **437 6455**
Performance Space: Club set-up with end stage *Seating:* 120, and some standing

Bookings: None. Advisable to arrive by 22 30, after which time a long queue forms and people are often turned away **Prices:** £4 **Concessions:** No
Perf Times: Saturday only 23 00-03 00 **Catering:** No **Bars:** 1 (waitress service with average prices 80p for a pint of beer, £1.20-£1.80 for cocktails, £4.50 for a bottle of wine) **Publicity:** Time Out listings

The Comedy Store lives in the Nell Gwynn Club, which serves as a Soho strip-club during the week. Based on the Los Angeles model of the same name, it is unique in London for providing aspiring comedians, young and old, with an opportunity to try out their jokes on an often unusually challenging public. It is policy to encourage audience participation, which takes the form of some very funny heckling, and brave audience members may spontaneously stand up and try their own act. There is also a gong, manned by compere Alexei Sayle, and if the comedian is not entertaining the audience recommends that he or she be thrown off the stage with shouts of 'Gong!', at which point Sayle sounds the knell, and the player is obliged to go. (In some cases, this happens after only a few seconds!) The atmosphere is intense — not for the softhearted — but this may be the only venue in London where you or anyone else may perform.

Underground: Tottenham Court Road (Central, Northern)
Bus: 1, 7, 8, 14, 19, 22, 24, 25, 29, 38, 73, 134, 176

Country Cousin

533 King's Road, SW10
Box office: **352 7161** Admin: **352 7161**
Performance Space: Supper club *Seating:* 127 (plans to extend to 300 by autumn 1980)

Bookings: Phone (entry *by reservation only*) **Prices:** £8.50 inclusive 3 course meal (service charge not included) and cabaret **Concessions:** No **Perf Times:** 23 00 & Sunday lunchtime **Catering:** Dinners served from 21 30, you may eat after the show **Bars:** Cocktail bar and waiter-service, but only with meals **Publicity:** Evening papers, Time Out, What's On

Country Cousin offers cabaret acts presented in five-night slots, with a drag show for Sunday lunchtimes. This Chelsea venue attracts both a gay and straight clientele and has plans to extend the premises in the summer of 1980. At time of going to press, Royal Shakespeare Company actresses Ruby Wax and Darlene Johnson were presenting their original *Johnson Wax Floor Show*.

Underground: Fulham Broadway (District)
Bus: 11, 22, 718 or 14 to Stamford Bridge

Rock Garden

6 The Piazza, Covent Garden, WC2
Box office: **240 3961** Admin: **240 3961**
Performance Space: Basement room of restaurant *Seating:* 50-60 (concentration on standing and dancing, up to 200)

Bookings: By phone, for restaurant only. Cheques accepted with cheque cards, no credit cards **Prices:** £1.50-£2.25 depending on the band, but with no entry charge if you're eating in the restaurant Monday-Thursday **Concessions:** ½-price Friday-Saturday if you eat in the restaurant, negotiable party bookings, and free entry to foreign press, musicians & record companies by advance arrangement
Perf Times: Monday-Saturday 20 45-03 00, Sunday 19 30-24 00 **Catering:** Rock Garden restaurant upstairs open 20 30-24 00 (last orders). Hot food downstairs to 01 00. No restaurant Sunday **Bars:** Yes, including cocktails, until 03 00
Publicity: Time Out, New Musical Express and London Evening papers

One of only two cellar rock clubs in London, the Rock Garden showcases many high calibre up-and-coming bands, and the management's progressive policy allows for booking of any band that sends them a good tape, regardless of 'name'. They obviously have a good ear, for among bands that started here before they became widely recognized are Dire Straits, Tom Robinson, The Police, and Gary Newman. Also, the Talking Heads had their first British booking here. As a result, the venue is much frequented by talent scouts and serious music listeners. (The majority of the bands here have already recorded and use the Rock Garden to help them to get the important exposure of playing a central London club.) Generally there is a different band playing every night, though there are 'regulars' who play twice a month, and music ranges from blues revival, two-tone selector specials, beat and 'good-time music'. Formerly a Covent Garden fruit warehouse, the Rock Garden attracts a 25-30 years crowd, and there is no admittance for under-18s.

Underground: Covent Garden (Piccadilly), Leicester Square (Northern, Piccadilly)
Bus: 1, 24, 29, 176 to Leicester Square Station or 6, 9, 11, 13, 15, 77, 77A, 77C, 168, 170, 172 to Strand

OPEN AIR

During the summer months a number of London's parks become open-air venues for concerts and operatic events. Children's shows, including mime, drama, clown and puppetry, run throughout August in some twenty-four central and Greater London parks. A small number of other venues of historical or architectural importance are also opened in spring and summer for concert performances. All these events are organized by the Parks Department of the Greater London Council which will be happy to provide information on request to: Booking Office (Room 89), GLC Parks Department, The County Hall, London SE1 7PB (01-633 1707), open 09 00-17 00 on Monday to Friday, and 09 00-12 00 on Saturdays during June and July only.

Bookings can be made in advance for most concerts and operas from the Parks Department either in person, by telephone (held 72 hours), or by post, enclosing a stamped addressed envelope. Cheques should be made out to Greater London Council. Bookings are not required for the free children's events.

As the weather is so unpredictable, the normal policy for the GLC's open-air venues is that decisions will be made just prior to the advertised starting times. No refunds will be made if a concert is started but is later abandoned. For visitors wishing to hear good music in pleasant surroundings, it is well worth while looking out for the Parks Department's publicity or contacting them direct.

Holland Park Court Theatre

Main entrance: Kensington High Street, opp. Kensington Odeon, W8
Tuesday-Sunday evenings (19 30) and Saturday matinees (14 30), mid-June to end-July for a mixed programme of orchestral music and Gilbert and Sullivan opera.

Prices: All seats unreserved. Concerts £1.75. Gilbert & Sullivan opera £2, children 50p. Catering: Wine bar and nearby park cafe for snacks, tea & coffee

Underground: High Street Kensington (Circle, District)
Bus: 9, 27, 28, 31, 33, 49, 73, 701, 704, 714, AV300, 311, 320, 322

Kenwood Lakeside

Hampstead Lane, Highgate, N6
Performance Space: Lakeside Concert Bowl *Seating:* 9,000 (deckchairs & on grass, on the other side of the lake)

Prices: Reserved & numbered deckchairs £2, unreserved deckchairs on the night £1.50, grass £1. Catering: Refreshments tent for bar, cold buffet and snacks. Coach House, Kenwood House, for snacks, tea & coffee.

Underground: Golders Green (Northern) or Archway (Northern) then Bus 210
Bus: 734

CINEMA

Perspective: Popular music fans will know that cinemas have become increasingly important as venues for live music concerts. Few other venues are large enough, or sufficiently well-equipped technically, to provide performance space for the well-known giants of the popular music business. Some cinema venues, like the Hammersmith Odeon, are becoming 'musts' for tours by groups such as Wings and The Who. Others, like the Dominion in Tottenham Court Road and Kilburn's Gaumont State, intersperse films with a wide range of live performances, from opera and ballet to folk and rock. In most cases where this policy of mixed cinema/live entertainment is pursued, the managements' intention is simple — to show films if they are likely to be block-busters, otherwise to respond to the demands of the live entertainment industry and to fit shows in as and when they can.

For those interested in the history of cinema and in its architecture, it is worth noting the style of many of London's picture houses, particularly those of the great era of cinema design, the 1930s, and seeing how readily they adapt themselves to present-day live performance. Many of the earlier ones — with their elaborate facades, neo-classical decor and red plush interiors — showed their debt to the music halls in which films were first shown. They even had orchestra pits, stages, and dressing rooms for the artists who preceded the film shows. In the 1930s, the introduction of sound brought about technical innovations and the development of three basic types of cinema design — the single-floored, flat or slightly-raked type of small cinema, the stadium type with a raised rear tier, and the 'super' cinema with a single balcony and a seating capacity of between 1,500 and 2,000. It is this last type which is so well-suited to today's popular music performances.

The purpose of this section is to remind readers of cinemas as venues, not to provide an exhaustive list of those cinemas which regularly or at intervals put on live shows. The following examples might be considered the main venues for live performances: film, however, is still paramount and there may be long gaps between live shows. Look out for publicity in all the major music papers, on hoardings and in the London and national press.

Dominion

Tottenham Court Road, WC1
Box office: **580 9562** (10 00-20 00)
Performance Space: Proscenium arch *Seating:* 1,995

Bookings: Personal or postal only **Prices:** £3-£10 **Catering:** Licensed bars and confectionery kiosks.

A varied mixture of films and live shows, ranging from leading ballet and opera companies to heavy rock groups.

Underground: Tottenham Court Road (Central, Northern)
Bus: 1, 7, 8, 14, 19, 22, 24, 25, 29, 38, 73, 134, 176

Hammersmith Odeon

Queen Caroline Street, Hammersmith, W6 9QH
Box office: **748 4081** (11 00-20 00 Monday-Saturday)
Performance Space: Large stage with extension *Seating:* 3,483 (on the flat)

Bookings: Postal and in person. **Prices:** £2.50-£5.50 **Catering:** Licensed bars, hot & cold snacks, confectionery

The Odeon is a key British music venue for rock concerts, jazz, country and western, and New Wave by top international artists. Some sporting events.

Underground: Hammersmith (District, Metropolitan, Piccadilly)
Bus: 9, 11, 27, 33, 72, 73, 91, 220, 260, 266, 267, 290, 701, 704, 710, 714, 715, AV300, 311, 320, 322

Kilburn Gaumont State

High Road, Kilburn, NW6
Box office: **624 8081** (10 00-20 00)
Performance Space: Proscenium arch, very large stage *Seating:* 1,810

Bookings: Personal or postal only **Prices:** Variable **Catering:** Licensed bar and confectionery kiosk

A building of special interest to enthusiasts of cinema architecture, serving as a venue for a mixed programme of rock concerts, opera, and individual performers.

Underground: Kilburn (Jubilee), Kilburn Park (Bakerloo), Brondesbury (British Rail), Kilburn High Road (British Rail)
Bus: 8, 16, 16A, 32, 176, 616, 708, 719 or 28, 31 to Kilburn High Road

Lewisham Odeon

Loampit Vale, Lewisham, SE13
Box office: **852 1331** (10 00-20 00)
Performance Space: Proscenium arch *Seating:* 2,850

Bookings: Personal or postal only **Prices:** Variable **Catering:** Confectionery only

Intersperses films with occasional live performances by rock bands or singers with wide appeal. Pantomimes at Christmas.

British Rail: Lewisham
Bus: 1, 21, 36, 36B, 47, 54, 70, 89, 94, 108B, 122, 151, 180, 185, 192, 705, 706, 729, 919

MUSIC

Perspective: The following short section lists London's main music venues. It includes those primarily used for classical concerts and two which promote popular music. Taken with all the other hundreds of venues in London where live music is performed, from colleges to cinemas, from pubs to community centres, they add up to a rich diversity of buildings offering a wide range of music to suit all tastes.

Fairfield Hall

Park Lane, Croydon
Box office: **688 9291** Admin: **681 0821**
Performance Space: Platform stage *Seating:* 1,930 maximum

Perf Times: Normally 20 00 **Prices:** Main concerts £1.60-£3.20 **Catering:** Fairfield Restaurant (688 9291) full service meals. Buffet open all day. **Bars:** 2

Policy: To appeal to the widest interests of the community with a broadly-based programme including pop, classical, jazz, light music, opera and variety.

British Rail: East Croydon or West Croydon (British Rail)
Bus: 12A, 50, 54, 64, 68, 109, 119, 119B, 130, 130B, 166, 166A, 194, 194B, 197, 233, C1, C3, C4, 403, 405, 408, 409, 411, 414, 455, 470, 483, 725, 726, OD853, 855, 857

Rainbow

232 Seven Sisters Road, Finsbury Park, N4
Box office: **263 3140** (10 00-20 00) Admin: **263 3140**
Performance Space: Converted cinema, proscenium arch *Seating:* 2,600

Perf Times: Variable **Prices:** £2-£10 **Catering:** Confectionery only **Bars:** 2

Policy: Operates entirely as a music venue, mainly for rock bands who can make good use of the very large stage.

Underground: Finsbury Park (Piccadilly, Victoria, British Rail)
Bus: 4, 19, 29, 106, 210, 221, 236, 253, 259, 279, 279A, W2, W3, W7, 735

Royal Albert Hall

Kensington Gore, SW7 2AP
Box office: **589 8212** (10 00-18 00 Monday-Saturday & Sunday when necessary)
Admin: **589 3203**
Performance Space: Circular auditorium, concert platform *Seating:* 5,000

Perf Times: Promenade concerts July-mid September 6 days p.w. Otherwise variable
Prices: Proms 75p-£4, others variable **Catering:** Buffet on each floor, cold snacks
Bars: Each floor

Policy: Home of the BBC's annual Promenade Concerts and a venue for a wide range of events, including conferences, displays, sports and popular concerts.

Underground: Knightsbridge (Piccadilly), South Kensington (Circle, District, Piccadilly)
Bus: 9, 52, 73, 701, 704, 714, AV300, 311, 320, 322

St John's, Smith Square

Smith Square, SW1P 3HA
Box office: **222 1061** (11 00-18 00 Monday-Friday) Admin: **222 2168**
Performance Space: Chancel of church *Seating:* 600

Perf Times: Mainly winter season at 19 30 Monday-Saturday, some lunchtime concerts
Prices: Variable **Catering:** Licensed refreshments in crypt before and during perfs

Policy: Classical concerts by chamber ensembles, orchestras, choirs and soloists. Also used by the BBC and record companies for recordings.

Underground: Westminster (Circle, District)
Bus: 3, 10, 77, 77A, 149, 159, 168, 507 or 11, 12, 24, 29, 53, 70, 76, 77C, 109, 155, 159, 170, 172, 184, 503 to Parliament Square

St Martin-in-the-Fields

5 St Martin's Place, WC2N 4JJ
Box office: **None** Admin: **839 1930** (Enquiries only)
Performance Space: Chancel of church *Seating:* 1,500

Perf. Times: Every Monday & Tuesday 13 00-14 00 **Prices:** Free (collection taken)
Catering: No

Policy: To provide opportunities for good musicians starting their careers, usually singers, solo instrumentalists, string quartets.

Underground: Charing Cross (Bakerloo, Jubilee, Northern, British Rail)
Bus: 1, 3, 6, 9, 11, 12, 13, 15, 24, 29, 53, 77, 77A, 77C, 159, 168, 170, 172, 176 or 88 to Horseferry Road

IN EXILE

IN EXILE

Almost Free

Perspective: From 1971 until 1980, the Almost Free, the new-plays production unit of the Inter-Action Trust, was housed in a ground-level theatre in Rupert Street off Shaftesbury Avenue. It was forced to move out because of redevelopment, and to enter a period of 'theatre-in-exile' using other venues until its planned return to Rupert Street (or an equivalent site) in 1983.

During its life in Rupert Street, when it was the home of the Ambiance Lunch-Hour Theatre Club, and (on a semi-permanent basis) of the National Student Company, its bookshop, exhibitions and programmes of short plays were a highlight of the fringe. Once a member, you paid whatever you could afford for a ticket to see a wide range of plays, many of them 'firsts' by established and (mostly) new writers. The big hit was Tom Stoppard's *Dirty Linen*, which transferred to the Arts, and broke fringe records, but other premieres have included work by Edward Bond, David Mercer and Wolf Mankowitz. The Almost Free has helped to introduce to Britain writers from abroad — Mustapha Matura, Martin Sherman (author of *Bent*), Peter Handke and Rainer Werner Fassbinder. Often, it has tried to group the plays into seasons, on a social or political issue (eg nuclear power, civil rights, sexuality) and has also helped others to form permanent companies (eg Gay Sweatshop, the Women's Theatre Group).

Ambiance, founded in 1968, and the Almost Free are part of Ed Berman's vast project, Inter-Action, which has become a model for the old and disabled. It runs street theatre, Professor Dogg's Troupe, children's theatre, a Fun Art Bus, and has more recently launched the British-American Repertory Company.

Open Space Theatre

Perspective: Claiming to have been deprived of new premises by the takeover of entertainment giant EMI, the Open Space is taking its case to the courts to get the permanent theatre it claims it was promised when its site in Tottenham Court Road was swallowed up for office-block redevelopment. Started in 1968 by Charles Marowitz and Thelma Holt, the Open Space took off in the heat of the fringe explosion, fuelled particularly by the visit to Britain of two US groups the year before, Cafe La Mama and the Open Theatre.

Marowitz had first directed in Britain at the Unity Theatre in 1958. He had made a name working with Peter Brook in the Royal Shakespeare Company's experimental *Theatre of Cruelty* season, drawing on the work of French pioneer Antonin Artaud, and as the director of Joe Orton's second play to be staged, *Loot*, at the Jeannetta Cochrane in 1966 as part of the London Traverse season.

The opening show at the Open Space, *Fortune and Men's Eyes*, transferred to the West End. This was followed by a crop of plays, lunchtime and evening, from leading fringe writers — Sam Shepard, Howard Brenton, Howard Barker, David Edgar, Mike Weller and Trevor Griffiths. Marowitz's 'collage' productions of Shakespeare became famous. The first had been *Hamlet* in 1964, but at the Open Space he directed a voodoo *Macbeth*, a black-power *Othello*, a Watergate-style *Measure for Measure* and a *Merchant of Venice* where Shylock is an oppressed Jewish nationalist.

Amid all the world premieres, from David Rudkin's *Ashes* to *Mecca* by Ted Whitehead, the finds (eg Brecht's *A Respectable Wedding*) and the valuable kicks against the establishment (eg bringing Dennis Potter's *Brimstone and Treacle* from the Sheffield Crucible when the BBC had banned it), the Open Space, even when it had been forced to move 'temporarily' to the old post office in the Euston Road, pictured on page 188, played a vital part in the capital's fringe theatre. It gave voice to new, non-naturalistic work and to original variations on the classics. Now forced to tour, it is to be hoped that a theatre will be forthcoming to house the Open Space in the near future.

THEATRE CONTACTS

A city which can boast as many theatres as appear in this edition of *Theatre London* can quite naturally also offer an impressive number of specialist theatre organizations. This section surveys some of the many useful contacts available.

Save London's Theatres Campaign is a voluntary organization devoted to preventing the destruction of London's principle playhouses. The campaign enlists the support of player and playgoer alike, and has already been instrumental in preventing the closure of both the Criterion and Shaftesbury Theatres. They can be contacted at British Actors Equity, 8 Harley Street, W1, where you may also obtain campaign tee-shirts and publicity in support of their work.

Collections worthy of investigation can be found at **The Theatre Museum,** which is presently in transit but scheduled to open at the old flower market in Covent Garden in the early 1980s. **Pollocks Toy Museum** at 1 Scala Street, London W1, is the home of the well-known cardboard cut-out toy theatres that make wonderful gifts for theatre afficionados. For those more interested in research, the **Westminster Reference Library** in Charing Cross Road (near Leicester Square), and the **Mander and Mitchenson Collection** (by appointment only) at 5 Venner Road, London SE26, both have invaluable resources.

Management Organizations for London's theatres fall into two distinct categories. The first represents the commercial and established tradition, recently amalgamated to form what is known in the profession by the acronym TMA/CORT/ATPM, which stands for the **Theatre Managers Association, Council of Regional Theatre** and the **Association of Touring and Producing Managers.** All are now housed at 1 Bedford Chambers, The Piazza, Covent Garden, together with the **Society of West End Theatre** (SWET), and can be extremely useful with professional enquiries. The other management organizations are those directly concerned with fringe, small-scale and alternative theatre, such as the **Independent Theatre Council** and the affiliated **Association of Community Theatre** (TACT). Current addresses for these organizations can be found through *Contacts* at 43 Cranbourne Street, WC2.

Trade Unions representing the theatre profession are **British Actors Equity** at 8 Harley Street, W1; the **National Association of Theatrical and Kine Employees** (NATKE) at 155 Kennington Park Road, SE11 4JU, and the **Musicians Union**, responsible for all musicians working in our theatres, at 29 Catherine Place, Buckingham Gate, SW1. All of these have information officers at their headquarters. Playwrights are represented by three organizations, the **Theatre Writers Union**, at 37 Goodge Street, W1P 1PD, the **Writers Guild of Great Britain** at 430 Edgware Road, W2, and the **Society of Authors, Playwrights and Composers,** at 84 Drayton Gardens, SW10.

The Actors Centre is a new professional organization presently based at the YMCA near Tottenham Court Road. It offers a wide range of classes and workshops, and is available to Equity members only. For further details write or call on The Actors Centre, c/o the YMCA, Great Russell Street, WC1.

For *Casting Information,* **Spotlight** is the bible — an annual series of volumes with pictures and agents' addresses of almost every actor and actress available for work in this country. In addition, *Spotlight* offers a mail forwarding system for all theatre workers on their files, and for persons wishing to write to theatre professionals whose addresses they do not have. (Just write to the person c/o *Spotlight* and they will send your letter to the relevant address on the same day.) The publishers also produce a very useful booklet called simply **Contacts** which lives up to its name, containing as it does key addresses and telephone numbers for all the ancillary organizations that serve the theatre profession. Their address is 43 Cranbourne Street, WC2.

Technical Theatre is something for which London has earned an unparalleled reputation, and some firms do have very useful information and publicity departments. **Rank Strand Electric,** which claims to supply most of the world with lighting equipment, and **Theatre Projects** (theatre design consultants and lighting and sound hire) are both very helpful to amateur and professional alike. **The Association of British Theatre Technicians** has recently moved to new premises at 4-7 Great Pulteney Street, W1, and provides both information services and technical training programmes.

The Arts Council of Great Britain is an independent organization which administers most of the central government funds allocated to the arts. Apart from this very important function, it has a comprehensive information service from which one can obtain news about current festivals and many aspects of the subsidised theatre. The Arts Council is at 105 Piccadilly, W1, and its new shop, at 8 Long Acre, WC2, sells Arts Council publications and many other interesting arts-related books, posters, pamphlets and journals.

The British Council was created in 1934 to promote a greater knowledge of the English language overseas and to develop closer cultural relations between Britain and abroad. It organizes overseas tours of theatre companies and eminent British theatre people, as well as hosting many outstanding theatre professionals from all over the world. For further information on its wide range of activities, contact the information department at 10 Spring Gardens, SW1A 2BN.

The Greater London Arts Association is responsible for promoting and assisting a number of the theatrical events you may come across in both central London and the outer boroughs. For up-to-date information about arts activities in all the 32 London boroughs, and a copy of GLAA's own newspaper, write to the Association at 25/31 Tavistock Place, WC1H 9SF.

The British Theatre Centre at 9 Fitzroy Square, London W1P 6AE is the home of a number of useful theatre organizations, but most notable is the **British Theatre Association**, formerly the British Drama League, which was founded in 1919 and has one of the most comprehensive script libraries in the country. It often organizes courses for amateurs, teachers and visiting professionals on all aspects of theatre, as well as publishing a quarterly journal called *Drama*.

Bookshops are an invaluable source of additional information about theatre in London and elsewhere, and apart from bookstalls at theatres, two specialist bookshops worth a browse are **French's**, 26 Southampton Street, WC2, and the **Ballet Bookshop**, Cecil Court, WC2. French's publish acting editions of scripts, and are generally able to obtain almost any theatre book still in print from anywhere in the world. They also stock magazines and theatre journals from most parts of the English-speaking world, and supply English-speaking amateur theatres with scripts, and very often control the performance rights as well.

ABOUT THE ITI

The International Theatre Institute was set up by a conference in Prague in 1948. It is a non-governmental organization affiliated to UNESCO, the United Nations Educational, Scientific and Cultural Organization.

British theatre people — notably J B Priestley — were prominent in establishing the ITI, and the Institute's biennial congress was held in London in 1971, but British membership lapsed shortly afterwards. In 1977, following the appeal of that year's Stockholm congress for Britain's re-entry, a group associated with the magazine *Theatre Quarterly* offered to establish a new 'associate' centre based in their Covent Garden offices, and this centre was promoted to full membership status by a unanimous vote of the 1979 congress in Sofia.

The ITI's aims are based on the premise that the theatrical arts are a universal expression of mankind, linking large groups of the world's peoples. The organization is dedicated to promoting international exchange, deepening mutual understanding, and increasing active co-operation between all theatre people.

The ITI has a small international office at UNESCO headquarters in Paris, and this co-ordinates the work of nearly sixty national centres worldwide. While each centre is guided in its work and structure by its own national traditions and requirements, all are concerned to facilitate contact between visitors from abroad and their professional counterparts.

The British Centre forms part of the registered charity European Theatre Co-ordinate Limited, whose trustees appoint an Executive Committee to oversee the work of the directorate. An advisory group helps to shape general policy guidelines, and its members form an essential link between the centre and the many branches of the British theatre it represents. A National Liaison Committee further assists the centre's work through its representation of British sections of the nine specialist theatre organizations associated internationally with the work of the ITI.

For notes on the work of the British Centre, and the address from which further information can be obtained, see the inside front cover of *Theatre London* — itself just one of the projects the Centre has undertaken to bring the theatre, its workers, and its audiences closer together.

FOR FURTHER READING

The reader wanting to discover more about London theatres of the past and present is confronted with two difficulties. Because playhouses — as buildings — have seldom received the scholarly attention paid to dramatic literature (and increasingly being paid to performance aspects of theatre), much of the material available is at best riddled with apocryphal anecdotage, or at worst just wildly inaccurate. And because London theatre has too often been regarded (wrongly) as synonymous with British theatre, there are virtually no studies which attempt to look at the importance of theatre to London as a local community, rather than as a capital city, conveniently representing a national culture in microcosm. Among the few general histories which focus on place as much as on performance are H. Barton Baker's pioneering *History of the London Stage and its Famous Players* (1899, revised edition of 1904 reprinted in facsimile by Blom, New York, 1969), and, more recently, James Roose Evans' readable but introductory *London Theatre from the Globe to the National* (Oxford: Phaidon, 1977).

The Historical Background

Although considerable attention has been paid to the influence of the Elizabethan and Jacobean theatres of London on the staging of the plays of the period, there was no comprehensive but concise guide to the playhouses themselves until the appearance of the splendidly accessible *The London Theatre Guide, 1576-1642*, edited by Christopher Edwards (Foxton Royston, Herts: Burlington Press, for the Bear Gardens Museum, 1979). Although not in the main a work of original research, this assembles in convenient format a mass of information otherwise widely scattered in scholarly sources. At the other extreme, the period from the Restoration through the eighteenth century is exhaustively (and exhaustingly) covered in the magnificent eleven-volume *The London Stage, 1660-1800* (Carbondale: Southern Illinois University Press, 1960-68), a monumental work including a near-definitive record of performances during its period. The introductions to the main chronological divisions of this work have been published separately in five paperback volumes, and contain sections on the playhouses of the period covered (Carbondale: Southern Illinois University Press, 1968). The two major theatres of the period, the patent houses of Drury Lane and Covent Garden, are the joint subjects of the excellent if slightly indigestible Volume XXXV of *The Survey of London* (London: Athlone Press, for the Greater London Council, 1970).

The interested reader could well contrast with this last another sturdy tome, Richard Leacroft's *The Development of the English Playhouse* (London: Eyre Methuen, 1973). Although, as the title suggests, much broader in scope, an important 'thread' through the volume traces the architectural development of Drury Lane and Covent Garden, in a series of 'cut-open' isometric reconstructions, visualized with unsurpassed clarity and amazing detail. A rather different contrast is with the works on Drury Lane and various other London theatres from the hand of W Macqueen-Pope, an amiable but thoroughly unreliable theatre historian who, together with his nineteenth-century counterpart E L Blanchard, helped to perpetuate a whole pantheon of myths about the histories of London theatres, which have all too often been handed down as fact by writers relying on secondary sources.

Pope's work comes in for waspish but justifiable criticism in the preface to *The Lost Theatres of London*, by Raymond Mander and Joe Mitchenson (London: Hart-Davis, 1968) which, with Errol Sherson's less dependable *London's Lost Theatres of the Nineteenth Century* (London: Bodley Head, 1925, reprinted in facsimile by Blom, New York, 1969), offers the fullest coverage yet of the boom years of the theatre building of the last century. A partially overlapping period is covered in a radically different way in Diana Howard's *London Theatres and Music Halls, 1850-1950* (London: Library Association, 1970). Eschewing narrative, this is a detailed and virtually comprehensive alphabetical listing of all buildings (including back rooms in pubs) used as venues for performances during its period, with architectural details, lists of managers, and a full bibliography for each theatre of contemporary and historical accounts. A pioneering work, inevitably open to correction in detail, this nevertheless includes the majority of still-extant London theatres, and should be the first source for any reader wishing to track down the basic 'curriculum vitae' of a playhouse, and to find a full guide to further reading about it. The only alternative source for factual 'bird's-eye views' are the entries under 'Londra' in Volume VI of the monumental *Enciclopedia dello Spettacolo* (Roma: Case Editrice le Maschere, 1959): it is a telling irony that this incomparable work of world theatre scholarship should be in Italian. The definitive bibliography of books *about* London theatres published up to 1900 is *English Theatrical Literature, 1559-1900* (London: Society for Theatre Research, 1970), by J F Arnott and J W Robinson, pages 111-50.

The Present

Before their explorations of the past, Raymond Mander and Joe Mitchenson had written in *The Theatres of London* (revised edition, London: New English Library, 1975) the fullest account in a single volume of surviving London theatres. Usefully conspective, this work is slightly flawed by its failure to attach authors' names to most of the plays mentioned, and by its lack of an index or bibliographical references — the latter fault, however, being remedied in most cases by reference to Diana Howard's listings.

Mander and Mitchenson have also written an introductory pictorial study of *British Music Hall* (London: Studio Vista, 1965), but neither this nor David Cheshire's *Music Hall in Britain* (Newton Abbot: David and Charles, 1974), which forms a valuable narrative complement (particularly strong in its use of documentary source material) focuses on the halls as buildings (Howard's work does include them, however). Nor are there many accounts — apart from *Theatre London* — of the contemporary explosion in 'illegitimate' theatre and smaller-scale venues, though the *Alternative British Theatre Directory* (Eastbourne: John Offord, annually) provides concise factual information on companies, venues and writers.

The periodical *Sightline* provides excellent brief accounts (technically-oriented, but not off-puttingly so) of new theatre venues in London and, indeed, throughout the country: it is the journal of the Association of British Theatre Technicians, and obtainable from the address listed in the 'Theatre Contacts' section. Previously the journal *TABS* had covered new theatre buildings in this way, and a useful anthology of these fully-illustrated articles appeared under Frederick Bentham's editorship as *New Theatres in Britain* (London: Rank Strand Electric, 1970).

Other Useful Sources

The past of popular and working-class entertainment is, ironically, but not unexpectedly, better covered than its present. Such pioneering studies as E. Beresford Chancellor's *The Pleasure Haunts of London* (London: Constable, 1925) and M. Willson Disher's *Pleasures of London* (London: Robert Hale, 1950), are now supplemented by Robert D. Altick's *The Shows of London* (Cambridge, Mass: Harvard University Press, 1978), a rare combination of the scholarly and the sumptuous with, unfortunately, an equally sumptuous price.

The indigent reader without access to academic or other institutional libraries can, however, find this and most of the other books mentioned here, plus a multitude of additional 'leads' to a variety of theatrical subjects, in the theatrical collection of Westminster Reference Library, located behind the National Gallery off Charing Cross Road. Though not available on loan, most of the books in the specialist theatre collection can be consulted on 'open access', and the staff are helpful in revealing the hidden riches of the book-stacks to genuine specialist enquirers. The opening of the Theatre Museum in Covent Garden, hopefully in 1981, will once more provide public access to the Enthoven Collection (formerly housed at the Victoria and Albert Museum), with its wealth of material on individual London theatres, and to much more besides. Finally, for the serious student and long-stay visitor, membership of the British Theatre Association (see 'Theatre Contacts') gives access to its own library, which is especially rich in out-of-print materials, though its helpful staff are hard-pressed on limited resources to keep pace with the increasing flood of scholarly works on the theatre of recent years.

SIMON TRUSSLER
Editor, Theatre Quarterly

GENERAL INDEX

Bold numerals indicate the main entry for each theatre or venue.

A

Aba Daba 87, 95
Abeng **16**, 47
Abrams, Oscar 65
Academy 164
Action Space **17**
Actors Centre 191
Actors' Company 133
Actors Soup Kitchen 116
Adelphi 10, **18**
Africa Centre **19**, 122
African culture 19, 47, 62
Afro-Caribbean 16, 65
Agents 191
Albany Empire **20**
Albery 10, **21**, 78, 135, 143
Albery, Sir Bronson 21, 26, 85
Albery, Donald 127
Aldwych 9, **22**,109
Alexandra Palace
 (Ally Pally) **23**
Action Group 23
Alfred Beck Centre 172
Almost Free 26, **189**
Alternative Theatre Co 31
Amateur 34, 35, 64, 84, 94, 107, 172, 176, 192
Ambassadors **24**, 104
Ambiance Theatre Club **189**
Anouilh, Jean 44, 53, 112
Antrobus, John 50
Apollo **25**, 70, 134
Arden, John 99
Arnhem Gallery 27
Arts, The **26**, 123, 189
Arts Council 10, 192
Arts Council Bookshop 192
Arts Education Schools 170
Ashcroft 10, **27**
Astoria **28**
Atkins, Robert 79
Avon Touring 116
Ayckbourn, Alan 34, 44, 53, 54, 70, 75, 76, 82, 106, 112
Arbuzov, Alexei 48
Ashford, John 60
Association of British Theatre
 Technicians 192

B

Baldwin, Nigel 93
Ballet 36, 100, 102, 111, 184
Ballet Bookshop 192
Ballet, London 24
Ballet, Lunchtime 24, 26
Ballet Modernes de Paris 167
Ballet Rambert 24, 63, 137

Bankside 30, 52
Barbican Arts Centre 9, **29**, 148, 166
Bargate, Verity 108
Barker, Howard 80, 118, 127, 190
Barking Drama Centre **173**
Barr, Ewen 43
Barrie, J. M. 44
Barrie, Shirley 122
Bart, Lionel 18, 73, 115
Barker, Nicholas 123
Baylis, Lilian 78, 102
BBC 23, 31, 40, 50, 95, 97, 130, 187
BBC Radio London 142
Bear Gardens **30**, 52
Beaton, Cecil 44
Bee and Bustle 84, 195
Behan, Brendan 115
Belt and Braces 36, 57, 135
Bennett, Alan 70
Berger, John 58
Berman, Ed 36, **189**
Beryl and the Perils 60
Birmingham Rep 75
Blitz **180**
Bolt, Robert 53, 75
Bond, Edward 23, 75, 99, 118, 127, 189
Bookshops 192
Bourchier, Arthur 59, 109
Bowsprit 55
Bread and Puppet 81, 99
Brecht, Bertolt 57, 73, 99, 115, 121
Brenton, Howard 20, 75, 108, 118, 190
British-American Rep
 Company 36, 189
British Council 192
British Theatre
 Association 192
British Toymakers Guild 89
Brixton Arts Theatre 19
Broadway 28
Brook, Peter 22, 85, 101, 127, 137, 167, 190
Bruce, Edgar 91
Brycbox **173**
Bryden, Bill 39
Bubble **178**
Buchanan, Jack 83, 111
Burbage, James 8, 30, 42
Burbage, Richard 8
Bush **31**, 56, 122

C

Cabaret 47, 111, 121, 174
Café La Mama 118, 167, 190
Campbell, Ken 39, 60, 118
Cambridge **32**
Capital Radio 10, 44, 138, 142
Central London Poly 108
Central School 63, 166
Chanticleer **164**
Charterhouse Ark **173**
Chat's Palace **33**
Children 62, 67, 89, 93, 103, 121, 122, 123, 124, 131, 137, 172, 173, 176, 183
Christie, Agatha 24, 104
Chubb, Kenneth 122
Churchill 10, **34**
Cinemas 184
Cochran, C. B. 83, 85, 104
Cockpit **35**, 55
Colleges 169
Collegiate **36**
Coliseum **68**
Combination 20
Comedy **37**
Comedy Store **181**
Common Stock 11
Community Centres 16, 20, 47, 62, 172
Compagnie des Quinze 26
Company of Three **38**
Congreve, William 59
Cons, Emma 78
Contacts 192
Contemporary Arabic
 Drama 19
Contemporary Dance
 Trust 167
Cooney/Marsh Group 10, 28
Cooper, Giles 26
Corbett **165**
Cottesloe **39**
Counterpoint Productions 117
Country Cousin **181**
Courtneidge, Cicely 83, 111
Covent Garden 100, 102, 113, 114, 191
Covent Garden Community
 Association 9
Covent Garden Community
 Theatre 11
Coward, Noël 21, 43, 44, 46, 53, 61, 85, 92, 102, 105
Crawford, Dan and Joan 66
Crazy Gang, The 69, 126
Cregan, David 80

197

Criterion 9, 10, 21, **40**, 117
Croft, Michael 107
Croft Theatre **174**
Croydon Warehouse **41**
Crunchy Frog Studios 128
Crystal Theatre of the Saint 60
Curtain, Shoreditch 8, **42**

D
Daubeny, Peter 83
Davies, Peter Maxwell 63
Deaf, Theatre for the 63
Devine, George 99
Diaghilev 68, 106
Dickens, Charles 52, 93
Dominion **184**
Donmar 10, 21, 127
D'Oyly Carte, Richard 83, 105
Drama 192
Drama Centre **165**
Drama Schools, Conference of 166
Drill Hall 17
Drury Lane Arts Lab 63, 118
Duchess **43**
Duke of York's 10, **44**, 115
Dunlop, Frank 137

E
Earl Russell **45**
East Fifteen 165
Edgar, David 190
Educational Stagecraft Centre 42
Elephant Lunchtime 169, 170
Ellacott, Vivyan 64
Embassy 8, **166**
Embassy Club **46**
Emmet, Alfred 94
English National Opera 86
English Stage Company 99
ENSA 113
Enthoven Collection 196
Equity 9
Evans-Late Joys 88
Evening News 141
Evening Standard 141
Exhibitions 23, 27, 29, 93, 97, 102, 124

F
Factory, The **47**
Fairfield Hall 27, 186
Fenn, Ann 116
Festival Ballet 101, 133
Fielding, Henry 114
Foco Novo 58
Folk Music 33, 62, 84, 95, 110, 184
Fonteyn, Margot 127
Foothills Theatre Company 76
Forces Theatre 49
Fortune 48

Fortune, Cripplegate 48
Fountain's Abbey 38
Frayn, Michael 58, 76
Freehold 81, 118
French's 192
Fringe Theatre Guide 143
Frohman, Charles 44
Fry, Christopher 53
Fugard, Athol 24, 41, 66
Fun Art Bus 189

G
Gaiety 18, 170
Gallagher, Tom 66
Garden, The 100
Garrick **49**, 44
Garrick, David 49
Gaskill, William 99
Gate 8, **50**, 88, 123
Gay Sweatshop 20, 64, 116, 189
Gay Times Festival 17
Gay's the Word **51**
GBS **168**
Gems, Pam 58, 108
George Inn 30, **52**
Gilbert, W.S. & Sullivan, A. 49, 105 106
Gielgud, John 63, 71, 92, 114
Gill, Peter 97
Gill, Richard 89
Globe 30, **53**, 92
Globe, Bankside 8, 52, 103
Golden Lane **170**
Goldsmith, Oliver 100, 114
Goodbody, Buzz 22
Gorky, Maxim 26
Grade, Lord 10
Granville-Barker, Harley 105
Greater London Council 10
Greenwich **54**, 121
Gray, Simon 82, 129
Greater London Arts Association 192
Greenwich Young People's Theatre 35, 42, **55**
Greet, Ben 52, 79
Griffiths, Trevor 190
Grillo, John 108
Group 64 35, 42
Group Theatre 8
Grove **56**
Guardian, The 142
Guildhall School 29, **166**

H
Hackney Marsh Fun Festival 33
Half Moon **57**
Hall, Anmer 131
Hall, Peter 9, 26, 75, 93
Halliwell, David 80

Hammersmith Odeon **185**
Hammerstein, Oscar 101
Hampstead Theatre Club **58**, 72, 80
Hampton, Christopher 37, 72, 99
Hare, David 37, 58
Harlequinades 8
Harris, Richard 58
Hastings, Michael 58
Hauptmann, Gerhard 73
Havel, Vaclav 80
Hengler, Charles 69
Her Majesty's **59**
Hicks, Seymour 53
Hicks Theatre 53
Hilton, Jack 18
Hippodrome, Greenwich 54
Holland Park Court **183**
Holman, Robert 31
Homerton Community Centre 33
Hooper, Ewan 54, 55
Hornchurch Theatre Trust 93
Horowitz, Israel 80
Hoxton Hall **174**
Hulbert, Jack 83
Hull Truck 31

I
ICA, The **60**
Ibsen, Henrik 70, 73, 114
Ilford Amateur Theatre 64
Incubus 81
Independent Theatre Council 191
Inner London Education Authority (ILEA) 35, 42, 55, 63
Institute of Contemporary Arts **60**
Inter-Action Trust 189
International Festival of Puppets 42
International Theatre Institute, ifc, 193
International Theatre Week 94
Intimate **61**
Intimate Repertory Company 60
Irish Theatre 110
Islington Entertainments 171

J
Jackson, Glenda 5
Jackson's Lane **62**
Jazz 33, 36, 93, 121, 129, 171, 174 186
Jeannetta Cochrane **63**, 190
Jenner, Caryl 26, 123
Johnson, Dr 52
Jones, Eamon 95

K

Kaleidoscope 142
Keeffe, Barrie 41, 107, 108
Kenneth More **64**
Kenwood Lakeside **183**
Keskidee **65**
Educational Trust 65
Kilburn Gaumont State 184, **185**
King's, Hammersmith 133
Kings Head 26, 46, **66**, 84, 125
King's Road 28

L

Late Joys 88
Late Night 180
LBC 142
Leigh, Mike 58, 76
Lenin 23
Leno, Dan 113
Leonard, Hugh 66
Lewisham Odeon **185**
Lime Grove Studios 31
Little Angel **67**
Little Theatre 38, **168**
Little Theatre Guild 94, 120
Littler, Sir Emile 83
Littlewood, Joan 38, 115, 165
Lloyd Webber, Andrew 83, 90
Logan Hall 169, **171**
Löhr, Marie 53
London Academy of Music & Dramatic Art **167**
London Casino 90
London Coliseum **68**
London Contemporary Dance Theatre 167
London Hippodrome 111
London International Jazz Festival 23
London International Mime Festival 35
London Mask Theatre 131
London Opera House 101
London Palladium **69**
London Pavilion 9, 10
London School of Contemporary Dance 167
London Symphony Orchestra 29
London Theatre Guide 143
London Theatre Studio 85
Longhouse, The **174**, 175
Lord Chamberlain, The 8, 26, 37, 106, 114
Lumiere and Son 31, 116, 165
Lyric **70**, 134
Lyric Hammersmith 56, **71**
Lyric Opera House 71
Lyttelton 21, 32, 39, **74**, **75**

M

Management organizations 191
Mander & Mitchenson 191, 195
Marowitz, Charles 63, 127, 190
Marylands Community Centre 47
Marx, Karl 87
Matalon, Vivian 58
Matura, Mustapha 16, 47, 118, 189
Matcham, Frank 71, 96, 126
Maugham, Somerset 53, 61
Mayakovsky, Vladimir 50, 73
Mayfair **72**
Menotti 67
Mercer, David 22, 66, 189
Mermaid 9, 10, 21, 37, **73**
Metropole, Camberwell 133
Miles, Sir Bernard 73
Miller, Arthur 44
Miller, Jonathan 54
Mime 35, 62, 81, 89, 174, 175, 183, 192
Molecule Club 73
Monstrous Regiment 9, 20, 60, 62, 116
Moonshine Community Arts **175**
Moore, Mary 40, 135
Moral Rearmament 131
Mortimer, John 71
Mountview Arts Centre **168**
Mountview Theatre School 168
Mouth and Trousers 136
Moving Being 81, 167
Mulholland, J B 133
Murcell, George 103
Murray, Melissa 17
Music Hall 20, 33, 63, 87, 88, 95, 121, 172, 176, 195
Musicians Union 191

N

Nash, John 114
Nash, Sir Thomas 60
National Student Company 189
National Theatre 9, 10, **74**, **75**, 78, 133, 141
National Trust, The 52
National Youth Theatre (NYT) 63, 92, 107
NATKE 191
Nell Gwynn Club 181
New Inn **76**
New, The, Bromley 34
New Princess 106
New Shakespeare Company 79
New Watergate Theatre Club 37
New Zealand, Government of 89
North London Poly **171**
Notting Hill Carnival 47
Novello, Ivor 18, 24, 53, 111, 113
Nuffield 116
Nunn, Trevor 127

O

O'Casey, Sean 48, 73, 110
Old Bull Gallery 175
Old Red Lion **77**
Old Vic 9, 10, 21, **78**, 102
Old Vic Company 78
Old Vic Youth Theatre 78
Olivier 21, 32, 39, **74**, **75**
Olivier, Lawrence 75, 78, 83, 85, 101, 168
Oliver, Peter 81
One in Ten 45
O'Neill, Eugene 24, 82
O'Neill, Terry 110
Open Air **79**, 183
Open Space 37, 46, **190**
Opera 36, 59, 100, 102, 111, 171, 184, 186
Oracle 143
Orange Tree 9, **80**, 135
Orton, Joe 63, 66, 76, 92, 190
Osborne, John 85, 99
Oval House 62, **81**
Overground **82**

P

Palace 31, **83**, 143
Palladium, The **69**, 126
Pantomime 88, 96, 133, 185
Parks Department (GLC) 183
Patrick, Robert 26, 66
Pembroke Theatre-in-the-Round 27
Penrose, Sir Roland 60
Pentameters **84**
People's Festivals 98
People Show 8, 31
People's National Theatre 43, 48
Permanent Wave 136
Phillips, Robin 54
Phoenix 10, **85**, 90
Picasso 32
Piccadilly 10, 21, **86**, 117
Pindar of Wakefield **87**, 95
Pinero, Arthur Wing 99
Pinter, Harold 22, 27, 93, 71, 76, 80, 84, 87
Pip Simmons Company 9, 81, 118
Pirandello 72

Place, The **167**
Players **88**
Playfair, Nigel 71
Plays and Players 142
Poetry 62, 84, 189
Poliakoff, Stephen 31, 37, 39, 60
Polka **89**
Pollocks Toy Museum 191
Pomerance, Bernard 58
Poplar Civic **176**
Priestley, J B 43, 61, 131, 193
Prince Albert Pub 50
Prince Charles 9
Prince Edward **90**
Prince of Wales 70, **91**
Project Arts Centre 60
Promenade Concerts 187
Prospect 32, 78
Puppetry 30, 47, 67, 89, 174, 183

Q
Queens 53, **92**, 138
Queen's Hornchurch **93**
Questor's 10, **94**, 120

R
Radio Times 142
Raffles, Gerry 115
Railway 84, **95**
Rainbow **186**
Rattigan, Terence 25, 40, 53, 66, 70, 85, 114
Raymond, Paul 101, 132, 134
Read, Herbert 60
Red Ladder 9, 62
Regent Theatre 28
Rice, Tim 83, 190
Richmond **96**
Riverside Studios 47, 56, **97**
Rix, Brian 49, 132
Rock Garden **182**
Roose-Evans, James 58, 194
Rose 8, 30, 52
Roundhouse 57, **98**
Royal Academy of Dramatic Art (RADA) 59, 168
Royal Albert Hall 187
Royal Ballet 100, 102, 133
Royal Court 10, 21, 37, 48, 51, 72, 83, 85, **99**, 105, 125
Royal Opera House 8, **100**, 141, 194, 195
Royal Shakespeare Company 9, 10, 21, 26, 27, 29, 63, 75, 127, 137, 166, 167, 190
Royalty 9, **101**
Royalty, Soho 105
Rudman, Michael 58
Ryton, Royce 82, 84

S
Sachs, Leonard 88
Sadler's Wells 8, 21, 78, **102**, 138
Sadler's Wells Ballet 100
St George's **103**
St John's Smith Square 187
St Martin's 10, 24, **104**
Saunders, James 58
Saunders, Peter 10, 125
Save London's Theatres Campaign 9, 191
Savoy **105**
Scottish Theatre Ballet 167
Seven Eighty-Four 9
Shaffer, Peter 37, 75, 76, 124
Shaftesbury 9, 22, 28, 30, 52, 63, 78, 79, 92, 93, 102, 103, **106**, 107, 109, 114, 120, 135, 191
Shaw **107**
Shaw, George Bernard 53, 61, 73, 79, 92, 99, 168
Sheridan, Richard Brinsley 100, 114
Show Biz 142
Sidewalk 81
Simon, Neil 70
Sixty-Nine Theatre 32
Sobell Sports Centre **176**
Society of Authors, Playwrights and Composers 191
Society of West End Theatre 143, 191
Soho Poly **108**
South Bank Poly 170
Spotlight 191
Sprague, W. G. R. 21, 22, 24, 53, 92, 104, 109, 135
Stage, The 142
Stage Centre 55
Stanley Halls, The **176**
Stoll, Oswald 68
Stoppard, Tom 26, 80, 85, 189
Storey, David 99
Strand 22, **109**
Sugawn **110**

T
Talk of the Town **111**
Tavistock Theatre Company 120
Teacher's Centre 35
Teatr Kozmo Mimzi 136
Temba Theatre Company 16, 19, 41
Tennent, H M 71, 92, 114
Terson, Peter 63, 107, 124
Theatre at New End 84, **112**
Theatre-in-Education 42, 54, 94, 173, 174
Theatre London 5, 191, 193
Theatre Museum 191, 196
Theatre Projects 192
Theatre Royal, Drury Lane 8, 43, 48, 59, 102, 104, **113**, 194
Theatre Royal, Haymarket 10, 37, **114**
Theatre Royal, Stratford East 47, **115**
Theatre Space **116**
Theatre-in-the-Square **117**
Theatre Upstairs 99, **118**
Theatre Workshop 49, 115, 135, 165
Theatro Technis **119**
Three Horseshoes 84
Tower 10, **120**
Toynbee Hall Theatre 42
Trafalgar Square Theatre 44
Tramshed **121**
Travers, Ben 22, 109
Traverse Theatre 63
Tree, Sir Beerbohm 59, 168
Tricycle **122**

U
Unicorn 26, **123**
Upstream **124**

V
Vanbrugh **168**
Vanbrugh, Sir John 59
Vaudeville 10, **125**
Victoria Palace **126**

W
Wakefield Tricycle 31, 87, 122
Warehouse 10, 41, **127**
Waterside **128**
Watford Palace **129**
Webber Douglas Academy 164
Weldon, Fay 80
Wembley **130**
Wesker, Arnold 98, 99, 125
Westminster **131**
Whitehall 90, **132**
Wilkinson, Chris 58, 66
Williams, Heathcote 108, 118
Wilson, Snoo 31, 60, 66, 118
Wimbledon **133**
Windmill 28, 70, **134**
Women's Theatre Groups 19, 20, 31, 173, 175, 189
Woolwich Theatre Co 121
World Theatre Seasons 22, 83
Writers Guild 191
Wyndham, Charles 21, 40, 135
Wyndham's 9, 10, 21, 80, **135**, 143

Y
York and Albany 136
Young Vic **137**